WE HAVE COME TO STAY

WE HAVE COME TO STAY

American Women and Political Parties
1880–1960

Edited by
MELANIE GUSTAFSON, KRISTIE MILLER, AND
ELISABETH I. PERRY

University of New Mexico Press
Albuquerque

Library of Congress Cataloging-in-Publication Data
We have come to stay : American women and political parties, 1880–1960 /
edited by Melanie Gustafson, Kristie Miller, and Elisabeth I. Perry.
p.   cm.
Includes bibliographical references and index.
ISBN 0-8263-1969-6 (cloth). — ISBN 0-8263-1970-X (pbk.)
1. Women in politics—United States—History.
2. Women political activists—United States—History.
I. Gustafson, Melanie S.
II. Miller, Kristie, 1944–
III. Perry, Elisabeth Israels.
HQ1236.5.U6W4   1999
320′.082—dc21   98-37401
CIP

UCD WOMEN'S CENTER

To
Our Political Foremothers

CONTENTS

INTRODUCTION

"Get into the parties," Carrie Chapman Catt told women in 1920, as the country anticipated the ratification of the woman suffrage amendment to the United States Constitution. Speaking as president of the nonpartisan National American Woman Suffrage Association, Catt argued that enfranchised women would gain greater influence if they became "partisan" and thus got "on the inside" of political parties. The *Woman Citizen* reported that Catt's speech "picked women up and faced them about completely in their feeling and conviction with regard to party affiliation." The suffrage newspaper overestimated the about-face. Many American women were already involved in party politics before the passage of the Nineteenth Amendment in 1920 and had been for a long time. Moreover women's use of a nonpartisan strategy did not end in 1920 but continued through organizations such as the National League of Women Voters as well as many other local and national groups. Students of American women's political history are now discovering that 1920 was less (to use historian Nancy Cott's term) the "great divide" than scholars once thought.

The essays in this book give weight to this insight. All based on research in primary sources, they explore women's participation in American party politics both before and after 1920, illustrating the many different ways women worked toward being "on the inside" of political parties and their uneven progress toward this goal.

While women's partisan traditions go back to the earliest days of the republic, our essays begin in the 1880s, when women began a systematic effort to find formal places in political parties. The book ends with the 1950s, before modern feminism began to grapple with new political challenges. We have ordered the essays chronologically to encourage readers to see this history as a whole, even though the essays are not meant to provide a straight or tight narrative of women's work in political parties. Instead, by showcasing important and fascinating episodes in women's political history, they prepare the way for new narratives both of women's participation in politics and of American political parties themselves and encourage more scholarship in this rapidly expanding field.[1]

Most studies of women's political activity have overlooked women in political parties. They have focused instead on the woman's rights and suffrage movements, the contributions of women's reform organizations to building the welfare state, and the political nature of legal or constitutional issues affecting women. Other studies have focused on who voted and how or on what offices women won or held. This scholarship has greatly enriched our understandings of women's political history, but there is clearly a need for new perspectives on this large and complex field.

We think that new perspectives can be gained from studying women in political parties. Most historians have assumed that parties were an exclusively male domain in which women's roles were severely limited or even nonexistent. Thus historians have often mentioned women only in ways that made them tangential to the story being told. This is especially true for the years before 1920 and for work on the two major parties, the Republican and Democratic. While men have certainly dominated party politics, women consistently challenged this masculine monopoly. Long before national woman suffrage, they entered parties, worked in campaigns, and sometimes held political office. By placing women at the center of inquiry, these essays reveal them as vital actors in party politics, especially in local and regional contexts, where they were most apt to find the opportunity and support to play such roles. The essays illustrate the ways in which political parties can be a rich resource for examining the challenges that women, both disfranchised and enfranchised, faced in their struggles for voice and power in the nation's political arenas.

There is more than one story to tell about women's activism in political parties. The American partisan tradition, for women as well as men, is complex and varied. Class, racial, and ethnic factors combined with larger political events and other social developments to determine the formation and impact of women's political action. Place and time are also critical to understanding women's partisan opportunities and choices. In some places, for example, women won the suffrage long before 1920. Some women's political work built on traditions established in their mothers' generation; others made innovative contributions that later generations would build on. In writing women's political history, scholars must take into account as many of these factors of difference, commonality, and tradition as they can discover and reconstruct.

They must also reframe the questions that historians have traditionally asked when they study the history of political parties. One historian has written that "Parties are institutions always in the process of deciding to act," and asks "how do they decide? How do they frame their platforms, stances, and activities, decide on candidates? Where did power reside in parties?"[2] Our essayists assert that women helped determine the issues debated and the strategies developed in political parties as people struggled for constituencies, votes, and offices. They also pose questions that focus on women's specific concerns: How and why do women choose to maintain or create separate spaces in parties? How are issues of equal representation resolved? Can strategies of separation and integration complement each other, or is there an inherent contradiction for women who choose both, either at the same time or at different times? When are notions of womanhood asserted in party politics? Why are some political issues and not others considered to be in the domain of women, and what are the consequences of such designations? As explored by our contributors, these and other questions and their answers open the door to more questions.

We begin the story of women's partisan efforts in the late nineteenth century. In the first essay of the volume, Melanie Gustafson writes about the establishment of the Woman's National Republican Association, the first national woman's party auxiliary. Founded by Judith Ellen Foster in 1888, this auxiliary organized voting and nonvoting women throughout the nation and laid the groundwork for the Republican women's party organizations of the twentieth century. Covering the same era but emphasizing questions of gender representation, Rebecca Edwards's essay shows how women's partisan activities in the 1880s and 1890s helped alter the class basis of political campaigns while supporting the reform agendas of middle-class men.

The next essays move into the first decades of the twentieth century, when women made gains in partisan politics at both local and national levels. Sherry Katz describes the activities of women in the Socialist Party in California. Describing an era of successful coalition building, Katz explains how Socialist women and feminists in the West came together to advance social reform legislation. In the East Lucretia Blankenburg mobilized clubwomen to create a reform coalition crucial to her husband's successful mayoral campaign in 1911. In his essay about Blankenburg, Drew VandeCreek shows that organized women could exert new leverage in partisan politics. Robyn Muncy's essay on the Colorado campaigns of 1912 argues that party competition in a three-way campaign created new opportunities for women in that suffrage state. But Muncy also explains the limitations of those opportunities by showing how women competed among themselves for a few political positions perceived as "women's" slots. The political culture of African American women in Chicago is the subject of the essay by Wanda Hendricks. Black women played a crucial role in the aldermanic election of 1914, Hendricks argues, and their influence did not go without notice.

The early twentieth century also saw women organizing in the national arena. In 1912 each of the major parties had for the first time a national women's political organization. In her essay on the 1912 election, Kristie Miller describes the activities of the Women's National Wilson and Marshall Organization. Founded by Democrat Daisy Harriman, it sought to appeal to women across party lines by promoting the candidates rather than the party they represented. Appealing to women's nonpartisanship and asking women to cross party lines was also the political strategy employed by Frances Kellor, the organizer of the 1916 Woman's Hughes Campaign Train. Molly Wood's description of the train's journey west reveals the tensions among partisan women in suffrage and nonsuffrage states.

Tensions arose between men and women, too, in the political parties. Anna Harvey and Elisabeth Israels Perry look at women's work in the political parties in New York state in the 1920s, but they approach this history from different perspectives. Harvey argues that the failure of women to gain equal access to party committees resulted from the strategies they chose, rather than from their political culture. With the story of Mary Garrett Hay, Perry demonstrates how loyalty to suffrage principles interfered with women's integration into the party structures. Kathryn Anderson, in her essay on Emily Newell Blair, also explores the complex nature of women's politics in the early suffrage era. She describes Blair as a woman whose feminist principles lost her opportunities to participate in partisan politics at the local level but who went on to play a role on the national stage.

In the 1920s and 1930s, more women ran for elective office, and our next essayists consider the relationship that emerged for women in those decades between party politics and electoral politics. Nancy Young's essay on Miriam "Ma" Ferguson describes a woman who served twice as governor of Texas in the 1920s and 1930s. Glenna Matthews writes about Florence Kahn's career in the U.S. House of Representatives from 1925 to 1937. Less concerned with transforming party structures, these elected women sought success through their ability to cooperate with men and by presenting themselves as politicians first, women second. But as both Young and Matthews demonstrate, gender mattered.

Most of the scholarship now available on women's contributions to politics in the 1930s focuses on women in voluntary associations or appointed political positions in the New Deal. Maureen Flanagan's essay describes the career of a contrasting figure, Republican Anna Wilmarth Ickes. Elected to three terms in the Illinois General Assembly beginning in 1928, Wilmarth Ickes pursued policies developed in women's organizations but was also successful in the male world of party politics. Elected women are also the subject of Elizabeth Salas's essay. Salas gives us portraits of three Chicana politicians from New Mexico who held office between 1920 and 1940. Soledad Chávez Chacón, Adelina Otero-Warren, and Concha Ortiz y Pino each developed different strategies influenced by an ethnic culture that valued strong family connections.

Paula Baker's essay shifts the focus back to party organization. Baker argues that an analysis of women in party political structures between the 1930s and 1950s is essential to understanding how party organizations changed and thus illuminates the larger issue of the presumed "decline" of political parties during this period. In the final essay of the volume, Jacqueline Braitman looks at women in California political parties in the 1950s. Braitman challenges the notion that women in political parties were marginal in the 1950s and notes that they continued to balance loyalties to both their parties and their gender-specific goals.

Taken collectively, these essays draw us toward new insights about American women's history and American political history. Women's different political styles influenced strategies that brought about important changes in the political landscape. Their activism had an impact on party structures, and their concerns colored party ideology. Such changes came slowly and unevenly. Sometimes men and women cooperated as they worked together in political parties, but often they were in tension with one another, continually negotiating with one another for power, influence, and place in American political life.

These negotiations often found expression in conflicts over definitions of partisanship. Both before and after 1920, women and men did not always agree on the meaning of loyalty to party. The portraits of Harriman, Kellor, Hay, and Wilmarth Ickes, for example, show women defining partisanship as drawing like-minded people together on certain issues to support candidates who upheld those issues. Men's declarations that women were unwilling to be partisan on male terms may have reflected men's strategy, conscious or unconscious, to limit the sharing of power. These essays show that the controversial and contested nature of partisanship as a form of political identity and activity did not disappear with the decline of popular politics in the late nineteenth century, nor is it a recent development of the late twentieth century.

This volume also establishes the centrality of issues of separation and integration to women's political lives both before and after 1920. These issues were difficult, and sometimes impossible, for women to resolve. National suffrage changed the terms of the debate but did not end it. After 1920 some women chose integration and struggled to create places within parties where they could work and share power equally with men. Other women chose separation, continuing women's long history of establishing separate gender institutions either completely outside or separated within the realms of politics dominated by men, including political parties. Yet others used both strategies, sometimes at once, sometimes alternately, depending on their changing opportunities and circumstances. Any story of women in politics must take into account women's struggle to resolve the tensions between these two strategies or risk ignoring the complexity of women's political experience.

We have taken the title for this anthology from Judith Ellen Foster's remarks to the male delegates assembled for the Republican National Convention in 1892. "We are here to help you," she said. "And we have come to stay." Happily, thanks to women's "staying" power, conditions have improved for women in politics since Foster delivered that speech. Women are no longer in politics just "to help," however. They want to exercise power themselves. It is our hope that this collection, by reclaiming a small part of women's historical experience in American political parties, will contribute not only to new understandings about women's past involvement in politics but also to the empowerment of political women today and in the future.

NOTES

1. Readers will be able to fill the gaps in this anthology with material from scholarly work that has already illuminated the field. J. Stanley Lemons's *The Woman Citizen: Social Feminism in the 1920s* offers a detailed treatment of women in partisan and nonpartisan politics for the immediate postsuffrage years; Nancy Cott's *The Grounding of Modern Feminism* focuses primarily on the national level and discusses many other issues than partisan politics; Felice D. Gordon's *After Winning: The Legacy of the New Jersey Suffragists, 1920–1947* is a study of women's postsuffrage activism in New Jersey; Susan Ware's *Beyond Suffrage: Women in the New Deal* examines women reformers' impact on the New Deal; Cynthia Harrison's *On Account of Sex: The Politics of Women's Issues 1945–1968* reconstructs the political prelude to the modern women's movement. For full bibliographical citations to the secondary works cited in the essays, see the *Works Cited* section at the end of this book. Some biographies of early twentieth-century women—for example, Eleanor Roosevelt, Ruth Mc-Cormick, Belle Moskowitz, Helen Gahagan Douglas, and Molly Dewson—hint at the broad extent of women's participation in party politics, notably at the local level, in third party movements, and in the steady increase of women in state and federal offices. Jo Freeman's forthcoming survey of women in party politics will supplement these studies.

2. Joel H. Silbey, *Partisan Imperative*.

CHAPTER ONE

PARTISAN AND NONPARTISAN
The Political Career of Judith Ellen Foster, 1881–1910

MELANIE GUSTAFSON

By the 1880s women's partisanship was an established fact. As Judith Ellen Foster declared from the podium at the 1888 International Council of Women in Washington, D.C., "Woman *is* in politics."[1] Although most women could not vote in the United States, strong partisan loyalties and commitments to diverse causes prompted and guided their partisan activism. However, women's work with political parties was never without controversy. And because the meanings of this activism were not always clear, numerous people attempted to define women's political place in the late nineteenth century. One of these was Judith Ellen Foster, an Iowa lawyer, temperance crusader, and staunch Republican.

When Foster declared that woman was in politics, she also formulated what she called "the only unanswered question" about women's politics: "What relation shall she hold to politics and what will be the result of that relation with all it involves?"[2] Drawing on observations from a recent trip to Europe and her own expectations in American politics, Foster posed a series of questions. Should women's relationship to politics be determined by the "mere accident of birth," as was Queen Victoria's? Should they find their power through their use of "favor and caprice," as did the ladies of the imperial French court? Or should they be like the English Primrose Dames, who labored for the government without the vote? Turning to the United States, she said that women seeking government protections were in the "position of supplicants," beggars asking for help. Should American women, who "seek governmental protection for temperance, for education, for philanthropy, for

1. Judith Ellen Foster, founder and president of the Woman's National Republican Association (State Historical Society of Iowa).

industrial education" continue as beggars, pleading for favors and protections from their government?

Her answer was a resounding *no*. American women needed the right to vote and the right to hold public office. They also needed to be active in political parties, which would give them direct political power and enable them to enact their issues into legislation. Foster carefully chose the last words of her International Council of Women speech, knowing they would be widely reprinted. She stated: "Gentlemen, we do not threaten. No, no, no. We are of you and yours." However, women needed the vote. They needed laws that would allow them to hold all elective and appointive offices.

To reach these goals, Foster promoted a political strategy for women that recognized their historical exclusion from partisan politics. It also recognized their aspirations to work with men in political parties.[3] Foster believed that women needed to engage in politics as both nonpartisans and partisans. Her strategy and her dedication to promoting both nonpartisanship and partisanship for women resulted in a political drama that played out in the national Woman's Christian Temperance Union [WCTU] and in the Republican Party in the 1880s. It was a drama that underscores the diversity of women's political commitments, loyalties, and tactics, as well as their struggle to elevate women collectively. It also highlights the passionate feelings that women invested in their politics and the powerful convictions that both divided and united women. It emphasizes as well the tensions felt by many political women seeking to define women's relationship to politics at the turn of the last century.

Foster was an active worker for the Republican Party. Her public career began soon after she moved to Clinton, Iowa, in 1869 to begin a new life with her second husband, Elijah Foster, a lawyer. While raising her children, Foster studied law and in 1872 was admitted to practice before the Iowa State Supreme Court. The Fosters established a law firm, "Foster and Foster," and worked side by side in the Iowa State Temperance Alliance. Judith Foster also became a member of the national WCTU, which used nonpartisan means to achieve moral temperance and legal prohibition. Superintendent of the Legislative Department of the WCTU since its founding in 1874, Foster had a close working relationship with President Frances Willard.

Foster easily balanced her partisanship and nonpartisanship until the early 1880s, when she learned that Willard, as part of her "Do Everything" strategy, planned for WCTU women to move into partisan politics as the Home Protection Party, merge with the Prohibition Party, and create a new party, the Prohibition Home Protection Party.[4] Foster opposed the plan and advocated a formal policy of nonpartisanship for the organization.

Though a Republican, Foster did not argue from her partisan position. Instead she argued that the WCTU should be nonpartisan because of the nature of the temperance question and the process of political change. She stated that temperance reforms "should be kept outside of *party* political action until the people through non-partisan agencies have secured so great popular support for these reforms that they may be safely championed by political parties." Different groups should educate and agitate, she asserted, and then legislation will be "secured through non-partisan measures. Then comes the machinery of the party and holds fast what has been secured through these other agencies." Nonpartisanship protected temperance legislation "from the varying fortunes of party politics," she concluded. Further she asked, "What has the WCTU to do with tariffs or free trade, with hard or soft money, with railroads or mines?"[5]

Willard saw things differently. She stated that if women worked with the Prohibition Party they would be "in at the birth" of bills and platforms, and they would help elect men who would forward their crusade.[6] "Moral suasion leads to legal suasion, and that involves in its national phases political suasion," Willard stated.[7] Since women were ignored by the major parties, Willard believed their only place was in the Prohibition Party.

Foster protested. At every WCTU annual convention from 1882 until 1888, Foster's resolutions that the WCTU enact a policy of nonpartisanship were debated and tabled. At the 1888 convention, in a move that everyone understood as total support for the Prohibition Party, the WCTU voted to back any party that endorsed prohibition and "Home Protection." Foster again sought to issue her protest but was refused a hearing.

Foster and her supporters attempted another avenue of protest. They refused to pay their dues to the national treasury, claiming that these were diverted to party political work. The WCTU responded by passing a resolution stating that anyone unfriendly to the Prohibition Party "is hereby declared disloyal to our organization." With Foster leading the way, a group of women bolted the national organization.[8] Foster and Ellen Phinney, of Ohio, established the Non-Partisan WCTU as a rival to the National WCTU.

Throughout the 1880s, the differences between Foster and Willard highlight women's passionate feelings about their politics and reveal the convictions that both divided and united women. In 1884 Foster wrote Willard, "I thought you loved and trusted me. I thought I had proved my devotion." Foster declared to Willard that she loved her, "as I have never loved any other woman. Even in this I say to myself, 'she did not *intend* to hurt, she was so intent on accomplishing the plans which to her seemed just and good that she looked neither to the right or to the left.' " Then Foster finally got to the point: "But better than I love any human friend I love the interests of our WCTU work." That love led Foster to her protests, her defection, and her attempt to recreate what she believed to be the original intent of the WCTU in her new organization, the Non-Partisan WCTU.[9]

To the WCTU women left behind, Foster wrote an open letter. She assailed them for personal attacks on her over the years as she had promoted a nonpartisan policy for the WCTU while maintaining her Republican loyalties. Why, she asked, were other women allowed to exercise their freedom of political action without censure while Republican women were "subject to impeachment?"[10] Foster may have been disingenuous about her reasons for promoting nonpartisanship in the WCTU, as some women seemed to think. She may have wanted to protect the organization as a bastion for Republicans. Or she may have honestly believed that nonpartisanship was the only course for such a large national organization of women with different partisan loyalties. She may also have believed her own analysis that legislation on moral questions such as temperance was best pursued and protected outside partisan politics. Whatever her motivation and purpose, her action split the WCTU.

The Non-Partisan WCTU proclaimed that it would "leave every individual member of our organization absolutely free to choose her party alliance and to follow her political convictions." "Every woman," Foster wrote, should "respect the conscientious convictions of every other woman. . . . [and] any abridgment of this is a violation of the spirit of political liberty which underlies the Republic." Because they lacked the power of the ballot, women were encouraged to use their "influence" in the moral and political crusade for temperance and prohibition.[11]

In the political culture of the late nineteenth century, women were not seen as inherently nonpartisan, but the word *nonpartisan* was increasingly associated with women and their political efforts. Rhetorically equated with the effort to infuse principles into the public sphere, nonpartisanship was already the structural basis of much of women's decades-long work in benevolent and reform organizations. The association between women and nonpartisanship was further reinforced by women's disfranchisement. So when Foster promoted nonpartisanship, she was embracing a term understood as part of women's political culture.[12]

The reunited woman suffrage movement also reinforced the association of women and nonpartisanship. The members of the National American Woman Suffrage Association declared in 1890 that they held a unanimous sentiment that the organization should keep "strictly aloof from all political alliances." Their awareness of the power of parties was also evident. Woman suffrage, they agreed, "can be gained only through the assistance of men in all parties."[13] Susan B. Anthony would invoke the term "all-partisan" rather than "nonpartisan" to describe their approach.[14]

Judith Ellen Foster, for all her promotion of women's nonpartisanship, was also a loyal Republican. So at the same time as she promoted women's nonpartisanship, Foster created a new space for women in partisan politics. Her efforts began in earnest in 1888. She attended meetings of "Anti-Saloon Republicans" in New York City and Chicago to support the call for a temperance plank in the Republican platform. In June the Republican Party adopted a platform that included only a weak resolution that the party "cordially sympathizes with all wise and well-directed efforts for the promotion of temperance and morality."

It did not call for the abolition of the liquor trade. It was also silent on the question of equal suffrage. Elizabeth Cady Stanton responded that "No woman with a proper self-respect can longer kneel at the feet of the Republican party."[15]

Foster ignored the party's silences and forged ahead. Her strategy was to establish a national organization of Republican women. When Benjamin Harrison received the party's nomination for president, Foster wrote him that she was "busily engaged making plans for the organization of Women's Republican Clubs." She declared that she hoped "this new departure may be useful" and that she had received the "kind approval and assistance of the National Committee."[16]

The approval came from James Clarkson, of Des Moines, Iowa, a member of the Republican National Committee and chairman of the National League of Republican Clubs.[17] Politically Clarkson and Foster were made for each other. They both had long histories in Iowa Republican politics. Both disdained independent factions within the party that led to third parties. Both were dedicated to making the party stronger. For Clarkson that meant a centralized, efficient way to educate voters using the National League of Republican Clubs, an arm of the Republican National Committee. The RNC created the educational propaganda. The league's clubs disseminated it.[18] Foster's Republican club for women would be one of these. With the party behind her, she established the national club, the Woman's National Republican Association [WNRA].[19] Its office adjoined the RNC's in New York City.

The national campaign of 1888 focused on the question of the protective tariff, and throughout the campaign Foster followed the party line and spoke in favor of it. Temperance was not on the agenda of the Republican party's national leaders, but it was on Foster's agenda. Her speeches were mainly attacks on the Prohibition Party, however. At a large Republican rally in Woodstock, Connecticut, Foster criticized the alliance of the Prohibition Party and the WCTU. She stated:

> It is boasted that the Third Party is the only political party which honors woman. Honors woman indeed! It appropriates her work and her influence to its own purposes and pays in fulsome flatteries; it gives to women seats in conventions and places their names on meaningless committees and tickets impossible of success. Flattery is cheap, full conventions are desirable, women's social and religious influence adds respectability to this propaganda.[20]

Foster knew that women and men would understand the use of the word *influence*. It represented not only women's formal exclusion from electoral

politics, because they were disfranchised, but also the desire to use their identification as uncorrupted authorities as leverage for themselves and their issues.
Influence could mean authority.

While Foster criticized Prohibition women for receiving only "flatteries,"
she herself was criticized for rewards of "sundry gifts of office, if not of money."
The Non-Partisan WCTU was seen as a front for the Republican Party. Elijah
Foster, the *New York Times* reported in 1891, was appointed general agent of the
Department of Justice "at a salary of $3,600 a year." The husband of Mrs.
Rufus Tilton, Foster's "chief lieutenant," was a clerk in the Second Controller's
Office "at a fat salary," and "other able supporters of the 'Non-Partisan Wom-
an's Christian Temperance Union,' have also comfortable berths at the public
crib."[21]

Foster did seek and receive rewards, including the government appointment
for her husband.[22] Working for the Republican Party had certainly changed
her life. The Fosters moved from Iowa to Washington, D.C. During campaign
seasons, she was either at the offices of the Woman's National Republican
Association or was traveling the country as a speaker and organizer. She was
never shy about promoting not only women in the party but also herself, her
family, and colleagues. She continually asked for and received various appointments from successive Republican presidents.[23] She asked President McKinley
for an appointment to the Industrial Commission.[24] McKinley appointed her
to inspect mobilization stations during the Spanish-American war. Roosevelt
appointed her to investigate the status of women in the Philippines with the
Taft Commission, as a U.S. representative to the International Red Cross
Conference, and to study the working conditions of women and children in
the U.S.[25] Taft appointed her a special agent of the Department of Justice to
inspect the prison system.

For all the rewards that were to come later, in 1891 Foster did not consider
that she made enough money from her Republican connections, so she established herself as a circuit lecturer. "After all these years of public service," she
wrote, "I am concluding that it is time I made money for myself."[26] Stump
speaking for candidates often led to the lyceum and lecture circuit and offered
speakers a way to make money between campaigns.

Foster's major partisan effort always was to increase women's presence and
influence in the Republican Party. It was an ongoing struggle, requiring constant reminders to the men of the party that women were able and willing
volunteers. To the delegates assembled for the 1892 Republican National Convention, Foster stated: "We are here to help you. And we have come to stay."[27]
During the 1892 campaign, the Woman's National Republican Association issued an appeal: "Republican Women: Please Take Action." It informed women

that the WNRA was officially recognized by the Republican National Committee and had been invited by the Executive Committee of the National Republican League to attend its next convention. All Republican women were encouraged to attend, because "such opportunities are rare in the lives of women."[28]

Republican women took action, and after the election Foster wrote President Harrison: "In this campaign, as never before, the Republican party has recognized its women sympathizers. With solemn joy I feel the responsibilities of leadership. I am doing the best I can."[29] But behind this public mask of optimism and cooperation was frustration. The Republican Party's continued silence on the questions of temperance and woman suffrage disappointed Foster, who wrote to a friend that she was "at a loss to understand."[30]

Foster's fame as a Republican organizer grew during the campaigns of 1892, 1894, and 1896, as she successfully organized African American and White women all over the Northeast and in the West.[31] In 1894 and 1896, the Republican National Committee sent Foster to Colorado to organize the newly enfranchised women of the state.[32] She stumped the state, and Republican women in Denver formed a "powerful organization," the East Capitol Hill Woman's Republican League. The victory of the Republican Party in Colorado increased not only Foster's fame in Republican circles, it also increased party leaders' understanding that voting women needed some attention paid to them.[33]

Assisting Foster in 1896 was Helen Varick Boswell, who had helped New York women establish their first Republican woman's club in 1895, the West End Woman's Republican Club. Boswell would take over the presidency of the Woman's National Republican Association after Foster's death. Boswell recollected years later that women got to know each other during campaign season, and afterwards "it seemed too bad to have the Republican women . . . separate."[34] The result was the formation of local Republican women's clubs that functioned before and after campaign seasons. During the campaign of 1896, the club women "spread the gospel of the Gold Standard" to residents of the tenement houses, a strategy that "became one of the greatest assets in political work and was followed in due course in every city by Republican women, and, when women had the vote, by Democratic women."[35]

Republicans won back the White House in 1896, with McKinley's election, and for the rest of her life Judith Ellen Foster saw her party hold a prominent place in American politics. But she was constantly disheartened by the fact that Republican men often ignored the women who had helped in the campaigns. In 1900, as she got ready to accompany Theodore Roosevelt for a campaign swing through the West, Foster wrote Ida Husted Harper that a new Board of

Charities for the District of Columbia had just been created by Congress. Everyone assumed a woman would be appointed to the board, but President McKinley "sent in the names of *five men* and *no woman!* A Jew, a Catholic, a colored man—but no woman!" Foster was appalled that a board to "inspect . . . poor, crushed and wicked women and girls" would not have a woman, and she regretted that it was "our noble and good and true McKinley" who had made the decision. Ever resourceful, she asked Harper to use the woman suffrage press to publicize that "a fine woman" who was in line for a position had been passed over. Ever the partisan, she warned Harper not to use her name or that of the "fine woman." "I don't want her to appear as a defeated candidate," and Foster didn't want to appear critical of McKinley.[36]

Foster knew that if she could not get rewards for women from her party, she could turn to women to pursue them. As much as possible Foster wanted to cooperate with political men and believed that women and men needed to "supplement each other's quality of ability" in the political realm.[37] But her actions indicate that she was also aware that women needed to rely on each other in politics. To maintain that reliance, create unity out of diversity, and see their issues become legislation, women cut across partisan lines. They joined together in nonpartisan organizations. Individual women could act in partisan ways and join political parties, but sometimes women's political impact was stronger by using nonpartisan methods.

There is no direct evidence that Foster believed only women should use nonpartisan means to advance their political interests. Men might also have been part of her vision of how the political process worked. In her first arguments against the affiliation of the WCTU and the Prohibition Party, she stated that it was "the people" who should use "non-partisan agencies" for their reforms. Then a party looking out for the interests of the people, convinced by the education and agitation of the people, would protect the legislation "from the varying fortunes of party politics." Foster's fight with Willard and her subsequent work with the Non-Partisan WCTU and the Republican Party occurred in an era when civil service reform, contests to machine politics, and new electoral laws were just beginning to have an impact in limiting or diminishing men's partisanship. It was a time when men as well as women promoted "disinterestedness" (or working for the collective good). Parties were still central to political culture, but strong partisanship was no longer central to men's sense of their total political experience. However, Foster's aim was to advance women in the partisan world, not to bring men into the nonpartisan world. The promotion of nonpartisanship for men was a challenge taken on by others.

Foster wanted women to work with men in the partisan arena, but she also knew that women's collective presence made a difference in politics. As women sought inclusion in political parties, and as they struggled for greater citizenship rights, Foster was always concerned that women not lose themselves, or what they had already developed and achieved, in the process.

During the last years of her life, Foster continued her work for the Republican Party. She was also active in the suffrage movement and guided the efforts of the Non-Partisan WCTU in its moral reform efforts and crusade for constitutional prohibition.[38] She was both a partisan and a nonpartisan woman. She died in 1910, ten years before the passage of the Eighteenth and Nineteenth Amendments to the U.S. Constitution.

Judith Ellen Foster died at the height of Republican dominance of national politics. Yet in two years, a schism in the party would lead to the creation of the Progressive Party and the loss of the White House to Democrats. In response to the strategic needs of a close three-way race in 1912, Helen Boswell transformed the Woman's National Republican Association into a more vigorous vehicle for women's influence in the party. The WNRA of 1912 was, according to the *New York Times,* "as well entrenched as the regular Republican machine . . . and it is no difficulty for them to reach just the kind of woman who can influence votes, if they don't actually cast them."[39] Being an integral part of the Republican machine was just what Foster was aiming for. And yet in 1912 the issue of women's nonpartisanship again was prominent in the campaign, as suffragists such as Ida Husted Harper spoke out against women's affiliations with political parties. The tension between women's partisanship and nonpartisanship would accompany women even into the postsuffrage era.

NOTES

1. Address by J. Ellen Foster, *Woman's Tribune,* April 1, 1888.

2. Ibid.

3. Judith Ellen Foster, "Woman's Political Evolution," *North American Review* 65 (1897): 600–609.

4. Judith Ellen Foster to Frances Willard, April 2, 1884, Woman's Christian Temperance Union Papers, microfilm ed. (Ann Arbor: University of Michigan, 1977), ser. 3, reel 13 (hereafter WCTU Papers).

5. *Woman's Tribune,* March 31, 1888; Judith Ellen Foster, "The Influence of Women in American Politics," in *What America Owes to Women: The National Exposition Souvenir,* ed. Lydia Hoyt Farmer (Buffalo: Charles Wells Moulton, 1893).

6. Ruth Bordin, *Frances Willard,* 374–75.

7. Frances Willard, "President's Annual Address," 1888 National WCTU Meeting, WCTU Papers, ser. 3, reel 2.

8. The controversy can be followed in the Minutes of the Annual Meetings, WCTU Papers, ser. 3, reel 2.

9. Judith Ellen Foster to Frances Willard, April 2, 1884, WCTU Papers, ser. 3, reel 13. See also Judith Ellen Foster to Frances Willard, November 16, 1888, WCTU Papers, ser. 3, reel 15, and *Boston Journal,* September 9, 1884.

10. *Union Signal,* June 12, 1888.

11. Speech by J. Ellen Foster, in *Transactions of the National Council of Women of the United States, Assembled in Washington, D.C., February 22 to 25, 1891,* ed. Rachel Foster Avery (Philadelphia: J. B. Lippincott, Co., 1891), 135–41.

12. On the concept of women's political culture, see Sklar, *Florence Kelley and the Nation's Work;* Nancy A. Hewitt, *Women's Activism and Social Change;* Lori D. Ginzberg, " 'Moral Suasion is Moral Balderdash.' "

13. Elizabeth Cady Stanton et al., *History of Woman Suffrage.* See also Ellen DuBois, "Outgrowing the Compact of Fathers."

14. Anthony wrote she was discouraged that "woman" seemed to care "more for her love of her political party, Republican, Democratic, or Greenback, than for her own political rights." Susan B. Anthony to Elizabeth Harbert, August 5, 1880, Elizabeth Harbert Collection, Huntington Library, San Marino, California. See also Susan B. Anthony to Jessie Anthony, August 1, 1896, Susan B. Anthony Memorial Collection, Huntington Library.

15. *Union Signal,* May 17, 1888; June 21, 1888; June 28, 1888; and September 13, 1888. Stanton et al., *History of Woman Suffrage* 4:19.

16. Judith Ellen Foster to Benjamin Harrison, July 19, 1888, Benjamin Harrison Papers, Library of Congress.

17. Judith Ellen Foster to James Clarkson, n.d. [Wednesday, 8th], James Clarkson Papers, Library of Congress.

18. Michael McGerr, *The Decline of Popular Politics,* 80–81.

19. It was also known as the Woman's Republican Association of the United States. The first secretary was Mrs. Thomas Chace, of Rhode Island.

20. J. E. Foster, "Republican Party and Temperance, Speech at Roseland Park, Woodstock, Connecticut, September 5, 1888," copy of what was probably a campaign leaflet, Main Reading Room, New York Public Library; *Union Signal,* 4 October 1888.

21. *New York Times,* March 8, 1891; *Chicago Times,* June 28, 1890.

22. Judith Ellen Foster to Elijah W. Halford, secretary to Benjamin Harrison, May 30, 1889, and undated notation by Halford, in the "President's Private Files," n.d., Benjamin Harrison Papers, Library of Congress. The issues of the *Congressional Directory* for 1889–93 and 1898–1906 list Elijah Foster appointments. In 1900 he became an assistant attorney in the Department of Justice.

23. J. E. Foster to Benjamin Harrison, December 24, 1888; January 1, 1889; and May 30, 1889, Benjamin Harrison Papers, Library of Congress.

24. John Porter to Judith Ellen Foster, July 1, 1898, William McKinley Papers, Library of Congress, reel 30.

25. Theodore Roosevelt to Judith Ellen Foster, June 25, 1907, Theodore Roosevelt Papers, Library of Congress, reel 346.

26. Judith Ellen Foster to Mr. Brigham, September 18, 1891, State Historical Society of Iowa, Des Moines, Iowa.

27. Judith Ellen Foster to Warner Miller, June 6, 1892. Reprinted in Francis Curtis, *The Republican Party,* (New York: G. P. Putnam's Sons, 1904) 251–52.

28. "Republican Women: Please Take Notice," Woman's Republican Association of the United States, flyer, 1892, Sophia Smith Collection, Smith College, Northampton, Massachusetts.

29. Judith Ellen Foster to Benjamin Harrison, September 6, 1892, Benjamin Harrison Papers, Library of Congress.

30. Judith Ellen Foster to Mrs. Callanan, August 17, 1893, State Historical Society of Iowa, Des Moines, Iowa.

31. On the recruitment of African American women into the party, see *New York Tribune,* September 27, 1892, and October 3, 1892; *New York Times,* November 8, 1892, and October 5, 1895.

32. Joseph G. Brown, *History of Equal Suffrage in Colorado,* 30; *Woman's Tribune,* December 28, 1895, and June 29, 1907.

33. James Clarkson, "How Women Voted in Colorado," *Woman Suffrage Leaflet* 6 (6) (December 1894), from an article published in *Clarkson's Iowa State Register,* November 16, 1894, James Clarkson Papers, Library of Congress.

34. Helen Varick Boswell, "Political Episodes," *The Woman Republican* 12 (19) (March 1935).

35. Helen Varick Boswell, "Political Episodes," *The Woman Republican* 12 (21) (May 1935).

36. Judith Ellen Foster to Ida Husted Harper, July 14, 1900, Ida Husted Harper Papers, Huntington Library, San Marino, California, box 3.

37. Judith Ellen Foster, "Woman's Political Evolution," *North American Review* 65 (1897); 600–609.

38. *Woman's Journal,* February 21, 1903, and Stanton et al., *History of Woman Suffrage,* vol. 4.

39. *New York Times,* August 11, 1912.

CHAPTER TWO

GENDER, CLASS, AND THE TRANSFORMATION OF ELECTORAL CAMPAIGNS IN THE GILDED AGE

REBECCA EDWARDS

During the presidential campaign of 1888, the WCTU's *Union Signal* featured the fictional account of Maria, a woman who began to follow politics and insisted on attending campaign meetings with her husband, John. Maria subscribed to the antiliquor goals of the Woman's Christian Temperance Union, and John was less than thrilled about her new activities. As Maria listened attentively to a speech, John "sat in stolid indifference, feeling that the fun had mostly gone out of politics." His public demeanor changed, and he sat frowning at the thought that on his way home he could not "stop at the free-lunch counter for a sandwich and a glass of beer." Grudgingly he deferred to his wife's wishes and voted for prohibition.[1]

Historians have recently suggested that some middle-class women, entering politics during the Gilded Age, used gendered arguments to bring attention to economic inequalities. Kathryn Kish Sklar, in particular, argues that "the novelty of women's activism after 1880 lay in its scale and in its capacity to implement class-bridging goals."[2] While this capacity was central to the work of socialists like Florence Kelley, much larger numbers of middle-class women joined politics as ardent Prohibitionists and Republicans. They relied on their position as "ladies" to claim a place in politics, and their work was part of a middle-class movement to regain control of the electoral process.

Nineteenth-century political culture had thrived on liquor, giant parades, and boisterous male recreation. By the 1890s elite men and women together issued a call for "purer elections" and more respectable behavior, through self-control for those who were willing, and by changes in the law for the recalcitrant.[3] Disapproving of men like John—especially among the working

THE 16 TO 1 BARGAIN COUNTER OF THE (BRYAN) FUTURE.

Shopping as it will be in the good times of high prices and cheap
silver dollars.

*2. This cartoon opposing Democrats' "free silver" plank, adopted by the convention that nominated William Jennings Bryan for president, emphasizes women's roles as consumers (*Review of Reviews, *November 1896, p. 541).*

class—Prohibitionists and Republicans sought to purge the "fun" from political campaigns. This effort was, in part, an attack on male privilege. It was also antagonistic to working-class traditions. In movements to reform electoral campaigns, the gender identities of women served to reinforce, rather than bridge, class differences.

Women had played public roles in elections since before the Civil War, and in the postwar decades they participated in rallies and even party conventions alongside men. Competition between the major parties became close and intense after 1874; the uncertain outcome of national campaigns increased men's willingness to accept women's aid, as did the appearance of new third parties that welcomed all volunteers. The Prohibition Party, revived in 1881 through the efforts of WCTU leaders, offered a particularly strong model for women's participation. Union President Frances Willard was a key strategist in the party's highest councils. Scores of women served as delegates to Prohibition conventions, and the party hired female campaign lecturers and in some areas nominated women for local office. Willard's campaign speeches circulated nationwide.[4]

Prohibition was not, of course, the sole issue of interest to women. In the South most Black women had been ardent supporters of Reconstruction. As southern Republicans lost ground, thousands of White women attended counterrallies to support Democrats who called for "White supremacy." By the early 1890s, western women played prominent roles in the People's Party; former labor organizers such as Mary Lease, of Kansas, and Eva Valesh, of Minnesota, were celebrated stump speakers until Populism's demise. Responding to third-party threats, Republican leaders commissioned Judith Ellen Foster to form a network of Republican women's clubs in 1888. Stumping from Boston to Colorado, Foster declared it women's moral duty to support the GOP. By 1910 the Woman's National Republican Association claimed one thousand local chapters around the nation.[5]

The Prohibition Party and Foster's WNRA were the broadest, most sustained efforts to involve women in electoral politics during the Gilded Age. Both groups based their arguments on domestic ideology; both emphasized women's special obligations as wives and mothers. Neither used this "maternalism" as a stand-in for working-class concerns. Rather through party Prohibitionism and the WNRA, thousands of women worked to assert middle-class control over elections. While differing in their views on women's rights, both organizations represented alliances of middle-class women and men, who together attacked the political culture of working-class men.

This agenda was manifest in the rhetoric of each party. Denouncing abusive husbands and fathers, Prohibitionists directed their ire largely toward the working class. Their portraits of alcoholism and domestic violence were often tinged with ethnic hostility toward Irish and German immigrants, and in the South toward Blacks. Antiliquor laws, the party argued, would "protect American homes" from saloons and their ultimate product, male irresponsibility. Republicans also sought, by different means, to encourage proper gender relations in working-class households. For WNRA spokeswomen—as for their party's male leaders—the overriding issue of the 1880s and 1890s was maintenance of high import tariffs. Republicans argued that the tariff raised men's wages, spared wives and daughters the necessity of wage labor, and thus offered "protection to the home." The overlapping rhetoric of "home protection" was not coincidental. Frances Willard, a former Republican, borrowed the term from tariff advocates; Foster, a former WCTU leader, used the antiliquor phrase for years before she founded the WNRA.[6]

I have elsewhere explored in more detail the implications of these highly gendered party ideologies.[7] Women in both camps worked on behalf of American womanhood, but high tariffs and antiliquor laws served the interests of particular classes—notably prosperous, native-born Protestants. Of interest here are the ways that women from this social stratum, entering politics to assert their goals in cooperation with men, helped change the practice of electoral campaigns. Not only through their beliefs but through increasing prominence at campaign meetings and the polls, women helped justify new arguments for curbing the electoral excesses of "ruffians" and "brawlers."

WCTU members were among the first middle-class women to station themselves at the polls to hand out literature and serve lunches. They met resistance in the 1880s, but by the following decade, outside the South, women's freedom to appear at the polls was widely accepted by men. Republicans, the party of the growing urban middle class, acknowledged the change more readily than did Democrats, and male GOP leaders began to recruit women in response to the Prohibitionist challenge. Like the WCTU, Republican women began to set up election-day lunch counters offering hot suppers, coffee, and campaign pamphlets rather than the traditional beer. By 1895 Republican women supervised ten election-day lunchrooms near various polls in New York City.[8]

These middle-class women entered politics as "ladies," often with the expressed purpose of "elevating" politics to a higher plane. As such their presence at campaign events brought change. Music was one of the first markers of the transition. Prohibitionists sang hymns at their conventions, ratifying nominations with "Blessed Be the Tie." Republicans, seldom so overtly evangelical, developed other customs. Female or mixed glee clubs supplanted brass bands at GOP meetings, offering such family favorites as "Home, Sweet Home." Some rallies began to feature piano or vocal recitals. When the Woman's Republican Campaign Quartette toured New York State in 1896, a newspaper reported that their music was "a decided innovation at the average mass-meeting, [being] selected almost entirely from the works of the most eminent composers—as, for instance, Beethoven, Mendelssohn, Neidlinger, and Hawley." Such performances were a startling contrast to the "hurrah" tunes of previous campaigns.[9]

The definition of political *receptions* also changed in the 1890s. Journalists had long used the term to describe any sort of greeting for a candidate or speaker. Some receptions had been rowdy celebrations at courthouses or railroad depots; at others local party loyalists enjoyed refined conversation and light refreshments. The latter definition gradually won out, with women leading the way. In 1896 the Women's Sound Money League and Women's Silver League held elegant receptions in Boston and Chicago. The Republican Women's League of Trinidad, Colorado, held an afternoon reception that was, according to a friendly newspaper, the hit of the political season. "The stage was pleasantly interspersed with selections by Nigro's orchestra and the colored trio," ran the report. "After the speaking the whole audience was made the guests of the Women's League and for an hour enjoyed refreshments, dancing, and social amenities." A Denver paper, also reporting on a GOP women's meeting, referred to the "brilliancy" of the occasion, describing the women's dresses and jewelry as well as the "trailing vines of clematis" that decorated the hall. In such accounts campaign journalists borrowed the conventions of the society page.[10]

Less accustomed than men to giving public addresses, some female campaign speakers brought notes with them to the podium, and the "political essay" became a recognized style of campaign address. Elizabeth Strong Worthington, an Oregon Republican, offered lectures instead of conventional speeches, interspersing her remarks with "a series of stereopticon views." In 1896 a Republican paper in Minnesota reported approvingly on events in Utah, where women had won full suffrage:

> The part which women voters are taking in the campaign in Utah has brought about a number of innovations. Especially is this true as regards the usual "rally" . . . [Previous] meetings have been confined to speeches by men, music from a brass band, preceded perhaps by a parade. Now the program includes speeches by men and women, selections by an orchestra, a recitation or two (comic pieces preferred), and the whole topped off by a ball. The ball has proved a great drawing card. . . . The new scheme has worked so admirably that the close of the campaign threatens to be a series of balls, with speeches as a mere incident of the evening.[11]

By reinterpreting old forms, middle-class women invented new events in the political sphere, drawing on models from their benevolent activities. One ladies' Republican club in Indiana raised money for their parade uniforms by hosting a "New England social." Women's Republican clubs in Colorado held numerous political tea parties. Lest afternoon tea be dismissed as too frivolous for politics, the speaker at a Denver gathering reminded her audience of a precedent, the Boston Tea Party of 1773.[12]

Middle-class men gradually accepted the presence of women as campaign allies and even voters. During the late 1880s and 1890s a number of states passed partial woman suffrage laws, usually for school suffrage. The trend offered women very limited political power, but it nonetheless brought them to the ballot box. By 1890 women held some form of suffrage in states and territories containing about 35 percent of the U.S. population. Women usually voted on the same days and in the same locations as men, depositing their truncated ballots in separate boxes.[13]

In some places these developments changed the polls' appearance and even location. After an Iowa campaign, WCTU leader Frances Willard wrote that in many towns Prohibitionist women had "decorated the city hall, engine houses, and other places where the ballot-box was set with pictures, mottoes, evergreens, and flowers." When Anna Howard Shaw visited Colorado in 1894, a year after the state adopted full woman suffrage, she remarked on the location of polls: "many of them in the sitting rooms or parlors of houses; not one in a saloon." Mary Bradford of Denver reported that she took her young daughter with her to vote, and that "while I was casting my vote the men gave my little one a flower. They always decorate the polling-places with flowers now." When Illinois granted women school suffrage, a diligent Republican in Chicago brought an armload of roses to his precinct headquarters and gave one to each woman who registered.[14]

Once female party organizers and voters occupied the polls, nonpartisan women's groups followed suit. In small towns from New York to Utah, church groups began to advertise election day suppers. These dinners first appeared in Indiana and Illinois during the 1880s, then spread to other parts of the Midwest, West, and Northeast. By all accounts they were popular: a ladies' aid society in Sundance, Wyoming, sold enough twenty-five-cent dinners to raise one hundred dollars for their church.[15] Once politically active women had appeared at the polls, families and churches began to occupy that public space.

At the polls women's appearance served as a catalyst for new rules, because their presence forced men to choose sides. When WCTU members were spat upon, hung in effigy, or otherwise rudely treated by men, other male bystanders rushed to the ladies' defense, even if they disagreed with their goals. When Omaha women joined a Prohibitionist parade, a spectator remarked that "there is no lady in that procession." "You must take that back," his neighbor responded. "My wife is there." An observer noted that "it was taken back forthwith." Male relatives, friends, and partisan allies played a key role in enforcing respectful behavior.[16]

Numerous witnesses observed that women's presence discouraged men from drinking, gambling, cursing, and fighting near the polls. A participant in Nebraska school elections remarked that women's presence "added a better feature to the election: I never saw a congregation at church more civil, and some of the men remarked that the men were not so rude." An Idaho lawyer declared that "the very presence of the ladies at the polls seemed to entirely eliminate many of the objectionable features of former elections." When female voters began to register in Illinois during the 1894 campaign, the *Chicago Tribune* observed that men stopped smoking and removed their hats.[17]

Some men, however, continued to reject middle-class standards of Protestant sobriety and self-control. Thus in the 1890s many states enforced new standards of male behavior through purity-of-election laws. Designed to end bribery and "clean up" politics, these statutes closed saloons on election day and often barred candidates from buying drinks for anyone during the campaign. Some laws required polls to close earlier in the evening; others outlawed bonfires and "excessive noise." Significantly Kansas passed a pure-elections law and a woman's municipal suffrage law in the same year. Utah cleaned up its elections four years after women won full suffrage. When New York passed a similar law in 1890, suffragist Lillie Devereux Blake wrote that ladies could feel safe appearing in public on election day. After touring its wards, she reported that "nowhere did I see any crowds of men, any disorder, or any drunkenness."[18]

Such changes were most striking in states where women won full suffrage, but they occurred to a lesser extent wherever women were politically active. Men's responses presupposed that the women entering politics were middle-class ladies, not women who were familiar with the inside of a saloon or wage-earning women who had always walked through rowdy streets in order to get to their jobs. A lady was a woman of sensitivity who needed protection from vulgar behavior. She was also a social arbiter who could affect a man's reputation if she saw him acting in an ungentlemanly way. These women exercised power at the polls because men perceived them as deserving of chivalry and as a "moral element" whose presence in the campaign served class and party interests. Evangelical and middle-class women and men reinforced each other's support for election-day temperance and decorum.

A related change in these years was widespread adoption of the Australian ballot, advocated by many young reformers. Prior to 1889 each party had printed its own ballots and circulated thousands. Aside from making ballot-stuffing temptingly easy, the system led to other abuses. Illiterate voters had to beware of fraudulent ballots: a favorite trick of southern Democrats was to print copies of their own ticket in Republican colors. Kentucky and Massachusetts were the first states to experiment with Australian ballots, in which candidates' names appeared on a single form. By the end of the 1890s, most states adopted the model. Observers agreed that it made voting more "fair and orderly."[19]

Adoption of the Australian ballot was not directly related to women's presence in politics, but there were intriguing connections. Young men who advocated the "Australian system" often supported limited woman suffrage as well. Old-fashioned politicians expressed parallel fears about Australian ballots and woman suffrage: both innovations would undermine party loyalty and lead to unpredictable ticket-splitting. Australian tickets made it easier for either male or female "scratchers" to choose candidates from different tickets without wrangling over multiple pieces of paper. Some suffragists supported the reform for this very reason. "Woman suffrage is coming," declared one southern judge, "but it is not likely to precede the Australian ballot or some other civilizing reform of our election laws. Under the Australian system, a woman can vote with as much modesty as she can go shopping or attend a charity meeting."[20]

A number of states adopted Australian ballots soon after they granted school suffrage to women. Colorado first experimented with the new system in school elections of the 1880s, which included women, before adopting it for men's national tickets. Voter education drives frequently accompanied the "Australian reform." From Maine to Utah local civic organizations sponsored "voting schools" for citizens, instructing them how to mark the ballots. These schools included many women who had partial suffrage and some who did not. An election school at California's San Bernardino County Fair, for instance, featured a mock voting booth for the edification of citizens. Though women did not have any form of suffrage, a local newspaper announced that on the last day of the fair, "ladies will be given a chance to demonstrate their ability to handle the ballot." Two years later a group of middle-class women in the same county organized a convention and endorsed a "women's ticket" made up of Prohibitionists, Populists, and the odd Republican.[21] The new Australian system, and perhaps women's experience in casting mock ballots, must have encouraged them to try this strategy.

Toward the end of the 1890s voter turnout in the United States began to drop markedly, and historians have long debated whether Australian ballots, pure-election laws, and other reforms contributed to the decline. Two other factors were certainly more important. In the South poll taxes, literacy tests, and other laws designed to disfranchise Black men proved overwhelmingly effective. And across the nation predictable elections reduced the significance of party loyalty. President William McKinley presided over a major economic recovery between 1897 and 1901; under his successor, Theodore Roosevelt, the GOP sustained its national popularity, and Republicans controlled the White House and Congress until 1910. Meanwhile Democrats maintained total control in southern states. With the partisan outcome of campaigns less in question, party loyalty simply did not matter as much as it had in the past.[22]

Voter apathy was not, however, solely a result of declining competition. The whole culture of elections had changed, as middle-class Americans abandoned mass politics and transformed its laws and practices. Men could no longer expect political managers to transport them to the polls and offer free drinks. Instead voters found they had to register in advance and decipher an Australian ticket. Men who tried to hang around the polls to drink, fight, and bet on the outcome might pay the price of a fine or a night in jail. The major parties' national headquarters increasingly sent out educational pamphlets rather than stacks of dollar bills. All these reforms created "dull campaigns" with fewer attractions for male participants.[23]

These changes took place first of all because of increasing divisions among social and economic classes, especially in the expanding cities. The Democratic and Republican parties had long linked men of different classes in shared political views, but these coalitions were fragmenting. Growth of the professional class—who increasingly valued efficiency, political purity, and genteel public behavior—gave its leaders the power to influence behavior at the polls. Their new power, in turn, reduced the clout of those beneath them on the economic scale. Legislators in office were all too happy to accelerate this process and solidify their status. In the wake of electoral reforms, declining voter turnout was slight among prosperous voters but precipitous among the poor.[24]

Though new campaign customs may have helped acclimate American men to the idea of women voting, they brought women little direct or immediate power. Politics had, nonetheless, became a more domesticated space, where middle-class men and women together enjoyed refined and sober entertainments. Americans came to view voting as a responsibility to be approached gravely—no longer an excuse for drinking, fireworks, and fights. Women's first entry into electoral politics was part of this movement to "purify" campaigns and "elevate" political life, goals that had complicated gender dimensions but that also benefited the growing middle class. The partisan involvement of well-to-do native Protestant women was, in its first expression, part of a cooperative movement by middle-class women and men to "protect the home." Their ultimate goal was to enforce respectability and temperance, in the public arena of electoral campaigns as well as in domestic life.

NOTES

1. *Union Signal,* November 1, 1888.
2. Kathryn Kish Sklar, *Florence Kelly and the Nation's Work,* xv; Sklar, "The Historical Foundations of Women's Power in the Creation of the American Welfare State, 1830–1930"; Theda Skocpol, *Protecting Soldiers and Mothers,* 529.
3. Michael McGerr, *The Decline of Popular Politics;* Reynolds, *Testing Democracy.*
4. Robert J. Dinkin, *Before Equal Suffrage;* Varon, "Tippecanoe and the Ladies, Too"; Rebecca Edwards, *Angels in the Machinery;* Ruth Bordin, *Frances Willard.*

5. Elsa Barkley Brown, "Negotiating and Transforming the Public Sphere"; Edwards, *Angels in the Machinery;* Dinkin, *Before Equal Suffrage,* 94–95; Gustafson, this volume.

6. Frances E. Willard, *Glimpses of Fifty Years* (Chicago: Smith, 1889), 401.

7. Edwards, *Angels in the Machinery.*

8. Frances E. Willard, *Woman and Temperance* (Hartford, CT: Park, 1883), 403–12; *Chicago Tribune,* October 19, 1895.

9. Willard, *Glimpses of Fifty Years,* 400; *Leslie's Weekly,* October 1, 1896, 231.

10. *Trinidad News,* October 25, 1894; *Woman's Journal,* October 13, 1894, 323.

11. *Boulder* [Colorado] *Camera,* October 8, 1894; *Seattle Post-Intelligencer,* October 18, 1896; *Minneapolis Journal,* November 2, 1896.

12. *Goshen* [Indiana] *News,* October 1, 1896; *Denver Times,* October 19, 1894.

13. Suffrage information by state in Elizabeth Cady Stanton, et al., eds., *History of Woman Suffrage,* vol. 4.

14. Willard, *Woman and Temperance,* 410; undated speech by Anna Howard Shaw, Harriet Hanson Robinson Papers, Schlesinger Library, Radcliffe College, Cambridge, MA; Stanton, et al., *History of Woman Suffrage,* 4:282–83; *Chicago Tribune,* November 7, 1894.

15. *Sundance* [Wyoming] *Gazette,* November 1, 1896; other sample reports in *Columbus* [Indiana] *Republican,* November 5, 1888; and Baker, *The Moral Frameworks of Public Life,* 39.

16. Baker, *Moral Frameworks,* 56; clipping (1890), *Woman's Tribune* scrapbook, Huntington Library, San Marino, California.

17. *Woman's Tribune,* September 1884; Cynthia A. Mann, "More Testimony from Idaho," *Political Equality Series* (NAWSA) 3 (6)(September 1898); *Chicago Tribune,* October 17, 1894, p. 1; *Wood River* [Idaho] *Times,* November 8, 1898; *Pueblo* [Colorado] *Chieftain,* November 6, 1894.

18. *Woman's Journal,* November 17, 1900, p. 361, and November 8, 1890, p. 357 (for Blake's quote); Michael Lewis Goldberg, " 'An Army of Women,' " 94–114.

19. L.E. Fredman, *The Australian Ballot,* 31–39, 46–47.

20. "Hon. Walter B. Hill on Woman Suffrage," (n.d.), Woman Suffrage Papers, Georgia State Archives, Atlanta; *Los Angeles Times,* October 17, 1894; John F. Reynolds, *Testing Democracy.*

21. *Silver* [Silver Plume, CO] *Standard,* May 6, 1893; *Los Angeles Times,* October 12–13, 1892; *Chicago Tribune,* October 3, 1894; Fredman, *Australian Ballot,* 53.

22. The causes of declining turnout are hotly debated; for an overview see Paul Kleppner, *Who Voted?,* 56–82.

23. McGerr, *Decline of Popular Politics;* Morton Keller, *Affairs of State,* 522–31; Reynolds, *Testing Democracy,* 61–65, 114, 159–60; Peter H. Argersinger, *Structure, Process, and Party.*

24. Kleppner, *Who Voted?,* 64–72; I draw here on Reynolds, *Testing Democracy,* and more broadly on Robert H. Wiebe, *The Search for Order;* Baker, "The Domestication of Politics"; and McGerr, "Political Style and Women's Power."

CHAPTER THREE

REDEFINING "THE POLITICAL"
Socialist Women and Party Politics in California, 1900–1920

SHERRY J. KATZ

On June 1, 1915, Los Angeles journalist Estelle Lawton Lindsey became the first woman elected to the city council of a major metropolis in the United States. Lindsey belonged to a well-organized network of socialist women that operated as an influential political force within California's radical and woman's movements during the Progressive Era. Backed by socialists, the labor council, and women's clubs, Lindsey ran as a candidate dedicated to the empowerment and welfare of women, children, and the laboring classes. Committed to bringing the "woman's point of view . . . the humanitarian point of view" to state policymaking, Lindsey argued that the "habit" of "men holding all government positions . . . won't be broken till women get in and do their share of it." In urging other women to run for office, she suggested that "suffrage without holding office [was] like apple pie with the apples left out."[1]

Lindsey's election epitomizes the determination and pioneering efforts of a new breed of female political activists—many of them aligned with radical third parties or reform tendencies within major parties—to incorporate women into partisan and electoral politics during the Progressive Era. Although the major parties remained largely uninterested in or hostile to the active participation of women prior to the achievement of national woman suffrage, third parties proved more hospitable, and thousands of women experimented with partisan politics through the Populist, Socialist, and Progressive Parties. Both before and after women's enfranchisement in 1911, California's socialist-feminists self-consciously challenged the boundaries that separated male partisan politics from female reform through activism in the Socialist Party. Their strong commitment to women's economic independence and its central place

3. Campaign card for Estelle Lawton Lindsey (Department of Special Collections, University Research Library, University of California, Los Angeles).

in their political vision, exceptional among women reformers, contributed to their unusual determination to enter partisan politics and serve as elected policymakers.[2] As party members and candidates for elective office, they championed a reconfiguration of the party's constituency, political agenda, and methods of influence, in an effort to combine the traditions of white, middle-class women's political culture with those of male partisan politics. They sought to expand the conception of "the political" to include the equal participation of women, the incorporation of gender-specific concerns in the agendas of parties and the state, and the integration of partisanship with coalition building in social policymaking.

The activities of these partisan women shed new light on the partial convergence of gendered political cultures, and the "two track system" of public policymaking they generated, during the Progressive Era. Historians have demonstrated that as women's social welfare services began to be taken over by the state, thereby "domesticating politics" and spurring the adoption of woman suffrage, men began to supplement their partisan activism with the pressure group politics women had long employed.[3] The experiences of Lindsey and her comrades suggest that partisan women played important roles in this process through their participation in parties and campaigns for office.[4]

This essay explores socialist women's campaigns for public office from 1912 to 1917 as a window into the process of women's incorporation into partisan politics. But first I provide a brief portrait of their social backgrounds and trace their political activism through the 1911 suffrage victory. During the 1890s, several generations of radical women, active in suffrage and temperance crusades, found in the "Cooperative Commonwealth" the basis for an egalitarian society guaranteeing women's freedom. These women were largely native-born and Protestant, fairly well educated, with backgrounds in professional and clerical occupations, and able to attain stable working-class or middle-class status. Although they shared the relatively privileged social locations of their mainstream colleagues in the woman's movement, socialist-feminists developed deep and life-changing identifications with the laboring classes and especially with wage-earning women. They insisted that gender equality required women's economic independence achieved through wage labor and state support for childrearing. Nurtured by a political climate congenial to radical proposals for ameliorating the economic inequalities engendered by California's speedy capitalist development and by a social context in which radicals shared the native-born and Northern European backgrounds of the majority of the state's political activists, they created a vigorous socialist women's movement. After the turn of the century, local activists built a network of independent socialist women's clubs, under the umbrella of the Woman's Socialist Union of California (1902–11) and worked within both the male-dominated socialist movement and the mainstream woman's movement. An effective political strategy that combined autonomy with integration helped them to achieve enormous influence in left-wing communities, feminist organizations, and social reform coalitions.[5]

From 1902 to 1911, the WSU represented the interests of socialist-feminists and enabled them to assert an independent-minded, militant, and well-organized presence within the Socialist Party. WSU leaders believed that one of their first tasks was to legitimize women's involvement in the party by demonstrating that women possessed the same capacities for partisan activism as did men. They emerged as the most prominent women in the party apparatus by serving in local and state leadership positions, writing for the party press, and participating in electoral campaigns. Socialist-feminists developed a distinctive program to recruit women and thereby enlarge and reconfigure the party's base. This program utilized the gender-specific styles and concerns of women's political culture to educate women in socialism and provide political training. They also attempted to expand the party's class-oriented agenda to include the feminist and "maternalist" issues central to their political vision, especially women's enfranchisement. Their relentless campaign to convince the party to participate actively in the struggle for woman suffrage finally paid off in 1911, when the party pledged itself to the fight just as victory seemed near. Meanwhile WSU activists established an influential left-wing constituency within the state's suffrage coalition that expanded the movement's base among the working class, devised new arguments linking economic and political emancipation, and introduced modern methods of "militant" agitation.[6]

From the first, WSU leaders demanded respect for women and their political initiatives. In 1903 they initiated a successful referendum that denounced the suggestion of a former officer that women be excluded from the party because they lacked, by nature or socialization, the "manly" qualities necessary to run a revolutionary political organization. While some of their male comrades viewed women's educational strategies and feminist agenda as positive additions, others contested the incorporation of women and their political traditions as threats to the party's identity as a masculine political institution. Socialist-feminists developed an independent style of partisanship that made loyalty to party contingent on support for women and their concerns.[7]

Socialist women responded to the victory of the state's suffrage amendment in 1911 with great optimism toward expanding their political influence within the party, the woman's movement, reform coalitions, and public policymaking. The Socialist Party's rising popularity, combined with competition from the state's progressives, prompted them to dissolve the WSU in favor of a party woman's committee, but their traditions of independent activism continued. As newly enfranchised voters, they embarked on a more ambitious effort to reshape their party's priorities in keeping with their political vision and activist traditions.[8]

After enfranchisement one of the principal ways Socialist women expanded the boundaries of the party, and partisan politics more generally, was through their campaigns for elective office. This essay will focus on electoral campaigns in Los Angeles County, where one-quarter to one-third of all state party members resided and where women constituted an unprecedented 30 to 42 percent of the membership from 1911 through 1914. Los Angeles was also a center of the "reformist" wing of the party, a stronghold of the WSU, and the region in which female activists achieved the greatest influence both before and after 1911.[9]

The Los Angeles party had run women for the Board of Education since 1902; after 1911 women ran for many other state and local positions, including City Council and State Assembly. Two women ran for State Assembly in 1912 and 1914, including Estelle Lawton Lindsey, who was narrowly defeated in 1914 but rebounded to win her City Council bid in 1915. In 1913 five women ran on a municipal slate of twenty, including Frances Nacke Noel and Mila Tupper

Maynard, for City Council, and Emma J. Wolfe for the Board of Education. All of these candidates represented the socialist-feminist constituency within the party and belonged to the left-wing network within the woman's movement. Noel, a German immigrant, was by 1908 a prominent clubwoman, suffragist, and the most influential woman in the county's labor movement. Maynard, a former minister and journalist, had been active in the suffrage movement during the 1890s and had returned to Los Angeles in 1911 to rejoin the suffrage campaign and local woman's clubs. Wolfe, a former nurse, dedicated herself to child welfare after her only daughter died in 1906; by 1912 she was the leader of the Child Labor Department of the California Congress of Mothers.[10]

These female candidates proudly asserted their qualifications for elective office as both the intellectual and political equals of men and as a group possessed of unique qualities central to a genuinely humanitarian society, including commitments to social welfare, nurturance, and morality.[11] The need for such affirmations of women's legitimacy as political actors indicated that Socialist women were, after ten years of party activism, still working to challenge "manliness" as the essential quality of "stern determined" party members. Fighting the stereotypes of women as incompetent in political affairs, "light-headed" thinkers prone to follow "sentimental humbugs," and focused on petty reforms rather than revolution, they simultaneously promoted women's maternalism.[12]

During their campaigns for City Council in 1913, Mila Tupper Maynard and Frances Nacke Noel issued a joint statement that spoke to men's apprehension of voting for women who might prove to be "impractical 'figureheads' " by emphasizing both the human competency and the special skills and concerns women possessed. Maynard and Noel stated emphatically that they were nominated for office because they were "Socialists of long established conviction" and "individuals believed to be capable of doing the work required and not merely because of [their] sex." They also discussed at length "why [they] believe[d] that women as women would be particularly valuable members of the Council." Women, they argued, had long taken the initiative in "progressive city affairs" and possessed the social housekeeping skills, common sense, and business ability to successfully manage their municipality.[13]

These female candidates certainly ran as representatives of the working class and emphasized the economic issues that remained central to the party, including support for organized labor, municipal ownership of public utilities and transportation, and eventual state control of the means of production.[14] But they emphasized the need to elect women to office as representatives of their sex, in order to further gender equality and to ensure that women's concerns would find representation and serious consideration in policymaking bodies. While Noel and Maynard established that they sought election as Socialists first and as representatives of "woman's distinctive interests" second, they appealed specifically to women voters, stressing their commitment to representing the interests of "all women of civic spirit" and especially of working-class women who lacked time to devote to municipal affairs. In her bid for State Assembly in 1914, Lindsey maintained that the election of women to office was an important consequence of woman suffrage and a measure of female political equality, for "as 50 per cent of the voters are women, there should be women in the legislature to represent the sex." All of these candidates argued that only by "admit[ting] women to a share in the government" would the needs of women and children be addressed and humanitarian legislation be passed.[15]

Socialist women strongly underscored a number of maternalist and feminist goals in their campaigns. These issues were all ones they simultaneously championed as activists in the woman's movement during the postsuffrage period: mothers' pensions, protective labor legislation, antiprostitution measures, and safe public amusements.[16] As a left wing of both the woman's movement and broader social reform coalitions, they advocated reforms they believed would prove "underminingly ameliorative," able to empower women and/or the working class and prefigure a socialist-feminist state. They became the leading proponents of labor legislation and unionization, the most outspoken advocates of a redistributive social welfare state, and the earliest supporters of birth control. In fact socialist women's influence on the legislative proposals advocated by mainstream women's groups helps explain why California was at the forefront of social welfare legislation for women during the Progressive Era. Socialist women's activism appears to offer an important reason why California devised better protection for women workers than most other states and debated more comprehensive and less oppressive mothers' pension programs than were considered elsewhere.[17]

The platform on which Socialist women campaigned not only challenged the legislative priorities of their party but also the ways in which their male comrades conceptualized the state and its functions. Socialist women insisted that the humanitarian concerns traditionally championed by women should be vitally important to all citizens and should become a major component of social provisions guaranteed by the state. Mila Tupper Maynard proposed that the significance of all public issues lay in their bearing on private lives and personal happiness. "After all, what are the harbor and municipal ownership and all that but efforts to enable the people in the homes to live fuller, better lives and to be better citizens?" Maynard argued that the social concerns of women, viewed as "side issues" by most men, were as significant to society as the traditional issues of male-dominated public life. Men had to realize, as did women, that the "function[s] of government" included providing for the moral, physical, and economic well-being of the nation's youths and children.[18]

In running as representatives of the woman's movement, organized labor, and the Socialist Party, these female candidates encouraged the combining of male and female political strategies: partisan loyalty and pressure group–based coalition politics. In Lindsey's 1914 bid for the Assembly, organizational support came from the party's campaign committee and a nonpartisan, ad hoc organization of local clubwomen. Always keen on bringing together what they considered the two great social movements of their day, the feminist movement and the labor/socialist movement, radical women constructed campaigns that attempted to further that goal. They believed that their multiple identities and commitments, their unique positioning between the feminist and socialist movements, and their long history of operating as a distinct constituency within larger political formations made them skillful coalition-builders in the service of social reform and eventual social revolution.[19]

Although they were partisan women, they sought to transcend the boundaries of class, ideology, and party affiliation in political activism. More devoted to socialist-feminism than the party itself, they occasionally bolted from the party if they felt partisan constraints bound them too tightly. Ironically, when Estelle Lawton Lindsey finally won election in 1915, she did so as an independent. Refusing to be bound by party discipline in matters related to her service on the City Council, she nevertheless captured the support of the socialist rank and file as well as of the labor and woman's movements. Frances Noel and Emma Wolfe also resigned from the party, in defiance of a stipulation that members never vote for candidates from other parties. Both believed that in some cases casting votes for progressives who had a chance of victory was the best way to further their political goals. Noel went on to serve on progressive Governor Hiram Johnson's Social Insurance Commission, which drafted a universal health coverage initiative defeated by the state's voters in 1918.[20]

As an independent political force within the party, Socialist women certainly enlarged debate about the appropriate political concerns and strategies for a left-wing political organization. Still the party seemed to be operating on two gendered tracks in the postsuffrage period. Many of the feminist and maternalist issues Socialist women championed were incorporated into party planks at election time. Although the public ownership and control of utilities dominated the 1913 municipal campaign, the party repeatedly pledged its commitment to improving the lives of wage-earning women, curbing child labor, and combating prostitution. At the opening meeting of the campaign, mayoral candidate Job Harriman demanded the election of women to public office, on the grounds that their "different psychology" would "put mother-love into our laws," making them "more humane, less brutal."[21]

But such actions appeared to have been motivated more by the initiatives undertaken by Socialist women and a desire to capture the allegiance of newly enfranchised female voters, rather than by a genuine shift in priorities. The party's three representatives in the State Assembly from 1912 to 1916, all from Los Angeles County, focused primarily on the passage of universal labor bills, measures to democratize voting and jury service, and on the defeat of proposals designed to extend nonpartisan elections, which eliminated party affiliations from the ballot and consequently put third-party candidates at a disadvantage. Clearly gender-specific reforms continued to be secondary to measures men regarded as more fundamental to working-class empowerment and economic transformation.[22]

In contrast Lindsey focused on measures intended to empower and protect women as well as the "great working masses of society" during her term on the City Council. She also self-consciously attempted to bring her fellow council members "around to the woman's point of view." As a leader of three social welfare committees, she championed public health measures, pressed for enforcement of the state's antiprostitution law, fought for greater city services for impoverished women, and secured the appointment of several female deputies assigned to investigate crimes against women and children. Along with council member Fred C. Wheeler, a prominent labor leader who had also resigned from the party over issues of party discipline, Lindsey worked toward improvements in the wages and working conditions of municipal employees and fought the Municipal Employment Bureau's attempt to furnish strikebreakers to private employers.[23]

While socialist men certainly participated in the labor movement and occasionally collaborated with middle-class progressives in advancing social reform, their engagement with pressure group, coalition politics tended to be circumscribed and limited. For men coalition building carried negative connotations associated with the "betrayal" of party purity or class interests. In 1915, for example, the two male party members elected to the State Assembly refused to caucus with progressives and introduced their own bills rather than unite with others in drafting like-minded proposals. Socialist women, by contrast, viewed themselves as loyal socialists even as they worked closely with nonsocialists, and they regarded coalition building as one of the most useful strategies for social change. After their breaks with the party, both Lindsey and Noel continued their vigorous participation in the mainstream woman's movement, as part of the left-wing network dedicated to expanding the political analysis and reform proposals of organized womanhood. Interestingly many of the men who more freely crossed the boundaries of class and party, such as Job Harriman and Fred Wheeler, either played leadership roles in organized labor or possessed particularly close ties to socialist-feminists and other women reformers.[24]

As partisan activists and candidates for office, socialist women participated in redefining "the political" in Progressive Era California. Through their campaigns for office, they attempted to integrate women, gender-specific concerns, and the concept of a "maternal" welfare state into partisan politics. As political candidates they also sought to build bridges between partisan electoral activity and the pressure group strategies of organized womanhood. Although their efforts to transform partisan politics through the Socialist Party were cut short by the onset of World War I and the subsequent decline of the organization, their activism suggests the significance of women's experimentations in partisan politics for the partial convergence of gendered political cultures in the early twentieth century.

NOTES

1. Letter from Estelle Lawton Lindsey, Los Angeles *Citizen*, March 30, 1917; Lindsey quoted in Bertha H. Smith, "Interesting Westerners," *Sunset* (January 1916): 28.

2. I want to thank Glenna Matthews for suggesting this connection to me. She discusses the importance of women's growing labor force participation to women politicians in the post–World War II period in Witt, Paget, and Matthews, *Running as a Woman*, chap. 2.

3. Chafe, "Women's History and Political History: Some Thoughts on Progressivism and the New Deal," 103; Baker, "The Domestication of Politics," 639–44.

4. The efforts of California socialist-feminists to incorporate women and their political culture into partisan politics prefigured a process that emerged on a much broader scale, and within the major parties, after 1920. While political parties adopted some of women's concerns and techniques, they also set new boundaries for women's participation and circumscribed women's power into the 1970s. For discussions of both the resiliency of gendered political traditions and the process of women's incorporation into partisan and electoral politics, see Cott, *The Grounding of Modern Feminism*, esp. chap. 3; Tilly and Gurin, *Women, Politics, and Change;* Witt, Paget, and Matthews, *Running as a Woman;* and Andersen, *After Suffrage.*

5. Katz, "Dual Commitments."

6. Ibid., chaps. 3–4; Katz, "A Politics of Coalition." I use *maternalism* to encompass proposals based on the valuation of women's socially constructed capacities for care, nurturance, and morality. See Koven and Michel, "Mother Worlds," 4.

7. Katz, "Dual Commitments," chap. 3.

8. Ibid., chaps. 5–6.

9. Ibid., 179–203, 418.

10. Ibid., chaps. 3–5.

11. Social-constructionists completely free of essentialist thinking were rare in this period.

WSU activists tended to argue for the social construction of gendered identities and characteristics, but they sometimes attributed women's special concerns to "natural" maternal functions.

12. For the stereotypes see Thomas Bersford, *Tactics and Strategy: Economic and Political* (San Francisco: Press of Eastman & Mitchell, 1903), 55–56.

13. Frances Noel and Mila Tupper Maynard, "Women Tell What They Will Do If Put in Council," *California Social-Democrat*, April 26, 1913.

14. "Socialist Women Appeal to Women," *Los Angeles Record*, May 5, 1913.

15. Noel and Maynard, "Women Tell"; Estelle Lawton Lindsey, in "Socialist Nominees for the Assembly See Victory Ahead," *Los Angeles Record*, October 27, 1914; Mila Tupper Maynard, in Estelle Lawton Lindsey, "City Should Provide Joys of Life and Save Girls from Preying Men," *Los Angeles Record*, April 23, 1913.

16. Lindsey, in "Socialist Nominees"; "Mrs. Lindsey Is Endorsed by Labor Council," *Los Angeles Record*, October 5, 1914; Noel and Maynard, "Women Tell"; Maynard, in Lindsey, "City Should Provide."

17. Sara [Bard Field] to [Charles Erskine Scott Wood], April 8, 1913, box 270, Charles Erskine Scott Wood Collection, Huntington Library, San Marino, CA; Katz, "Dual Commitments," chaps. 6–8; Katz, "Socialist Women and Progressive Reform."

18. Maynard, in Lindsey, "City Should Provide."

19. Estelle Lawton Lindsey campaign card, [1914]; Frances Noel, "Trade Union Movement Helps to Americanize," [Los Angeles *Citizen?*], [1916]; and "Mrs. Noel's Report on Women's Clubs," n.p., [1914], Knox Mellon Collection [a collection of Frances Nacke Noel materials held privately by historian Knox Mellon; hereafter cited as Mellon Coll.].

20. Shaffer, "Radicalism in California," 182–83; "Socialists Put Mrs. Lindsey Out of Party," *Los Angeles Examiner*, March 20, 1915, box 527, Socialist Party of America Papers, Duke University; clipping on Noel's resignation, [Los Angeles] *Citizen*, n.d., Mellon Coll.; Emma J. Wolfe, "Women and Politics," *Western Comrade* 4 (November 1916): 19. For Noel's stint on the Social Insurance Commission, see Katz, "Dual Commitments," 561 n. 77.

21. T. W. Williams, "An Open Letter to the Women Voters of Los Angeles," *California Social-Democrat*, May 24, 1913; Harriman, quoted in Arthur R. Andre, "Big Auditorium Rally Opens Socialist Campaign," *California Social-Democrat*, April 19, 1913.

22. Shaffer, "A History of the Socialist Party of California," 124, 129–37, 150–51.

23. Zoe Hartman, "A City Mother," *Independent* 88 (November 27, 1916): 356; Smith, "Interesting Westerners," 28; [Los Angeles] *Citizen*, July 9, September 10, and December 3, 1915; September 3 and December 22, 1916; March 30 and April 20, 1917; City Council Minute Books: 101: 218, Los Angeles City Council Archives, Los Angeles.

24. Shaffer, "History of the Socialist Party," 132–40; Katz, "Dual Commitments," chaps. 4, 6–8, and conclusion; Sitton, "John Randolph Haynes," 21–23.

CHAPTER FOUR

UNSEEN INFLUENCE
Lucretia Blankenburg and the Rise of Philadelphia
Reform Politics in 1911

DREW E. VANDECREEK

In April of 1917 Lucretia Blankenburg looked back at her long career as one of Philadelphia's preeminent reformers, a career that had culminated with her husband Rudolph's 1911 election as mayor of Philadelphia. On this day, she recalled, "Mr. Blankenburg and I consecrated ourselves to his service for the city. . . . I think we proved the city could be run on business principles." "It was characteristic of Mrs. Blankenburg that she said 'we,'" the Philadelphia *Evening Bulletin's* reporter noted, "for in every activity of her husband's she has kept pace with some interest of her own."[1] Mrs. Blankenburg's reference to her husband's political service reflected gender roles that denied women a place in public life. In the last decades of the nineteenth century, Rudolph Blankenburg led Philadelphia's male reformers in the electoral realm, while his wife became a leading clubwoman. But a close examination of Lucretia Blankenburg's life reveals how she and many other Philadelphia women more than kept pace with male reformers. Women proved to be the decisive factor in electing Rudolph Blankenburg mayor in 1911. Their maternalist emphasis on "civic housecleaning" provided the dark horse reformer with a powerful new campaign appeal. More importantly the dense network of women's clubs and organizations that Lucretia Blankenburg had helped build served as her husband's de facto political organization during the campaign's home stretch. As his machine rival relied upon regular Republican organizations and funds, Rudolph Blankenburg drew upon clubwomen's volunteer efforts and their feminine claim to the moral high ground. Nevertheless women remained largely invisible in the campaign. Machine Republicans never knew what hit them and, indeed, male reformers failed to give women credit for their efforts.

Old Dutch Cleanser

Chases Dirt

CONTRACTOR RULE!

SCANDAL

JOBBERY

RUDOLPH BLANKENBURG

FINE FOR CIVIC HOUSECLEANING

4. Above, *A pro-reform cartoon portrays Rudolph Blankenburg as a vigorous female housecleaner. This image mirrored the label of the popular national brand "Old Dutch Cleanser"* (Review of Reviews, *November 1896, p. 541*).

5. *Lucretia Blankenburg as First Lady of Philadelphia* (The Blankenburgs of Philadelphia, *Blankenburg, 1929*).

This essay records women reformers' contributions to reform's 1911 victory in Philadelphia. But it also reexamines the bases of maternalist politics itself.

The Centennial Exposition of 1876 brought the nation to Philadelphia to marvel at the massive Corliss steam engine and its other harbingers of industrial modernity. But it also spurred the residents of Philadelphia to civic activism. The Quaker City had become, in the words of a later muckraking journalist, "corrupt and contented." While the Centennial Exposition largely joined in this chorus, it also drew a number of Philadelphia's elite citizens to notice their city's shortcomings. Among their leaders were the young Rudolph and Lucretia Blankenburg, she a daughter of leading Philadelphia Quakers, he a German immigrant intent upon taking his new political freedoms seriously.

Lucretia Longshore was born in 1845, the daughter of a teacher and one of the nation's first woman physicians. Her parents became leaders in Philadelphia's reform community, working for women's rights and the abolition of slavery, and named their daughter in honor of Lucretia Mott. Young Lucretia observed the discrimination and poor treatment her mother received as a pioneer among physicians and resolved to continue her fight for equal opportunity. Her family's life also brought out other talents in the young woman. The Longshores' busy careers thrust many household duties upon their daughter, who managed the home and discovered that she did it well. "Here I learned to buy and sell," she recalled. "I kept my mother's books. My father, too, cooperated in every way. It is impossible to make a success of public life unless the family cooperates."[2]

Hannah Longshore's medical career inspired her daughter's later reform work, but Lucretia did not follow in her mother's professional footsteps. After one year's training, she abandoned medicine and enrolled in bookkeeping classes at Philadelphia's Bryant and Stratton Commercial College. In 1865 Lucretia's life took another major turn when young Rudolph Blankenburg knocked on the family's door bearing a relative's letter of introduction. The son of a German Reformed minister, he had been educated for the ministry himself. He was a large, hearty man with a booming voice and a ready smile. After finding employment as a traveling salesman for the textile house of William H. Horstman and Sons, he married Lucretia in 1867.[3]

The Blankenburgs made a dynamic couple. First they turned their attention to the business world. In 1875 he channeled Longshore family capital toward the inauguration of his own textile business, producing yarns, quilts, and spreads. A natural promoter and leader, he easily made new business contacts and quickly built his mill into a larger concern. Lucretia Blankenburg kept the firm's books and directed many of its financial dealings. Her natural abilities as a manager and her bookkeeping training made her a valuable business asset and freed Rudolph for the personal and promotional work he performed so well.[4]

The 1876 Centennial Exposition provided an opportunity for the Blankenburgs to take up the reform work they had often discussed. The exposition relied upon volunteers to organize the proceedings, and upon the event's completion these citizens carried their organizing zeal to the causes of charitable relief and political reform. Rudolph Blankenburg stepped to the fore. In 1878 he became one of the founding members of the new Society for Organizing Charitable Relief. Three years later he took his place on the new Committee of One Hundred, an organization of national Republicans devoted to challenging the city's political machine for municipal control. The Committee of One Hundred and its succeeding organizations enjoyed few electoral successes. Nevertheless Rudolph became a popular reform leader in Philadelphia. His persistent optimism and good cheer in the face of unremitting political setbacks earned him the sobriquet "the warhorse of reform."[5]

While Rudolph labored in the realm of Republican electoral politics, Lucretia Blankenburg became a leader among Philadelphia's clubwomen and reformers. She also began bookkeeping instruction in the New Century Club's night school curriculum and founded a new organization for the city's working women.[6] Prevailing class boundaries prevented elite women from welcoming working and immigrant women into their own organization, but Lucretia Blankenburg led the way in organizing the New Century Guild for working women. The parent club could not financially support the new guild for long, so Lucretia set about to secure its financial stability. After considerable research she led the club to purchase two houses on Arch Street in downtown Philadelphia. The club succeeded in renting one at sufficient profit to allow it to provide the other as the new guild's clubhouse; the properties were eventually sold at a large profit, providing the New Century Guild with an endowment of twenty-five thousand dollars. Lucretia Blankenburg's considerable business acumen had helped create a new organization that came to boast over seven hundred members, its own clubhouse, a library, assembly hall, and cafe.[7]

Upon joining the New Century Club in 1878, Lucretia Blankenburg also renewed her long-dormant interest in woman suffrage. In 1892, after years of grass-roots organizing and activism, she became president of the Pennsylvania Woman Suffrage Association, a post she held for sixteen years. In 1908 the General Federation of Women's Clubs elected Lucretia its auditor, and she led the effort to bring that organization around to the support of woman suffrage. Work in the New Century Club and woman's suffrage movement trained Lucretia Blankenburg to move on to other reform activities. Unlike the partisan political world, the new network of women's organizations offered an arena for a viable career in reform.[8]

Lucretia first organized the Smoke Nuisance Committee. She recalled that "after careful study of the question we discovered that the smoke nuisance could be abated by the use of mechanical appliances." Committee members visited offending businesses and persuaded many of them to install appliances. "Our argument," she recalled, "was based on the facts that housekeeping was the largest industry in Philadelphia, that the destruction of clothes and household furnishings by smoke cost thousands of dollars annually, and that smoke-laden air was irritating to the lungs and should be eliminated as far as possible."[9] The members of the committee employed the Progressive Era's familiar maternalist appeal to "civic housecleaning" and efficiency. Yet an analysis of their appeal reveals none of the usual references to morality, children, and caregiving. Rather Lucretia Blankenburg characterized housekeeping as a business, discussing cost and efficiency. Experience as a bookkeeper and businesswoman influenced her interpretation of housekeeping itself and enhanced her feminine political appeal. These activities must significantly affect our understanding of women and Progressive politics. While many brought their experiences as mothers and caregivers to the political realm in order to argue for a new maternalist state apparatus, others like Lucretia Blankenburg drew upon their business experience to demand efficiency and accountability from businessmen and politicians.

In the 1890s Philadelphia's clubwomen began to gain real influence in the electoral arena. In 1894 Pennsylvania Republican boss Quay selected the young Boies Penrose to become the next mayor of Philadelphia. Penrose was possessed of an appreciable intellect and equally considerable appetites for food, drink, salty oaths, and other pleasures. In Philadelphia's seedy political climate he made no attempt to conceal his activities. But the Penrose candidacy proved "more than the women of the city could tolerate." A committee of women circulated a petition declaring that "We, the women citizens of Philadelphia, ask for the nomination of a candidate for Mayor whose private life shows a high moral standard and whose mature character and experience in business affairs will ensure a good administration." Many leading women, including Lucretia Blankenburg, signed the petition, as did a number of reform-oriented Republican men. Rudolph Blankenburg, in a typical stroke of promotional genius, printed hundreds of oversize yellow posters of the petition and attached them to fences and billboards around the city on the eve of the Republican nominating convention. The posters omitted the word "women" in the bold-faced type, but included all two hundred signatures. Republican officials could

plainly see that these leading Philadelphia Republicans found Penrose of-
fensive and unprepared for office. In the city convention they nominated
Charles F. Warwick for mayor.[10]

The successful derailment of Penrose's mayoral candidacy marked a rare
electoral victory for the city's reform community. For fifteen years Philadelphia's reformers failed to build upon this political triumph. But they continued
to share common goals and build a strong partnership that would later bear
fruit. As early as 1890 Rudolph and Lucretia Blankenburg had succeeded in
opening elite reform functions to women as well as men. These events then
became opportunities to compare notes, share ideas, and formulate plans. In
this atmosphere the Philadelphia reform community grew and prospered.
Women reformers, assured of their place in the larger effort, moved forward to
new innovations that would prove useful in the future.[11]

When Rudolph Blankenburg announced his intention to run for mayor of
Philadelphia in 1911, almost no one gave him a chance to win. The warhorse of
reform was sixty-eight years of age. Boies Penrose, who had secured election to
the United States Senate in the Republican sweep of 1896, now administered
the Pennsylvania machine with fearsome precision. Yet Blankenburg swept to
victory. Why? A major rift in the Republican Party explains much of the
result.[12] But electoral success in 1911 remained a daunting challenge. Penrose
had perfected the techniques of fraud and intimidation and commanded a
legion of loyal voters and political operatives. Philadelphia's electorally oriented
reformers had built their Keystone Party around a minuscule group of elite
professionals and men of affairs and lacked any viable political organization. In
these circumstances the reform community's two wings came together as never
before to seize their rare opportunity and secure the election of Rudolph
Blankenburg. Philadelphia's clubwomen stepped into party politics and provided the Blankenburg campaign with its political style and organization.

Blankenburg's fortunes benefited from the familiar technique of women's
influence in the home. Clubwomen steadily lobbied their husbands, sons, and
uncles on behalf of his candidacy. Inventive women reached out into the Black
and working-class communities, and domestic servants carried Blankenburg
campaign literature into the homes they served. In the public realm the Blankenburg campaign drew upon the suffrage movement's growing momentum
and proven political style. Blankenburg marshaled massive marches and rallies,
often organized largely by women who had orchestrated the suffrage movement's own use of these mass techniques.[13]

In addition to these women's activities, the Blankenburgs crafted a feminine
aspect for Rudolph's hale-and-hearty political image. On the stump he emphasized maternalist themes of good city management and civic purity. Blanken-

burg women organized schoolchildren's clubs for their candidate and circulated photographs of an angelic-looking Rudolph accompanied by an adoring circle of children.[14] Finally Rudolph himself appeared in feminine form in an influential cartoon published on the front page of the reform-oriented Philadelphia *North American*. In addition to "the warhorse of reform," he had also come to be known as "Old Dutch Cleanser." In a novel twist on contemporary advertisements for housecleaning products, the cartoon portrayed Rudolph, labeled "Old Dutch Cleanser," in a Dutch peasant woman's garb complete with wooden shoes, sweeping the scoundrels from Philadelphia. Captions of "Chases Dirt!" and "Fine for Civic Housecleaning" accompanied the illustration. Blankenburg supported his promises for civic housecleaning with a well-publicized alliance with Frederick Winslow Taylor and his followers in industrial management. "Old Dutch Cleanser" promised to use the tools of Scientific Management for good government.[15]

Women also provided Rudolph Blankenburg with his political organization. Their clubs provided a ready-made network of volunteers for a candidate without party machinery behind him. For nearly a decade before the election, the women of the Philadelphia Civic Club (where Lucretia Blankenburg was also a member) had organized the city's Black, immigrant, and working citizens on a ward-by-ward basis for the ostensible purposes of civic education. In 1905 women reformers and clubwomen had also formed a Women's City Party to parallel the men's City Party. In 1911 these organizations sprang to life as electoral entities. Clubwomen formed the Women's Permanent Committee for Good Government. Women from a number of clubs made house-to-house canvasses of the city, raised funds, and organized motor pools and other logistics on behalf of the Blankenburg campaign.[16]

Lucretia Blankenburg undoubtedly organized many of these activities on her husband's behalf, yet she remained hesitant to elaborate upon her role in the election. Later she revealed her ambivalent feelings when she recalled how the city's women mobilized for the campaign: "When they did that, I felt that I ought to step aside and keep quiet." But she went on to admit that "of course they met with me often and I suppose I sort of egged them on."[17] In part this attitude reflected her reserved nature. While an intrepid organizer and leader, Lucretia Blankenburg remained disarmingly self-deprecating. Certainly this posture reflected the era's prevailing constructions of feminine modesty. But Lucretia's reticence also reflected a native shrewdness in political affairs borne out immediately upon her husband's election.

Although women helped her husband's campaign in many ways, Lucretia Blankenburg also realized that Rudolph needed the support of other regular Republicans. To take an active role in campaign activities would risk marking her husband, already running an innovative campaign appealing to women, as unmasculine and hence suspect in the all-male electoral realm. Her strategy worked. Despite Rudolph's creative use of feminine imagery, machine leaders declined to attack him as ineffectual or effeminate. This in part reflected Rudolph's vigorous and hearty presence on the stump and his citywide popularity. But it also reflected his wife's reticence.

Only upon Rudolph Blankenburg's election did machine Republicans wake up to his unusual political partnership. While the city's machine newspapers mouthed platitudes about cooperation, Penrose's spokesmen issued histrionic press releases proclaiming that Mrs. Blankenburg, and not her husband, would run the new administration. Of the country's major newspapers, only the *Chicago Tribune* gave the story any credence. It ran an article asking "Woman as Ruler in Philadelphia?" "Rudolph Blankenburg yesterday was elected mayor," it began, "but it will be theories of his wife, a suffragist, which will be put into practice during his term."[18] This attack vividly illustrates the type of response Lucretia Blankenburg assiduously avoided during the campaign. While she remained in the shadows, Rudolph reaped the benefits of the clubwomen's organization and a feminine political style without tangible backlash.

Machine Republicans simply failed to notice Philadelphia clubwomen's large-scale organization on behalf of Rudolph Blankenburg. From the perspective of their all-male political clubs and party events, the women's organization seemed invisible. But machine men were not alone in failing to discern the real causes behind Rudolph Blankenburg's election. Giddy with victory, reform men marveled at the outcome. United States Senator Robert LaFollette of Wisconsin, himself a warhorse of reform, wrote to congratulate Blankenburg upon his victory "without organization." The morning after Blankenburg's election, the pro-reform *North American* concluded that "All the organization he had was the volunteering of the men of the mills, and the shops, and the college."[19]

Philadelphia's male and female reformers built parallel organizations in the years between the Centennial Exposition of 1876 and the 1911 mayoral election. Although they shared a similar agenda emphasizing municipal efficiency, public morality, and woman suffrage, the period's prevailing gender roles and women's wholesale exclusion from the franchise effectively divided them. While Philadelphia's male reformers struggled to challenge the city's powerful Republican machine, Lucretia Blankenburg and the city's clubwomen honed their political skills in the fight for woman suffrage and turned their clubs to other political ends. In 1911 this shadow organization of clubs and clubwomen broke through into electoral politics and propelled Rudolph Blankenburg to the mayor's office. Their practiced maternalist appeals to morality and efficiency provided the Blankenburg campaign with its central theme. The city's women also used their persuasive powers to promote the warhorse of reform. But most importantly the clubwomen provided Rudolph Blankenburg with the army of volunteers only political parties had been able to provide in the past. Thus the clubwomen of Philadelphia blunted the Republican machine's greatest advantages, allowed their candidate to make the most of his opponents' disarray, and recorded a rare victory for reform in the Quaker City.

Unfortunately the same assumptions that blinded machine Republicans and municipal reformers alike to these women's political roles have afflicted recent work in women's history. As scholars have turned to consider women's political activities in the years before the Nineteenth Amendment, they have emphasized women's activities within their separate sphere, primarily their unique ability to influence political discourse, policymaking, and state building, without investigating the possibility of women's grass-roots electoral activities. This has led to the elaboration of a new argument emphasizing two Progressivisms in America, one a primarily masculine corporate liberalism built around the model of the business enterprise, the other a feminine progressivism (with a small "p") built from women's nineteenth-century concerns for caregiving, social welfare, and social purity. It candidly assigns the blame for modern America's ills to the corporate liberalism of Theodore Roosevelt and Woodrow Wilson, while concluding that "almost everything that we find admirable about the Progressive Era appears to have been associated in one way or another with women reformers carrying out the politics associated in the nineteenth century with women's domestic concerns."[20]

This scholarly dichotomy succumbs to the same assumptions and ideal types that obscured Lucretia Blankenburg and the Philadelphia clubwomen's role in Philadelphia politics for so long. While research for this essay has illuminated Blankenburg's important political work, it has also revealed new aspects of the politics women built before the Nineteenth Amendment. Women's experiences in business exercised an unseen influence upon the development of their politics in the Progressive Era. Some, like Lucretia Blankenburg, found their way to responsibility in private firms. Gilded Age women's clubs also provided opportunities for women to hone their business acumen. In new organizations such as the Smoke Nuisance Committee, they anchored the familiar feminine "housekeeping" metaphor in basic appeals to efficiency and cost. When we uncover women's complex political ideas and their roles in partisan politics, the idea of "two progressivisms" begins to unravel; men and women often worked together, as partners with common ideals and motivations, in the quest for a modern American order.

NOTES

1. "Blankenburgs Wed Fifty Years Tomorrow," Philadelphia *Evening Bulletin,* April 17, 1917.

2. "Woman's Rights Champion Sees Dreams Fulfilled: Mrs. Blankenburg Tells of Her Lifelong Work Furthering the Feminine Interests," *Philadelphia Record,* March 22, 1925. See also Lucretia Blankenburg's autobiography in *The Blankenburgs of Philadelphia* (Philadelphia: John C. Winston and Co., 1929), 107. For brief biographical sketches of Lucretia Blankenburg, see Edward James *et al., Notable American Women* 1:170–71; *Notable Women of Pennsylvania* (Philadelphia: University of Pennsylvania Press, 1942), 222–24; *The Biographical Cyclopaedia of American Women* (Detroit: Gale Research Company, 1974), 171; and Helen Christine Bennett, *American Women in the Civic Work* (New York: Dodd, Mead and Co., 1919), chap. 9.

3. See *The Blankenburgs of Philadelphia,* 108; for details of Lucretia's educational experiences, see the *Notable American Women* biographical sketch.

4. On the origins of Rudolph Blankenburg and Co., see *The Blankenburgs of Philadelphia,* 113; Helen Christine Bennett, "Lucretia Blankenburg, Assistant Mayor of Philadelphia," *Pictorial Review* (December 1912): 21; "Rudolph Blankenburg," *Dictionary of American Biography,* 357.

5. See *The Blankenburgs of Philadelphia,* 8–14; "Rudolph Blankenburg," *Dictionary of American Biography;* Bonnie Fox, "The Philadelphia Progressives," 375. For details on the impact of the Centennial Exposition and the rise of new civic associations in Philadelphia, see "Blankenburg Had Made War 30 Years on Political Evils," Philadelphia *North American,* November 3, 1911; *The Blankenburgs of Philadelphia,* 5 and 113–14; "City Mourns for Mrs. Blankenburg," Philadelphia *Evening Bulletin,* March 29, 1937.

6. *Notable American Women,* 1:171; Bennett, "Lucretia Blankenburg," 21.

7. See Bennett, "Lucretia Blankenburg," 21, and a similar account in Bennett, "Lucretia L. Blankenburg," in *American Women in the Civic Work,* chap. 9; also see her memoir in *The Blankenburgs of Philadelphia.* Also see significant obituaries in the *New York Times, New York Herald-Tribune,* and all of the major Philadelphia newspapers, all dated March 29, 1937.

8. Lucretia Blankenburg did not enter reform activities as an accomplished public figure. When called upon to present her first paper before the New Century Club, she demurred and asked a friend to read it instead. But work in the suffrage movement trained her for public life. Susan B. Anthony offered her public speaking lessons, and the basic political activities of the movement provided increased self-confidence. See *The Blankenburgs of Philadelphia,* 114–15.

9. *The Blankenburgs of Philadelphia,* 120–21.

10. See *The Blankenburgs of Philadelphia,* 15–16, for quotation and an account of this episode.

11. See *The Blankenburgs of Philadelphia,* 14–15.

12. For details of the Republican schism, see "John Burt, Big Vare Supporter, Turns in for Blankenburg," Philadelphia *North American,* October 10, 1911; "Vare Leaders from 15 Wards

Out for Blankenburg," Philadelphia *North American,* October 13, 1911; "Revolt of Vare Men Hits the Northwest; Blankenburg Gaining," Philadelphia *North American,* October 26, 1911; see also the *Evening Bulletin* of November 8, 1911, which reported "Blankenburg Strong in South Philadelphia." For general accounts of the campaign and Blankenburg's election, see Fox, "Philadelphia Progressives," and Donald Disbrow, "Reform in Philadelphia under Mayor Blankenburg." For an exhaustive electoral report of the Philadelphia wards, see the Philadelphia *North American* of November 9, 1911, as well as the *Evening Bulletin* of the same date.

13. For details of the women's campaign for Rudolph Blankenburg, see "Women Organize to Assist Blankenburg, Will Conduct Feminine Campaign in Behalf of Fusion Nominee," Philadelphia *North American,* October 24, 1911; "Women Send Out Last Blankenburg Appeal, Urge Their Sisters to Join in Fight for Good Government," Philadelphia *North American,* November 6, 1911; "Women in the City Election," Philadelphia *North American,* September 10, 1911; "Women's Committee Visits Mayor-Elect," Philadelphia *North American,* November 9, 1911. See also *The Blankenburgs of Philadelphia,* book 1, chap. 7, and book 2, chaps. 5 and 7; Bennett, "Lucretia L. Blankenburg."

14. For an account of these activities and a copy of the photograph, see Helen Christine Bennett, "Interesting People: The Mayor of Philadelphia," *American Magazine* (November 1913).

15. Philadelphia *North American,* November 9, 1911.

16. See Julie Johnson-McGrath, "The Civic Club of Philadelphia" and "The Octavia Hill Association."

17. Bennett, "Lucretia Blankenburg," 22–29; Philadelphia *Public Ledger,* November 9, 1911.

18. "Woman as Ruler of Philadelphia?" *Chicago Tribune,* November 9, 1911. The article announced that Lucretia had declared that "Now I will have the opportunity of putting some of my theories into practice." A review of local newspapers finds no such public utterances by Mrs. Blankenburg.

19. Philadelphia *North American,* November 9, 1911.

20. William Chafe, "Women's History and Political History," 105; for similar arguments see also Kathryn Kish Sklar, "Two Political Cultures in the Progressive Era," and Maureen Flanagan, "Gender and Urban Political Reform."

6. Helen Ring Robinson (The Denver Public Library, Western History Collection).

CHAPTER FIVE

"WOMEN DEMAND RECOGNITION"
Women Candidates in Colorado's Election of 1912

ROBYN MUNCY

In 1912 Colorado promised much to partisan women. Female Coloradans had been voting for nearly twenty years; a new law guaranteed them equal representation on many mainstream party committees; and Colorado was in the midst of a hotly contested election, which showcased the surprising power of a new third party. This essay explores the fortunes of women as candidates under these particularly favorable conditions.

The evidence from Colorado supports two major arguments. First, the battles of partisan women for representation in party hierarchies and on ballots succeeded best when intense electoral competition sent parties scurrying for every vote they could muster. Second, when those efforts failed, they were sometimes deflected by male leaders; they were, however, more subtly discouraged by the notion that the political field was divided between women and men. Most Coloradans—including its political women—seem to have believed that some seats or offices were reserved for women and that the rest belonged to men. This kind of thinking pitted women candidates only against other women and men only against other men; it granted women the status of genuine political actors but perpetuated the sense that they were nevertheless different sorts of political actors from men. Given the history of politics as a male domain, for women to be different was for them to be inferior, less essential political players.

In 1912 many conditions favored the participation of Colorado's women in electoral politics. Women had been voting in that state since 1894, when the Populist threat to Republican domination prompted Republicans desperately to stump for women's votes. To attract women Republicans inaugurated a system of male and female cochairs in their ward committees in Denver and Boulder and appointed gender-integrated teams to organize the state's counties.[1]

This precedent for integrating women systematically into Colorado's party structures later received statutory blessing. In 1910 Colorado became the first state to ensure by law the equal representation of women and men on all major committees of the mainstream political parties: a new primary law, not in effect until 1912, forced the two major parties to select through open primaries a committeeman and a committeewoman in each precinct. These precinct officials then constituted each ward organization and each county's central committee, which meant that ward committees and county central committees had equal numbers of women and men. The innovative election law also required that each committee of a party at the county and municipal levels have a chair and vice chair, one of whom had to be a woman.[2]

In addition to demanding equal numbers of women and men on many party committees, the new primary law aimed to break the hold of party insiders on nominations for office. Instead of allowing party caucuses to slate candidates for general elections, the law forced the major parties to hold primaries, and it required that parties put on the primary ballot anyone who received the requisite number of signatures on a petition for candidacy or who received 10 percent of the vote in a party assembly held before the primaries. Party insiders thus could not restrict the number of names that appeared on the primary ballot and certainly could not control who survived the primary to appear on the general election ballot. New parties, which did not yet qualify to participate in the primaries, could put candidates on the November ballot only by petition.[3]

In 1912 the Progressive Party was just such a party, created by Republicans who had hoped to nominate Theodore Roosevelt for the presidency. When Republican regulars instead nominated William Howard Taft, TR's supporters formed the Progressive Party. The new party advocated such political reforms as the initiative, referendum, and recall as well as such social justice measures as mothers' pensions, workmen's compensation, and factory safety laws. The party moreover supported women's suffrage and maintained that women should participate on a basis of "absolute equality" with men.[4]

The strength of the Progressive Party meant that, in Colorado as elsewhere, three parties offered viable presidential candidates in 1912. Republicans offered the most conservative option. Democrats, partly in response to Roosevelt's dynamic candidacy, nominated Woodrow Wilson for president, thus aligning the Democratic Party with progressive impulses as well.

In Colorado the threat of deserting to Roosevelt gave Democratic women the most power within their own party during the 1912 election. Even despite the Progressive Party's explicit commitment to women's advancement, Democratic women did at least as well as Progressive women in becoming candidates for office. Indeed the Democratic Party hierarchy granted its imprimatur to more female candidates than did the Progressive Party. Moreover the process of nominating candidates revealed attitudes that kept women from competing equally with men in either party.

At the state level Progressive Party activists believed women to be appropriate candidates only for offices connected with education. Through petition the state Progressive Party put fifteen names on the November ballot, and only two of the fifteen were women. For superintendent of public instruction, a position long held by women in Colorado, the party offered Ida M. Casady, of Flagler; Mrs. Frederick Dick, of Denver, was nominated as one of three regents to the university. The party's candidates for governor, lieutenant governor, and attorney general were all men.[5]

At the local level women were considered legitimate candidates for a wider range of offices, including state representative and state senator. In Denver each party could put eleven candidates for state representative on the general election ballot and three candidates for state senator. To consider possibilities for such local offices, the Progressive Party of Denver held two nominating conventions in September 1912. At the first of these conventions, attorney Gail Laughlin was accepted as a nominee for state senator from Denver, and Dr. Maude Sanders as nominee for one of the state representative positions.[6] Both women were ardent prohibitionists, suffragists, and clubwomen as well as professionals.[7]

That these women were nominated by acclamation was not insignificant. It meant that in this open forum, women did not openly *compete* for their places on the ticket; they had only to *accept* nomination. The popular juvenile court judge Benjamin Lindsey first recommended Laughlin and Sanders to conventioneers, an event that one newspaper reported this way: "Judge Lindsey suggested that, as a matter of courtesy, the nominations for representative and senator be given to women."[8]

Lindsey's own representation of his role in this nominating convention reveals that even he—long a champion of women's rights and an elected official who believed his own success was largely due to women voters—thought of women as different sorts of political actors from men. "I made a speech in the first convention," he explained, "calling attention to the fact that because the Progressive Party was the only party for suffrage, and because of Col. Roosevelt's attitude, and for many other reasons, that I thought our party should be particularly and unusually generous in recognizing the women in placing them on our ticket."[9] It was, of course, never "generosity" that put men on party tickets. Lindsey went on to boast that when the convention decided to name only one senator and one representative at the first meeting, he "personally nominated Miss Laughlin for senator and Dr. Saunders [*sic*] for representative, and was afterwards roundly scored by some of the men."[10] Apparently not all of the men in the Progressive Party were feeling quite so "generous" as Lindsey, who was himself a candidate for his position as juvenile court judge in Denver. He claimed that "being a candidate myself and the national committeeman, I decided to limit my nominating speeches to women candidates alone. . . . "[11]

While it is impossible to know exactly what Lindsey meant by this last statement, he seems to indicate that as a candidate himself, he needed to exercise statesmanship in his role at the local convention, to appear, that is, to be above any factional fray. He believed that he could do so by openly supporting only women candidates. Even in Lindsey's mind, then, female politicos remained apart from the gritty power seeking that created factional conflict; their political identities continued—even within gender-integrated party operations—to separate them from men.

This notion of gender difference ruled the process of further nominations as well. At that first convention of Denver's Progressives, after Laughlin's and Sanders's nominations had been confirmed, many other names were put forward as possible nominees for the ten remaining state representative positions, district attorney, constable, justice of the peace, and district and county judges. Instead of taking a vote on these suggestions as they came up, the conventioneers decided to appoint a committee to make final recommendations from the convention suggestions for nominees to these offices. This committee of sixteen was all male. On the list of contenders were four women, all of whom had been suggested as possible candidates for representatives from Denver. They were Mamie Piquette, Mrs. M. J. Davis, Alice Disbrow, and Hattie Howard. In addition to the four women, the convention suggested twelve men, for a total of sixteen, and the committee had the freedom to name ten of those sixteen to the ballot (because at that time Denver sent eleven representatives to the state house). Ultimately no additional women found their way onto the ballot from Denver: Dr. Maude Sanders remained the only woman among eleven candidates nominated for state representative. The all-male committee thus nominated the ten remaining candidates from the twelve men they were allowed to consider for state representatives. They nominated none of the four women.[12] According to Lindsey, members of the committee privately expressed the opinion that "women had enough places on the ticket."[13] No one on the committee countered that there were already plenty of men on the ticket; men were taken to be the standard candidates and women the extras.

In this case, moreover, women themselves were in no way ambivalent about running for office, but male intransigence kept them from it. Although Lindsey claimed that he had been told at the second convention that "the women were satisfied, since they had gotten a state senator, etc.," both Alice Disbrow and Hattie Howard continued to desire places on the ticket and tried unsuccessfully to rouse support at the second convention.[14]

The importance both of having women on the nominating committees and of intraparty competition for winning women's nominations is revealed by the actions of Colorado's Democrats in 1912. Despite Woodrow Wilson's nomination for president, some progressive Democrats in Colorado were determined not to work directly with the regular state Democratic Party—often pejoratively called "the machine." These progressive party members met in August 1912 to choose candidates for the Democratic primary. The committee on candidates for this break-away group included five women out of the total of eleven members. This gender-mixed group not only proposed a woman for state senator—Helen Ring Robinson—but also recommended five women for the eleven state representative spots.[15] State laws required this group to collect a specified number of signatures to put its slate of candidates on the Democratic primary ballot; it succeeded in putting all its women candidates on that ballot.[16]

These moves by the insurgent group pressured other Democrats, gathered in August 1912 at the official Democratic state assembly, also to nominate more than the usual number of women. By law anyone who received support from 10 percent of those gathered at the assembly had to be put on the primary ballot. The Democratic state assembly, attended by Democratic Party regulars and a few progressives, nominated six additional women for state representative. In the end, out of a total of forty-two candidates for the eleven state representative spots on the Democratic ballot, eleven were women (26 percent of the candidates).[17]

In this closely contested primary election, the male leadership of the Democratic Party—both progressive and regular—was remarkably open to female candidacies. In a last minute attempt to gain support for particular candidates on the primary ballot, the executive committee of the Denver Democratic Party endorsed candidates for all local offices. These endorsements not only supported Katherine Williamson, the one woman running for U.S. Congress—a huge leap from any previous place offered to women—but also supported three of the women running for the eleven state representative positions from Denver.[18]

This was a step ahead of even the progressive newspaper, the *Rocky Mountain News,* which also endorsed candidates in the Democratic primary election. The *News* vetted all candidates for local office to see which of them was truly progressive, and on that basis it endorsed two Democratic women running for the eleven state representative spots. It further endorsed one woman for state senator but did not support the woman running for U.S. Congressman-at-large.[19]

Denver's progressive Democratic newspaper and Democratic Party regulars thus supported more women for office than leaders of the Progressive Party. This amazing twist occurred because of pressure exerted by Democratic women in a party that was torn by factional strife and threatened by the Progressive Party. Both regulars and progressives in the Democratic Party believed they needed to appease as many party members as possible; all knew that if the Democratic ballot did not satisfy a large enough constituency, local Democrats could desert to another party in November.

With this leverage women members pushed at all levels for greater representation within the party. The formula they used for increasing their power followed the logic embedded in the primary law: women asked that the party cede them a greater portion of seats on committees or slots on the ballot. That is, they asked for set-asides, for slots that would be designated for women only. At a caucus of several hundred progressive Democrats in early August, for instance, women demanded that at least one state senator and five state representatives nominated by the party be women.[20] Later, in a huge meeting of Denver Democrats to select delegates to the state nominating assembly, a female party leader "asked that women be given a representation of ten delegates at large instead of the five they formerly have had."[21] This strategy worked: under pressure from women members, the leadership of the Democratic Party of Denver endeavored to put an extraordinary number of women on ad hoc committees as well as on the ballot.[22]

After the primary voting was over, however, only one of the three women nominated for state senator from Denver and one of eleven nominated for state representative made it onto the November ballot. These two women went on to win their November elections, but the leadership of the Democratic Party had clearly not controlled the votes of the majority of their members, who rejected, for instance, the recommendation of more than one female candidate for state representative.[23] In this case leaders and activists in the party felt the pressures of intraparty factionalism much more keenly than did the average party voter, male or female. The result was that women could win concessions from the leadership and the larger group of party activists who attended conventions, but they still could not force the hand of the much larger group of Democratic voters.

Women primary candidates fared so poorly in part because even women politicians themselves seemed to see women as running only against other women candidates. This understanding of political competition was revealed, for instance, in the Democratic primary for state senator. Democrats put nine people on the primary ballot for state senator from Denver, three of them women: Alma Lafferty, Helen Ring Robinson, and Harriet Wright.[24] In the primary, each voter was to mark the ballot for three state senators, and no legal barrier prevented voters from voting for all three women. As the election approached, Dora Phelps Buell, a progressive Democrat and seasoned politician, tried to rouse support for her favorite candidate, Harriet Wright. In arguments on behalf of Wright, Buell insisted that she was very "anxious to defeat" Alma Lafferty, long associated with the Democratic machine in Denver, and she believed that "Mrs. Wright is so much stronger in every way than Mrs. Robinson." Wright, according to Buell, was a more consistent progressive and would be more reliable for progressive causes in the Senate.[25] Buell did not explain why Wright would be a better candidate than any of the men running for the state senate: this omission revealed her belief that Wright was running only against other women on the primary ballot, not the many men also in the field at the time. The ballot itself, of course, did *not* separate men from women candidates; in fact men and women were running against each other in the primary. Nevertheless Buell saw the political field as divided between male and female candidates, with the larger portion of the field reserved for men.

Although we have no evidence as to how many Democratic voters, male or female, voted for more than one woman for state senator, anecdotal evidence suggests that Buell's assumptions accorded with those of the larger electorate. On primary election day, reporters interviewed people at the polls, and one male voter explained. "If the women hadn't been represented so heavily [on the primary ballot], I think a few of them would have had a better chance. The men are not going to stand for women trying to hog everything, you know."[26]

Of those three Democratic women running for state senator, only Robinson made it to the general election, and she went on to become the first female state senator in Colorado's history. A journalist and clubwoman, Robinson claimed that the Senate needed her precisely because she was different from men, and her candidacy received support not only from the Democratic Party but also from the Woman's Senatorial League, formed specifically to elect her.[27]

In the Republican Party, too, women activists had greater success pressuring other party activists than in convincing the larger membership to send women to office. In the primaries a few progressive Republicans ran—despite formation of the Progressive Party—in an effort to get control of the Republican Party itself. Because the Progressive Party had already siphoned off most progressive Republicans, the intraparty strife was not nearly so intense as it was in the Democratic Party, but it existed nonetheless. In this situation twenty-two candidates appeared on the Republican primary ballot for the eleven state representative positions from Denver, and five of them were women, a slightly lower percentage of women than in the Democratic primary. Republican voters, however, were even more reluctant to nominate a woman for this office than were the Democrats. Not a single woman from the Republican Party survived the primary. Furthermore the Republicans did not even put one woman on the primary ballot for the three state senatorial positions.[28]

Still women did much better in the hotly contested election of 1912, with its inter- and intraparty competitions, than they would do in the much more staid election of 1916. By the fall of 1916, not only had the Progressive Party mostly bowed out of Colorado politics, but a violent coal miners' strike had produced a huge Republican victory in the by-election of 1914, when the majority of Colorado voters gravitated toward the Republicans' promise of "Law and Order." With international relations the focus of the national election and law and order the center of local concern, the two mainstream parties suffered little internal strife and worried not at all about third-party threats.

In this context women candidates made a particularly poor showing. Denver's Republicans and Democrats put only men on the primary ballot for state senator; of nineteen Democratic candidates for state representative from Denver, only one was a woman; of thirty-four Republican candidates for those positions, only two were women. Neither of the Republican women won a place on the November ballot, and the one Democratic woman who did, lost in the general election.[29]

In conclusion one of the most successful mechanisms for women's inclusion in party politics was the requirement by law that women occupy half of the positions on the major committees of each mainstream party. This practice carried over into other areas of party activity: for instance, in order to get onto smaller committees or the ballot, women activists often convinced men to cede women some portion of the slots. When that was agreed, women's participation in electoral politics genuinely increased.

But this very method for assuring women's participation also solidified the limitations on that participation. In this situation women competed only against other women for the slots on the ballot or seats on the committee that had been designated their portion. The rest continued to be construed as men's portion, and it was, of course, always the larger and more powerful portion. Men continued to compete only against other men and were thus able to continue to envision the standard political actor as male—with women as a deviation from that standard—and most areas of political endeavor as belonging only to men.

Moreover Colorado's political women expanded their portion of the electoral pie only under extraordinary circumstances. In 1912 unusually intense intraparty rivalries and interparty competition sent parties stumping for every vote they could win. In this context men had an incentive to meet some of the women's demands for greater representation on the ballot. Otherwise those same men clearly had no motive for further opening their domain to women.

NOTES

1. Rebecca Edwards, *Angels in the Machinery,* 105.

2. "Primary Election Notice," *Rocky Mountain News,* August 31, 1912, pp. 9–10; Marguerite J. Fisher, "Women in the Political Parties," 89; John R. Eyre and Curtis Martin, *The Colorado Preprimary System,* 20.

3. Eyre and Martin, *The Colorado Preprimary System,* 20–25.

4. Quotation in "To the Women Voters," 1912, folder 2, box 13, Theodore Roosevelt Collection—Progressive Party Papers, Houghton Library, Harvard University; John Allen Gable, *The Bull Moose Years,* chap. 1.

5. "Bull Moose Fill Ticket Vacancies When Peace Fails," *Denver Republican,* September 2, 1912, box 331, Benjamin Lindsey Papers, Library of Congress (hereafter BLP); "A List of Nominations, *Rocky Mountain News,* November 1, 1912, pp. 8–9.

6. "John A. Rush is Repudiated by Moosers," *Rocky Mountain News,* September 3, 1912, p. 1.

7. Barbara Sicherman, et al., *Notable American Women,* 410–11; James Alexander Semple, comp., *Representative Women of Colorado* (Denver: n.p., 1914), 111.

8. "John A. Rush is Repudiated by Moosers."

9. Lindsey to Mrs. Disbrow, September 28, 1912, box 39, BLP.

10. Ibid.

11. Ibid.

12. "Lindsey Slapped on Wrist," *Denver Times,* September 3, 1912, and "Boatwright Named District Attorney by Bull Moosers," *Denver Times,* September 18, 1912; both box 331, BLP.

13. Lindsey to Mrs. Disbrow, September 28, 1912, box 39, BLP.

14. Ibid.; Lindsey to Mrs. Hattie Howard, September 28, 1912, box 39, BLP. Disbrow did make it onto the ballot as a nominee for state representative from the Progressive Party; "A List of Nominations," *Rocky Mountain News,* November 1, 1912, pp. 8–9.

15. "Progressive Democrats Bolt," *Denver Republican,* August 10, 1912, box 331, BLP.

16. "Primary Election Notice," *Rocky Mountain News,* August 31, 1912, pp. 9–10.

17. "Both Assemblies Dominated by Same Machine," *Rocky Mountain News,* August 9, 1912, p. 1; "Primary Election Notice," *Rocky Mountain News,* August 31, 1912, pp. 9–10.

18. "Evans-Speer Gang Picks Candidates to Support at Tomorrow's Primary," *Rocky Mountain News,* September 9, 1912, p. 1.

19. "*News* Marks Sample Ballot," *Rocky Mountain News,* September 6, 1912, p. 3.

20. "728 Votes Claimed by Platform Men in Assembly Today," *Rocky Mountain News,* August 1, 1912, p. 5.

21. "Wait Hour after Hour in Hope Platformists Will Relent," *Rocky Mountain News,* August 3, 1912, p. 2.

22. Ibid.

23. *Abstract of Votes Cast,* [in Colorado] (Denver: Smith-Brooks Printing Company, 1913).

24. "Both Assemblies Dominated by Same Machine," *Rocky Mountain News,* August 9, 1912, p. 1.

25. Dora Phelps Buell to Ben Lindsey, September 1912, box 39, BLP.

26. Alice Rohe, "Women Show Men How Real Enthusiasm Wins Votes for Candidate," *Rocky Mountain News,* September 11, 1912, p. 3.

27. "State Needs Women in Law-Making Body," *Rocky Mountain News,* September 4, 1912, p. 12.

28. *Abstract of Votes Cast,* 1913.

29. *Abstract of Votes Cast,* [in Colorado] (Denver: C.F. Hoeckel Blank Book and Lithographing Company, 1916).

CHAPTER SIX

AFRICAN AMERICAN WOMEN AS POLITICAL CONSTITUENTS IN CHICAGO, 1913–1915

WANDA A. HENDRICKS

In June 1913 the Illinois legislature passed the bill that enfranchised female residents twenty-one years of age and older. Women voted for presidential electors, mayors, aldermen, municipal court judges, sanitary trustees, and most local officers. Women could not vote, however, for governors and other state officers, members of the legislature, county or district judges, congressmen or senators.[1] The legislation had immediate impact. First it propelled the state into the national spotlight, because Illinois was the first state east of the Mississippi River to politically empower a significantly large female voting constituency. Second it expanded and advanced women's ability to participate in municipal affairs. Finally and most importantly, the legislation lay the foundation for African American female voters in the racially segregated second ward of Chicago to profoundly transform the electoral process in that area.

This essay examines both the creation of a political culture by African American women and the essential role that these female political constituents played in the local patriarchal world of Chicago politics, prior to the great Black migration to the city during the final years of World War I, when employment opportunities increased. For the two years between 1913 and 1915, Black women created political organizations, educated themselves on the intricacies of politics, developed strategies, and centered themselves in the debates concerning the direction of Black progress. The overwhelming success in the second ward primarily stemmed from the passage of the suffrage legislation and its emphasis on electing local officials, the increase in the number of Black residents and their confinement in the racially segregated ward, and the orga-

7. *From left to right: Virginia Brooks, "Mrs." Belle Squire, Mrs. Ida Wells Barnett (Chicago Daily Tribune, March 4, 1913; Illinois State Historical Library).*

nized efforts of women and their devotion to a reform ideology that emphasized racial advancement.

The slow steady growth of the Black populace contributed to more than a doubling of the population over a six-year period. In 1910 the Black population in the ward numbered 10,709, approximately one-fourth of the inhabitants. By 1916 the number had climbed to 24,865, making Blacks the largest minority population.[2] To assist the escalating numbers of "newcomers," Black women engaged in the progressive social reform club movement to feed, clothe, and shelter the poor and destitute. Eventually they expanded their social activities to include political involvement. Traditionally reform work was by definition part of women's responsibility and required women to merge private domesticity in the home with public domesticity in their neighborhoods. Under the aegis of traditional reform, however, women did not vote for officers engaged in the process of running the city. But the suffrage bill changed that by expanding the traditional notion of a woman's place and allowing men and women to share the same space in municipal affairs. Moreover Black women acquired the necessary tool linking them to a racially based, politically conscious culture that encouraged racial responsibility.

The "passion for organization" that lecturer, author, clubwoman, and second ward resident Fannie Barrier Williams alluded to in the essay "Colored Women of Chicago" was not unique only to Chicago women, but their passion certainly contributed to their success in municipal politics.[3] Civic duty, social responsibility, and race pride motivated women to unite for a common cause and devote countless hours to providing for the poor and destitute. It was also civic and social duty that engaged women in the politics of racial responsibility Enfranchisement, according to Williams, was an "important responsibility" that was going to "lift colored women to new importance as citizens," primarily because "they now have an effective weapon with which to combat prejudice and discrimination of all kinds."[4] For African American women like Williams who suffered under the oppressive duality of racism and sexism, exercising the right to vote offered the most expedient means of eradicating two foes—"prejudice and discrimination."

African American women throughout the city began the first step in developing a political culture when they mobilized their forces and organized several exclusively female suffrage clubs. Some of the associations included the Aloha Political Club, the Colored Women's Party of Cook County, the Mary Walker Thompson Political Club, the 3rd Ward Political Club, the Woman's 25th Precinct Political Club, and the Alpha Suffrage Club.[5] The most prominent, successful, and earliest of the clubs was the Alpha Suffrage Club, headquartered in the second ward. Organized in January 1913 and directed by the dynamic Ida Bell Wells-Barnett, the club had by 1915 become a major force in the election of the first African American alderman in the city.[6]

Wells-Barnett's interest in politics began soon after the end of the Reconstruction period, in the aftermath of the Civil War. As African American men systematically lost the franchise in southern states, she came to realize that limits on the franchise retarded Black social, economic, and political equality. Disfranchised African Americans were not only oppressed but were persecuted American citizens as well. In her essay "How Enfranchisement Stops Lynching," she attempted to illustrate the relation between oppression and the franchise. One part of the essay focused primarily on the atrocities that Blacks experienced at the hands of White supremacists precisely because they lacked the ballot. She argued that

> With no sacredness of the ballot there can be no sacredness of human life itself. For if the strong can take the weak man's ballot, when it suits his purpose to do so, he will take his life also. Having successfully swept aside the constitutional safeguards to the ballot, it is the smallest of small matters for the South to sweep aside its own safeguards to human life. Thus "trial by jury" for the black man in that section has become a mockery, a plaything of the ruling classes and rabble alike. The mob says: "This people has no vote with which to punish us or the consenting officers of the law, therefore we indulge our brutal instincts, give free rein to race prejudice and lynch, hang, burn them when we please." Therefore, the more complete the disfranchisement, the more frequent and horrible has been the hangings, shootings, and burnings.[7]

Disfranchisement, for Wells-Barnett, quite simply marginalized Blacks and made them pawns in the hands of southern White supremacists.

Another part of the essay focused on the positive influence that political empowerment had on shaping state policy. She suggested that it was the combination of the election of a Black to the state legislature, the passage of an antilynching bill, the cooperation of the Republican governor, vigilant law enforcement officers, and the anger of Black Illinoisans that curtailed lynching and mob rule in the state.[8] Indeed the differences between this midwestern state and its southern counterparts were striking. Chicago, the sprawling, second largest city in the country, was located there. Several prominent African American men were involved in politics, casting ballots, holding office, or belonging to Republican clubs. And women had some access to politics through their participation in school board elections.[9]

Wells-Barnett's concerns for enfranchisement were not limited to Black men. For African Americans to benefit fully from the franchise, Wells-Barnett surmised that Black women should also be included in the process. To encourage women to support suffrage, she traveled throughout the state promoting the cause for the state central committee during the last decade of the nineteenth century. While touring she found to her dismay that "in only a few instances did I see any of my own people." Because so few Black women attended the forums and had limited knowledge of the suffrage issue, she concluded that "if the white women were backward in political matters, our own women were even more so."[10] The combination of disfranchisement and lack of interest in female suffrage, Wells-Barnett reasoned, rendered Black women in the state just as powerless as their southern male counterparts. To rectify the problem, she began to develop a plan to create an organization solely devoted to educating African American women on the importance of the vote.

More than a decade passed before she and a White colleague, Belle Squire, created the African American Alpha Suffrage Club, the first in the city. African American women warmly embraced it. By 1916 nearly two hundred women had joined the organization and pledged to perform their civic duty by voting. The Suffrage Club developed a socially responsible agenda that educated members on the intricacies of the voting process and devised strategies to aid the community in its quest for political empowerment. The ultimate objective of the club, according to Wells-Barnett, was teaching Black women how to use their "vote for the advantage of ourselves and our race."[11]

But the assumption that African American men would readily embrace them for their views often fell short of their expectations. Many men, threatened by women's push into the male domain, were reluctant to ally themselves with them. Scholar Deborah Gray White contends that their reluctance stemmed from the fact that the political forum afforded Black men the only public means of exercising real power in the Black community. Unlike women, whose status in the community primarily stemmed from their club network, men had limited access to community ventures. Men's organizations seldom did public domestic housekeeping, because that duty was thought to be intrinsic to women's natural ability. For men to move into that arena meant redefining gender roles. So men secured their position in the community in the only public venue left solely to them, precisely because women lacked the ballot.[12] Because Black men in midwestern cities like Chicago exercised their voting rights relatively free from persecution, many enjoyed favorable membership in predominantly White organizations, and some were elected to political offices. The expansion of women's roles into municipal politics threatened their political stronghold.

As Alpha Suffrage Club members prepared for their first aldermanic primary, in 1914, they met some fierce opposition from men. Each week that members gathered at club headquarters to discuss their progress and share information, the main topic of the business meeting was usually the strain of confronting antisuffrage men. The hostility from many men was so fierce, some of the women recounted, that they were ready to cease their canvassing. They encountered "jeers" from men who "told them they ought to be at home taking care of the babies," while others confronted men who "insisted that the women were trying to take the place of men and wear the trousers." Wells-Barnett, of course, refused to allow them to bow to the pressure. She encouraged the women to continue their activities.[13]

Not all men resented the empowerment and creation of a political culture among women, however. Some, like the editor of the Black weekly the *Chicago Defender,* applauded the women's dedication to reform and to the race. Early in the primary campaign, its headlines glorified women's roles as both race loyalists and as municipal housekeepers. The February 1914 headlines boasted: "Women to Show Loyalty by Casting First Ballot for Cowan for Alderman. Second Ward Women Determine to Use Their Power to Better Themselves and Strengthen the Race. Assert Men Needed Their Assistance. Garbage Question, Children's Playgrounds, Ventilation in Public Places, Supervision of 'Movies' Important Matters to Them."[14] It was the traditional "women's issues"—children, housekeeping, and morality, combined with race loyalty—that encouraged the editor of the paper to recognize the potential influence women could have in the political arena.

Nearly three thousand women cast ballots in the 1914 primary. Many voted for the Black independent candidate, William R. Cowan. Endorsed by the Alpha Suffrage Club over the Republican machine's White candidate, Cowan's slim defeat by less than two hundred votes signaled a distinct shift away from both the Republican Party and voting for White candidates. Black women took a grave risk by endorsing the independent over the Republican candidate, because quite simply they broke with tradition. The vast majority of African Americans held the party of Abraham Lincoln in high regard and allied themselves with it despite their inability to gain access to key positions either in the party or in municipal government that directly affected Black wards. Even more importantly, the women's attempt to deny the party's hegemonic control over the selection of candidates without the approval of the Black community demonstrated both an unwavering commitment to self-determination and a direct assault on the party's dominance. The women who voted for Cowan did so because he was African American. Party affiliation took a back seat to race loyalty. The progress of the race necessitated that they vote along race lines, to meet their goal of electing an African American male to a key position in the municipal government.

Even those men who questioned women's right to the ballot had to concede that in their first venture into the electoral process, women in the ward had succeeded in unnerving the Republican Party and illuminating the importance of racial solidarity. The Black weekly the *Broad Ax* charged that "Cowan and his followers woke things up . . . for he received 2700 votes more than one thousand of that number being cast by the ladies." Moreover, the paper opined, the only conclusion that could be drawn from the election was that the supporters of the Black independent candidate "plainly brought to the front one thing and that is that within the next two or four years at the longest a high class popular solid Colored man of affairs can and will be elected to the City Council from that ward."[15]

The machine and Black men with political aspirations took note of the implications of the vote and concluded that if enough African Americans embraced independent candidates, then the split vote would open the door for other party candidates to win. Ultimately, of course, neither the Republicans nor African Americans would reap benefits.[16] Hoping to avoid the loss of its lock on the Black vote, recognizing the shift in the women's votes, and viewing the disgruntlement of loyal Black ward advocates as a clear sign of departure from the normal routine, party officials courted organized African American women.

Two representatives attended one of the weekly meetings of the Alpha Suffrage Club. The visit legitimized this female electorate, made them central players in ward politics, and offered them the opportunity to unmask their ultimate goal—that the party relinquish its practice of endorsing only White candidates in this heavily populated Black ward. After some negotiation, the representatives assured members that the party would back a Black candidate upon the first opening on the City Council. Unsure that the representatives had the authority to affirm the party's position on this issue, the women "wanted to know when there would be another vacancy."[17] Assurance that at least one of the two aldermanic posts in the ward would become available within the year did not appease them. Instead they asked "How could we be sure that the organization would keep its promise?"[18] The solution to their query, one of the representatives declared, was for club members to join forces with other organizations with the same agenda, present their idea to party leaders, and win their pledge. Before the year ended, a seat on the City Council did become available.[19]

The Republican ward machine promoted the candidacy of Black party loyal Oscar Stanton DePriest. A recognized name to both ward constituents and to Alpha Suffrage Club members, he was one of the emissaries from the Republican Party who had visited the club after members supported the Cowan bid for

City Council. DePriest was also a well-known figure in the community. He migrated to the city from Kansas in 1889, became a successful businessman, and established himself as a respected Republican Party member. He served two terms on the Cook County Board of Commissioners and helped build a strong Black male Republican faction.[20]

Because the party delivered on its promise to back a Black candidate, the clubwomen delivered on theirs, despite the fact that three Blacks ran in the primary. In the hotly contested election of 1915, they backed DePriest. Even when there was another opportunity to resurrect and endorse the independent candidacy of William Cowan, Wells-Barnett recoiled and argued that the scheme was conjured up by "this nameless white man" who "had not been prompted by the desire to 'secure a better man for nomination'. It simply was to get two colored men to fight against each other, and the result would be that neither one of them would secure the place."[21]

In spite of her concerns, DePriest became the first African American alderman in Chicago.[22] He was victorious primarily because a large Black voting bloc, steeped in a heightened sense of racial consciousness, stimulated electoral mobilization. And African Americans allied across gender lines, creating a broad-based, self-determined coalition that voted to elect one of their own to the City Council. Because women in the ward cast nearly one-third of the total ballots for him, DePriest announced in the national publication *The Crisis* that "I favor extension of the right of suffrage to women," because the women in Chicago "cast as intelligent a vote as the men."[23] His declaration illuminated the civic role of African American women to a national audience and signaled to men that voting had little to do with gender and more to do with race loyalty. The "intelligent" voters, according to DePriest, had cast their ballot for him, the "race man."

In subsequent years, Black women constituents remained integral players on the Black political landscape. The electoral success in the 1915 campaign fulfilled rising African American expectations and set a precedent. Because Blacks had developed a racially motivated political consciousness, the Republican Party could not retreat from continuing to support the candidacy of at least one African American in the ward. Long after DePriest's victory, Black men maintained a lock on at least one of the second ward City Council seats. Louis B. Anderson won the seat in 1917, and Robert R. Jackson claimed the position in 1918.[24]

African American women won a considerable measure of acceptance in Chicago politics primarily because of their tenacity, the passage of a suffrage bill by the state legislature, the creation of organized suffrage clubs, the development of a distinct politically conscious plan, and the adoption of a progressive reform agenda. To appease Black men who felt threatened by their presence, they highlighted the traditional women's role as municipal housekeepers. And they proved their race loyalty by voting for the "race man." Blending what seemed to be the disparate concepts of race, gender, enfranchisement, and urbanization to formulate a new paradigm for group politics provided the opportunities to bridge gaps, merge voices, and consolidate energies into a powerful political bloc. As a result gender conflict was suppressed, creating a male-female alliance that kept in check the resistance of the Republican machine to African American leadership of their own people.

To successfully place race and sex unity in a contextual framework that benefited women and men was not a simple task. Yet these women succeeded because of self-determination and a strong belief in creating opportunity for African Americans. Unorganized, politically powerless Black men and women were vulnerable, but organized, politically shrewd Black voters were powerful. Urbanized Chicago, with its large enfranchised and racially segregated communities afforded Ida B. Wells-Barnett and politically active African American women the laboratory to explore the possibilities of how the ballot could work for Black women and men. It offered the opportunity for the dynamic convergence of a Black female political force with an astute Black male voting populace steeped in racial consciousness. Racial discrimination forced them into some of the poorest segregated communities, yet it was the segregation that enabled black men and women to successfully develop challenges to the White power structure.

Forcing Blacks, regardless of class, to reside in racially stratified neighborhoods ensured the numerical growth of potential Black voters. And the rise in racial consciousness obligated Blacks to pursue self-determination. This blossoming racial pride opened the door for the collective response that was instrumental in political mobilization. Black women seized the moment to center themselves in the political discourse and demonstrated their ability to reshape, redirect, and strengthen their community's political influence.

NOTES

1. John D. Buenker, "Illinois and the Four Progressive-Era Amendments," 222–25.

2. *Thirteenth Census of the United States*, 512; *Chicago Daily News Almanac and Year Book for 1916* (Chicago: Chicago Daily News Co., 1915), 586.

3. Fannie Barrier Williams, "Colored Women of Chicago," *The Southern Workman* 63 (October 1914): 565.

4. Williams, "Colored Women of Chicago," 566.

5. Ford S. Black, *Black's Blue Book: Directory of Chicago's Active Colored People and Guide to*

Their Activities, 1917 (Chicago: Ford S. Black, 1917), 55–57; Ford S. Black, *Black's Blue Book: Business and Professional Directory* (Chicago: Ford S. Black, 1916), 55; *Chicago Defender,* February 21, 1914.

6. For a discussion of political reform activity among African American women, see Anne Meis Knupfer, *Toward a Tenderer Humanity,* 46–64.

7. Ida Wells-Barnett, "How Enfranchisement Stops Lynching," *Original Rights Magazine* (June 1910): 42–53, rept. in Mildred I. Thompson, *Ida B. Wells-Barnett,* 269.

8. Thompson, *Ida B. Wells-Barnett,* 270–75.

9. Adade Mitchell Wheeler and Marlene Stein Wortman, *The Roads They Made,* 106; *Thirteenth Census,* 505. See also Harold Gosnell, *Negro Politicians;* Allan H. Spear, *Black Chicago;* Willard B. Gatewood, *Aristocrats of Color,* 119–24.

10. Alfreda Duster, ed., *Crusade for Justice,* 244–45.

11. Katherine E. Williams, "The Alpha Suffrage Club," *Half Century Magazine* (September 1916): 12; *Alpha Suffrage Record,* March 18, 1914 [1915], Ida B. Wells-Barnett Papers, Joseph Regenstein Library, University of Chicago; Duster, *Crusade for Justice,* 345; Wanda A. Hendricks, "Ida B. Wells-Barnett and the Alpha Suffrage Club," 263–75.

12. Deborah Gray White, "The Cost of Club Work," 253.

13. Duster, *Crusade for Justice,* 346.

14. *Chicago Defender,* February 21, 1914.

15. *Broad Ax,* February 28, 1914.

16. Duster, *Crusade for Justice,* 346.

17. Ibid., 346–347.

18. Ibid., 347.

19. Ibid.

20. Gosnell, *Negro Politicians,* 163–95; Spear, *Black Chicago,* 78–79.

21. Duster, *Crusade for Justice,* 348.

22. See Wanda A. Hendricks, " 'Vote for the Advantage of Ourselves and Our Race,': 171–84.

23. Oscar DePriest, "Chicago and Woman's Suffrage," *The Crisis* 10 (1915): 179.

24. Gosnell, *Negro Politicians,* 75–76.

CHAPTER SEVEN

"EAGER AND ANXIOUS TO WORK"
Daisy Harriman and the Presidential Election of 1912

KRISTIE MILLER

"With a suddenness and force that have left observers gasping, women have injected themselves into the national campaign this year in a manner never before dreamed of," wrote a reporter for the *World* on August 11, 1912. In the presidential election of 1912, national women's groups for the first time represented all major parties, working in the six woman suffrage states and campaigning for women to use their influence with male voters in the states where women lacked the vote. The Republicans had sponsored a national women's organization as early as 1888, the Democrats had formed a national group early in the summer of 1912, and the Progressives had endorsed woman suffrage. But the *New York Times* considered the Women's National Wilson and Marshall Organization, founded by Florence Jaffray ("Daisy") Harriman to urge women of all political persuasions to support Woodrow Wilson, as the "most ambitious . . . in the way of work."[1] Her activities as head of the WNW&MO signaled a new level of political participation for women.

The Women's Democratic League of New York, headed since 1904 by Nellie Fassett Crosby (identified in the press as Mrs. John Sherman Crosby), became a national organization in June 1912. The National Women's Democratic League (NWDL) planned to mount a nationwide letter campaign on behalf of Democratic candidates, as well as to give semisocial affairs like bridge parties and teas to spread the Democratic word and to raise funds for the general campaign.[2] Less than two months later, in late July, Daisy Harriman, with the approval of William F. McCombs, chairman of the Democratic National Committee, formed the Women's National Wilson and Marshall Organization

8. Florence J. "Daisy" Harriman during World War I (Phyllis Darling, private collection).

to support the Democratic ticket.[3] She opened an office on Fifth Avenue in New York City on August 8. Typical of the wide media coverage she received was the observation by the *New York Times* that the office "gave every appearance of being a bustling political headquarters."[4] Shortly thereafter the Republicans and Progressives also established New York offices run by and intended to influence women.

Even before opening their office, the WNW&MO claimed a hundred members, not including the committee. "Women have come in of their own accord, eager and anxious to work," marveled the *New York Times.*[5] Their work was to be national in scope, drawing on a list of fifty thousand women from all over the United States—teachers, professionals, and members of women's clubs. In each state local women were to organize branches and hold discussions to study the tariff issue, immigration laws, local option, and "other questions with direct influence on home and good citizenship."[6] The WNW&MO would provide weekly letters on talking points and would book women speakers all over the country. In the suffrage states, the organization would operate through existing local Democratic women's organizations.

Press clippings show that branches of the WNW&MO were active on the eastern seaboard, in the West, and in the Midwest. Maryland, the District of Columbia, Tennessee, and Texas also formed clubs, as did southern women living in New York City. Daisy Harriman traveled to Chicago to inaugurate the club in that city, and Dr. A. B. Schultz-Knighton headed a Chicago Colored Woman's Wilson & Marshall League.[7]

Daisy Harriman, married to J. Borden Harriman, a cousin of railroad magnate E. H. Harriman, was socially prominent, but she had also been active in reform circles in New York after the turn of the century, including campaigns to distribute pure milk, fight tuberculosis, and improve housing. As founder and president of the fashionable Colony Club, she had invited New Jersey Governor Woodrow Wilson there to lecture on government; by 1912 she was convinced that he would and should be "the next president of the United States." Wilson's aide, Archibald Alexander, suggested to her that since Wilson had improved laws protecting women and children in New Jersey, "there ought to be a women's organization to help elect him." Harriman claimed that she was "at the bottom of the list" of possible chairs, but that as Jane Addams and other prominent women had joined the newly formed Progressive Party, and Ida Tarbell felt she could be more effective writing, she was the only one available.[8] Harriman saw a need for a women's organization that was not identified with the Democratic Party, which is why they named the organization after the candidates.[9] She believed all women should stand for certain measures, "irrespective of parties"—protective labor laws, especially those affecting women and children, recreation facilities for children, infant and maternal care, eradication of tuberculosis, and "clean government."[10] Nellie Crosby promised that the NWDL, although separate, would be "perfectly harmonious." Crosby noted that the two organizations had different aims: the NWDL was working "a little more slowly" than Harriman's group, who "frankly declare themselves a temporary organization." Crosby wanted to be a factor "in the election of subsequent Democratic presidents" as well.[11]

As a social reformer, Harriman preferred Democrats to Progressives, whom she accused of having appropriated many traditionally Democratic principles. She argued that even if Theodore Roosevelt could be elected, he would not have a majority in Congress and could therefore get no legislation passed. Furthermore she claimed that TR lacked Wilson's stability, coming dangerously close to the negative campaigning she elsewhere claimed was beneath the women.[12]

A more significant problem for many women who shared Harriman's interest in progressive reform was the issue of suffrage. The Progressives had endorsed woman suffrage in their platform. Daisy Harriman noted that most of the women she would have liked to have in her organization, like Jane Addams, "had gone to perch on the suffrage plank."[13] Sometimes Harriman tried to dismiss the importance of suffrage as an issue, claiming that Wilson's position on the tariff and his legislative record should have been "enough to win over all women."[14] She argued that in any case, Roosevelt was not in a position to promise suffrage, that the Democrats were more likely to have a congressional majority that could pass suffrage laws. (She either did not know or would not admit that the southern Democrats, one of whom was Woodrow Wilson, were vehemently opposed to woman suffrage, not least because it would raise the question of suffrage for the African American community in the South.)[15]

Harriman wanted the WNW&MO to appeal not only to women of all political backgrounds but also to "those who favor the vote, those who don't have it but want it, and those who don't want it."[16] The organization was predicated on the notion that, outside of the six suffrage states, women could use their indirect influence over the men in their families, persuading them to vote for Wilson and Marshall. Harriman admitted that the notion of "indirect influence" was like a "red rag" to some women, since it was but a poor substitute for the direct ballot. However, she insisted that there was no need "for women to sit back and say they can't do some good in politics until they have the vote." Women who wanted the vote could, by cooperating with men in the campaign, "demonstrate that they deserve the vote." She may have been mistaken in this assumption. Wilson came late to the support of women voters.

He did not endorse suffrage at the state level until 1915 and endorsed the federal amendment only after the militant campaign waged during the war by Alice Paul's Congressional Union.[17]

Women who did not want the vote still had the "responsibility of indirect influence," according to Harriman. "Women who oppose equal suffrage say a woman has enough influence in her home to see her husband votes correctly," she noted. "Here is where they can prove it." She believed that party alignment was weakening and that women also had the chance to influence young men who would be voting for the first time. Women could influence other women, too, and were urged to persuade the wives of prominent Democratic men to join the Wilson and Marshall clubs. Members were also instructed to "interview wives of intelligent workingmen and interest them in lessening the high cost of living."[18]

At first the WNW&MO stressed Governor Wilson's legislative record. One of their first actions was a mass mailing of one hundred thousand that included a long list prepared by Daisy Harriman of laws passed during his administration for the protection of working men and women. These included a ten-hour day for women and employers' liability laws as well as health measures.[19] The letter also addressed what emerged as the main theme of her campaign, the high cost of living; it explained how expenses would be reduced through a lower tariff under a Wilson administration. Enclosed with the letters was a membership coupon. Membership was free but the organization solicited contributions of from ten cents to five dollars. They also sold Wilson and Marshall stamps and certificates in amounts of from one to one hundred dollars. Campaign finance reform was another popular topic with women; by helping to fund the campaign, women hoped to keep it "free of sinister influence."[20]

Daisy Harriman next took to the hustings. An hour after her official election as president of the WNW&MO on August 20, 1912, she addressed a crowd of several hundred in Union Square in downtown New York City. She was surprised to see that most of the crowd were men and boys, with only a dozen or so women. Nevertheless, in her nervousness, she stuck to her prepared speech and addressed the audience as "You housekeepers!" Although she was speaking to the voters themselves, she asked the men to pass her remarks along to their wives. Her nervousness was understandable; she alluded to the time, not long before, when women speaking in public had been physically assaulted: "Even if you wanted, you could not throw an egg at me, because they are too expensive." Again she stressed Wilson's legislative record and the high cost of living. At the end of the speech, she and other women began tossing campaign buttons to the crowd, who swarmed up onto the platform and, in their eagerness to grab buttons, pushed the women aside, nearly knocking them down.

Nevertheless Harriman pronounced the occasion a "great success."[21] As time went on Harriman became a more confident speaker. She spoke in Far Rockaway, despite a report that "residents down there think that it is a terrible thing for a woman to speak in public." She had to defuse a hostile audience at one meeting "by tact and argument"; an account of another meeting reported that a man "with socialistic tendencies" failed to disconcert her. One man demanded to know how she, a wealthy woman, dared address a meeting of common people. Harriman replied that her father had been an immigrant (from England, be it noted) who had earned his fortune by his own efforts.[22]

Although there was a hint of *noblesse oblige* in some of her pronouncements, such as when she urged "those people who have had greater advantages in culture and self-restraint to go out and meet half-way those others who have seen a vision but may need the counsel of more tutored minds," Harriman was aware of the needs of the working class. She was a strong supporter of unions. She planned a series of meetings for Tuesdays at noon, to give working women the opportunity to attend, and suggested that nurseries be provided at political gatherings.[23]

Some reporters had suggested that the tariff was not a particularly compelling topic, especially for women, but the WNW&MO found a way to dramatize it. At the end of August, a "Tariff Exhibit" opened on Union Square, consisting of a three-room apartment furnished for a family of four. Inside, everyday articles, from sewing machines to soap and tooth powder, were tagged with their current cost and with what their cost would be under a lower tariff. By mid-September the exhibit was said to be drawing as many as twelve thousand visitors daily; Nellie Crosby alternated with Harriman in presiding over it. Harriman hoped that the Housewives Committee, which had organized the tariff exhibit, would "become national in scope and a permanent organization after [the campaign]." This inspired the Republicans to mount a rival exhibit on another side of the square.[24] Publicizing technical issues in a vivid, accessible form was a Progressive Era technique for getting public support behind social reforms.

Although the tariff exhibit was designed to appeal to women's interests, on a designated Housewives Day only a few women appeared, in contrast to a large number of men. Daisy Harriman, the featured speaker, criticized protectionism, personalizing the tariff issue by drawing from her own experience in reporting on a strike in Lawrence, Massachusetts: "Conditions were very bad and wages low in the woolen mills, and wool is our best protected industry." She asked the men to tell their wives and sisters to visit, seeming again not to realize that, as male voters themselves were in her audience, she could appeal directly to them. It may have been difficult for her to redefine the role she had envisioned for herself as someone who educated women to use their influence with men. However, it is possible that Harriman may have been trying to recruit future female voters. The press noted that "Although Mrs. Harriman says that women will exert an indirect influence, her methods are extremely direct."[25]

If Harriman and other women were confused about their new role as political activists, the press was equally ambivalent; it was sometimes snide, sometimes gushing, but admiring more often than not. Many reports suggested the incongruity of women in politics. "Modishly clad figures made their way into stern committee meetings," noted the *Peoria Star*. Some reporters included descriptions of the women's clothes. Some belittled the women's work, perhaps at times unconsciously: "Between speeches a band played ragtime tunes after the manner of real political meetings," one paper noted at the first Union Square meeting. Progressive women were called "Moosettes." A headline declared "Parasols Now 'In the Ring.' "[26]

More stinging were dismissals of the seriousness of "society women." During the scuffle at the Union Square meeting, it was reported that "not a few feared to use their bejeweled hands to beat off impulsive ones." Another paper speculated that "Women in social circles which forbid their being present at department store bargain sales must have some excitement occasionally." Harriman rebuked the press on several occasions for identifying her as a "society woman" and offered this careful presentation: "I am not a society woman and do not wish to be referred to as one . . . It is ridiculous the way so many people speak . . . as if members of this alleged class was [sic] addicted to nothing less than amusing themselves . . . Women who go a great deal in society [are] earnest, serious, thinking folk and vitally interested in bettering conditions but they do their work quietly." Her social status may not have been a liability. Just as the suffrage movement recruited elite clubwomen to give their cause respectability in the public eye, Daisy Harriman's social status may have helped to make women's political activity more acceptable to both women and men.[27]

More often press coverage was positive and predicted that women's campaign activities were just the beginning of their political involvement. The *New York American* looked forward to "All thoroughgoing school reform and all the social and political regenerations that are to come through the wider use of the initiative of women. It is not what Mr. Wilson or Mr. Roosevelt or any other public man may say of these matters that counts . . . What counts is the sudden and intense inspiration of Mrs. Harriman and women of her sort." The *New York Evening Sun* noted the "strenuousness with which the three big bureaus at the three national headquarters [the NWDL had been put in the shade] are vying with each other for the support of their sisters this fall as if woman suffrage were already an accomplished fact throughout the Union instead of in only half a dozen states." Perhaps because of the novelty of women campaigners, Harriman got extensive press coverage, often more than male speakers at the same event. Papers all over the country ran many of the articles sent out from the WNW&MO office in New York, some of which Harriman had written herself. Her message was clearly reaching large numbers of both men and women through the media.[28]

An ongoing debate at this time was whether women would improve politics or politics would improve women's lives. Many men ignored the question of whether women, like men, had a right to participate and evaluated their activities only in light of their potential for good. A reporter for the *Chicago Examiner* wrote: "If women in politics are merely going to debate the old issues that men have debated for generations, then advent of the woman means nothing but increase in the number of debates." The *New York Clubfellow* asked peevishly: "Are they in earnest or only in love with being in the limelight?"—as if to suggest that women could be admitted into politics only if their motives were purer than men's.[29]

It is difficult to gauge the extent to which the WNW&MO influenced the election, even though William McAdoo telegraphed Harriman after the election that it was "not possible to exaggerate the importance and effectiveness of your personal efforts, nor overestimate the value of the work of the WNW&MO which you formed." It is easier to see that the organization helped Daisy Harriman achieve some of her own political aims. It gave her a forum to promote two of her causes: the use of public schools for voting and civic meetings and health care reform for children. Ten days after Harriman was named chair, the WNW&MO called on women "in every city and town" to lobby for the use of schools as polling places and for community assemblies. Schools, according to Harriman, would provide "in each neighborhood a place where men and women could meet on equal ground to examine public questions." Perhaps she thought that if women were going to enter politics, it was preferable to have a neutral place where men had not already made themselves at home. A committee was formed in Manhattan by August 31 to ask for the consent of the Board of Education.[30]

Harriman also believed that health was a "vital" issue for women. In this she was supported by the General Federation of Women's Clubs, which, at their biennial conference earlier in the summer, had criticized the Department of Agriculture for being under the influence of special interests. Harriman, who had been working for a number of years to ensure the distribution of pure milk and eggs and to eradicate the conditions that bred tuberculosis, said "No function is so essential as women's function as protector of the food supply, protection of sanitary and hygienic working conditions and the general conservation of human life." On September 9 Wilson met with Harriman at the Colony Club to form a WNW&MO Bureau of Health Conservancy that would lobby Congress to pass pure food laws. Although this issue benefited Wilson—the president of the Bureau of Health, Dr. Harvey W. Wiley, proposed campaign documents to show that both Roosevelt and Taft had opposed pure food legislation—it seems to have been at least as much a case of Harriman and the other women using Wilson for their own political ends. Men who hoped women would raise new issues in the political debate thought that by discussing these topics Harriman had made "an inspiring beginning."[31]

In addition to using the WNW&MO to lobby for issues of national concern, Harriman used the extensive media exposure her position gained her to lobby for local New York issues as well. In late October she won media coverage for her endorsement of a request before the Board of Estimates for appropriations to build a separate house of detention with separate facilities for segregating younger women. Reformatories were needed, not workhouses, Harriman said.[32]

By 1912 women, especially middle-class and elite women, were finding fulfillment in political activity. Harriman noted that "The time has come when women have more to do than just to sit around a bridge table or sewing basket . . . We must get out and make the world better." Whatever the effect of her organization's activities on the election, her work in the 1912 campaign was the beginning of her own life in politics. The following year President Wilson recognized her with an appointment to the Federal Industrial Relations Commission, the first to a federal commission for a woman. This position led to other appointive offices during World War I. She remained active in partisan politics, working in 1913 for the fusion candidacy of John Purroy Mitchel, and in the 1920s and 1930s for Democratic candidates at the local and national level. In 1937 President Franklin Roosevelt named her minister to Norway, where she distinguished herself during the Nazi invasion.[33]

NOTES

1. *New York Times,* September 9, 1912. All references except where noted are from 1912 newspaper clippings in the Florence Jaffray Harriman Scrapbook, private property of Mrs. Phyllis Darling (hereafter HS). Where a date or place is not given for a clipping, I have included the HS page number.

2. Unidentified clippings, August 26, 1912, HS 20.

3. *New York Tribune,* August 7, 1912.

4. *New York Times,* [August 7, 1912].

5. Ibid., August 9, 1912.

6. *Bayside Watchman,* August 23, 1912.

7. *Baltimore Sun,* September 30, 1912; *New York Tribune,* August 20, 1912; *Sacramento* [California] *Star,* October 12, 1912; *Dallas News,* October 18, 1912; *Elizabeth* [New Jersey] *Journal,* October 18, 1912; *Chicago Evening American,* September 17, 1912; *Chicago Journal,* October 18, 1912.

8. Mrs. J. Borden [Florence Jaffray] Harriman, *From Pinafores to Politics* (New York: Henry Holt, 1923), 111–12; *Seattle Intelligencer,* August 21, 1912.

9. *New York Tribune,* August 7, 1912.

10. *Morning World,* August 6, 1912; *New York Herald,* August 16, 1912.

11. Unidentified clipping, August 25, 1912, HS 48.

12. *Morning World,* August 11, August 19, 1912; *National Monthly,* untitled article by Daisy Harriman, HS 27.

13. Harriman, *From Pinafores to Politics,* 112.

14. *Morning World,* August 8, 1912.

15. See Sara Hunter Graham, *Woman Suffrage,* 114.

16. *National Monthly,* Harriman article.

17. [Boston] *Globe,* August 12, 1912; *National Monthly,* Harriman article; Graham, *Woman Suffrage,* 114.

18. [Boston] *Globe,* August 12, 1912; *Chicago Interocean,* September 18, 1912; *Hackensack* [New Jersey] *Record,* August 21, 1912.

19. *New York Herald,* August 12, 1912; *New York Times,* August 9, 1912.

20. [Boston] *Globe,* August 12, 1912; *New York American,* August 24, 1912; *Detroit Times,* August 19, 1912; *New York Herald,* August 10, 1912; *New York American,* August 30, 1912.

21. *Tucson Citizen,* August 20, 1912; *Morning World,* August 21, 1912; [New York] *Post,* August 20, 1912; *Portland Express,* August 20, 1912; *New York American,* August 21, 1912.

22. *New York Times,* August 14, 1912; *New York American,* September [4?], 1912, HS 32; *Brooklyn Eagle,* September 10, 1912.

23. *Morning World,* August 11, 1912; *Chicago Examiner,* September [18?], 1912, HS 40; *Morning World,* August 20, 1912; *Lincoln* [Nebraska] *Star,* August 21, 1912.

24. *Chicago Examiner,* September [18?], 1912, HS 40; *New York Evening Sun,* September 26, 1912; *Brooklyn Eagle,* September 8, 1912; *New York Telegraph,* October 19, 1912.

25. *New York Times,* September 14, 1912; *New York Herald,* August 16, 1912.

26. *Peoria Star,* October 18, 1912; *Press,* August 21, 1912; *Lincoln* [Nebraska] *News,* October 18, 1912; unidentified clipping, HS 43.

27. [Unidentified city] *Press,* August 21, 1912; *Grand Rapids News,* August 23, 1912; *Cincinnati Enquirer,* August 23, 1912; see Graham, *Woman Suffrage,* 36–37.

28. *New York American,* August 30, 1912; *New York Evening Sun,* August 20, 1912; *Brooklyn Eagle,* September 10, 1912.

29. See Graham, *Woman Suffrage,* 28; *Chicago Examiner,* October 10, 1912; *New York Clubfellow,* October 16, 1912.

30. McAdoo telegraph, November 6 [1912], HS (loose); *New York Tribune,* August 30, 1912; *New York Telegraph,* August 31, 1912.

31. *Houston Chronicle,* October 9, 1912; *New York Times,* September 9, 1912; *Chicago Examiner,* October 10, 1912.

32. *New York Herald,* October 20, 1912.

33. *Newark Morning Star,* August 29, 1912; see also Graham, *Woman Suffrage,* 74.

9. *Woman's campaign train for Hughes (Bain Collection, Prints and Photographs Division, Library of Congress).*

CHAPTER EIGHT

MAPPING A NATIONAL CAMPAIGN STRATEGY

Partisan Women in the Presidential Election of 1916

MOLLY M. WOOD

In September 1916 Maud Howe Elliott, veteran campaigner and delegate to the 1912 Progressive convention, received a long-distance call from her former colleague in that campaign, Frances Kellor. Kellor, a well-known social reformer, had been busy all summer organizing women to work in the upcoming presidential election for Republican candidate Charles Evans Hughes. She asked Elliott to "please plan to go on our Woman's Hughes Campaign Train which will go across the country in October."[1] The women on the campaign train, which traveled through twenty-one states in October 1916, wanted to educate the American public, especially other women, about the relatively unknown Republican candidate and hoped to convince voters to cast their ballots for Hughes in November. As the organizers of the train later stated, the Hughes Campaign Train was an "eleventh hour attempt to rally the women of the country to the cause of Mr. Hughes."[2] Completely organized, funded, and staffed by women, the Hughes train was a unique example of women's partisan political activity before the passage of the Nineteenth Amendment. In a well-meaning effort to appeal to all women who might potentially support Hughes, however, the campaigners actually succeeded in alienating many women across the country.

The women who arranged, promoted, and campaigned from the Hughes train in 1916 faced a distinctive set of problems stemming from their assumptions about the role they and other women across the country would play in the election. For a variety of reasons these women believed Hughes would make a better president than the incumbent Woodrow Wilson, and they championed as their only goal the successful election of Hughes to the presidency. They also believed that the majority of women nationwide were politically uneducated. If women were interested or involved in politics at all, they believed, it was solely at the local level. The role of the women campaigners, therefore, was to educate women across the country about Hughes's favorable stand on issues of national importance, such as labor, Americanism, and preparedness.[3] The campaigners expected women to embrace this political education on the importance of "national" issues and either vote for or otherwise lend their support to Hughes.

The "campaign strategy" adopted to achieve these goals reveals much about the obstacles partisan women faced in a national political campaign at this time of transition—when many women in the West were already exercising their right to vote, but before most women in other parts of the country felt themselves to be part of the "official" national political process. In order to promote the "national" issues that would supposedly affect all citizens, the women campaigners decided to avoid addressing potentially divisive matters such as partisanship, state and local elections, and woman suffrage. They believed they could convince women voters that they were totally committed to one goal—electing Hughes—and that this solidarity in the face of differences over other issues would be enough to convince voters to drop their petty concerns and do what was best for the nation. The women pledged not to take part in any local elections, and they hoped to appeal to women of all political persuasions. By taking no public stand on the suffrage issue during the campaign, they hoped to win the support of women who both opposed and supported suffrage. The campaigners formulated a "campaign strategy" that reveals remarkable insight into the problems they would face in tackling a nationwide audience of women. They anticipated and attempted to resolve divisive issues, but they failed to foresee other problems and to gauge accurately the response women across the country would have to their efforts.

In 1916 Republican and Progressive leaders had agreed to run a joint compromise candidate, Republican Charles Evans Hughes, and set about the difficult task of mounting an effective challenge to the popular incumbent.[4] Just after the Republican convention at Chicago adjourned, a group of Republican and former Progressive women approached Hughes about forming a women's committee to act in conjunction with the new men's Hughes Alliance, which was being formed for the sole purpose of uniting Republican, Progressive, and independent voters to elect Hughes. Hughes "heartily approved" of the plan for a women's committee, and Frances Kellor assumed duties as temporary secretary of the fledgling organization. In preparation for the first organizational meeting of the committee, Kellor sent a letter to three hundred women throughout the country, inviting them to join. One hundred and thirty-five women accepted membership.[5]

Kellor and her committee went to work raising money and setting goals for the campaign as soon as they began to receive positive responses to their appeal. While pledging to work in "closest possible cooperation" with the "various phases of the men's" Hughes Alliance, the Women's Committee retained sole control over its own work and immediately initiated a campaign to raise $100,000 for Hughes.[6] On July 7 fifty-six members of the Women's Committee met and made Frances Kellor its permanent chair. Kellor emphasized that the Women's Committee was first and foremost a *temporary* organization, formed to offer a "medium through which all citizens dissatisfied with Wilson might cooperate in order to elect Hughes."[7] Kellor and the other women assumed that with the proper "education" on the issues of greatest national importance, "all citizens dissatisfied with Wilson," especially women, could cooperate to put Hughes in the White House.

The Women's Committee took on the impossible task of trying to appeal to all women who were not already unswervingly attached to Wilson or the Democratic Party. Since the Women's Committee was not a permanent organization of Republican women, and in order to appeal to the largest number of potential supporters, the women campaigners officially disclaimed the issue of partisanship. The committee professed to be "non-partisan and non-factional in character," and members pledged not to become involved in any local elections.[8] They insisted that every "effort will be made to unite women throughout the country of all parties . . . "[9]

Clearly, however, the committee women were partisan. They sought, after all, "to work in entire harmony and cooperation with party committees and with other organizations in behalf of presidential electors pledged to vote for Charles Evans Hughes . . . "[10] Perhaps they were not all lifelong Republicans, but they endorsed and worked diligently for the Republican candidate.[11] The organizers of the Women's Committee felt, however, that being outspokenly "partisan" would be too divisive. If the women campaigners claimed to be a new Republican women's organization, they believed too many potential voters and campaign workers would turn away. By following an official declaration of nonpartisanship, they hoped to win votes from Progressives, independent or undecided voters, and possibly even a few Democrats. The committee claimed to be nonpartisan because they wanted to appeal both to those women like themselves who were already politically conscious and perhaps had already identified themselves with a particular party and to those many women who remained politically unaware and uneducated, those who had not yet "committed" to a party. Finally they also hoped to attract women Kellor referred to as "club women"—women who generally eschewed party politics and remained "above" the political fray. The strategy of downplaying partisanship shows an insightful recognition by the women campaigners of the various stages of political awareness and activism among women across the nation. The mistake they made was in assuming that women with so many obvious differences could be "united" for Hughes and in blatantly ignoring the one issue that automatically came to mind wherever women and politics mixed in 1916.

From its inception the committee believed women voters would play a vital role in this election. Noting that "there are nearly four million women voting this year," they emphasized the importance of carrying a "constructive campaign . . . which will appeal to women voters" to the suffrage states. There the Women's Committee went to work immediately, sending field organizers off to assess the situation.[12] These field organizers, as well as committee members in each state, devoted their time to winning votes, primarily women's votes, for Hughes. Through the summer they publicized Hughes's support for legislation protecting women and child workers and for "social legislation and other subjects of particular interest to women."[13]

Kellor recognized early on, however, that "different policies would be necessary in suffrage and non-suffrage states."[14] In nonsuffrage states, the committee's goals were not well defined. First of all the organization of branch committees could not take place until a men's Hughes Alliance had already been established, and this impeded the women in many states.[15] But in those nonsuffrage states where a Women's Committee was active, members concentrated their efforts on advancing education about campaign issues and spreading Hughes propaganda. They had the more difficult and challenging job of educating nonvoting women about "the issues" and encouraging them to be active and to persuade the men in their lives to vote for Hughes. Women campaigners who worked in suffrage states, on the other hand, had the clear task of winning women's vote for Hughes. Katharine Bement Davis, a longtime Republican and the first woman appointed to a cabinet-level position in New York City government, summed up the role women across the country should play in this election by stating that women who do not vote must do the job of education, while "women who vote do their part by voting."[16] As the women campaigners worked through the summer in both suffrage and nonsuffrage states, however, no one mentioned a word about woman suffrage as a campaign issue.

While the suffrage issue remained quiet over the summer, the campaigners faced other problems. Reports from Women's Committee organizers in many states were not encouraging. There was, as feared, a "general preoccupation with the state and local tickets," which resulted in a "marked lack of interest in the national situation."[17] The committee members needed to come up with a plan to reassert their commitment to "national" political work—a strategy to get the public interested in the presidential election, as opposed to local elections, and enthusiastic about their candidate in particular. By September 17 the Women's Committee had financed and completed arrangements for a women's campaign train to travel across the country. The train would carry "prominent women in various fields," who would strive to unite women of every belief "under the banner of Republicanism."[18] Many of the women aboard the train were "known throughout the country" as "writers and speakers."[19]

As chair of the Women's Committee, Frances Kellor assumed primary responsibility for organizing the campaign train. Maud Howe Elliott later referred to her as "the soul of the enterprise."[20] In recruiting women to go on the train, Kellor turned to many of her former colleagues in the Progressive campaign of 1912. In that year the Progressive Party had welcomed women and promised them an "equal voice" in managing the party.[21] Kellor and others like her had responded eagerly to this opportunity. Katharine Bement Davis, Mary Antin, Margaret Dreier Robins, Mary Elizabeth Dreier, and Maud Howe Elliott, who had all worked for the Progressives in 1912, responded to Kellor's call in 1916.[22] Kellor and others on the Women's Committee had been disappointed in the Republican Party's dismissal of women as significant political workers. When they formed the Women's Committee, they were careful to publicly emphasize the "cooperation" of the committee with the men's Hughes Alliance, but they really expected and received complete autonomy in decision making. These were women who had firsthand experience in a presidential election and because of their positive experience with the Progressive Party fully expected that their important role in politics would continue in 1916.

The campaigners were prepared, they thought, for the political challenges they would face, but they did not foresee the reaction that women across the country would have to their endeavor.

To their great surprise, misconceptions about some of the women campaigners and the membership of the Women's Committee aroused considerable hostility. Davis discovered that branches of the Democratic National Committee wired dispatches containing information about some of the members to local Wilson leaders in each city where the train was scheduled to stop. A telegram that reached Fargo, North Dakota, for example, stated that the committee in charge of the train included such members as "Mrs. Stotesbury, whose husband is a Philadelphia partner of Morgan and Co." and Mrs. John Hays Hammond, "wife of the multi-million dollar mining man."[23] While writers of the telegram acknowledged that women who were actually making the trip were largely professional women, they were still indignant that members of the Women's Committee included "Mrs. Daniel Guggenheim of Smelter Trust" and "Mrs. Cornelius Vanderbilt, who reputedly inherited millions in railroad capital." The train was widely attacked as the "Women's Billionaire Special."[24]

Vast sums of money were indeed contributed to the Women's Committee by some of the wealthiest members of the committee over the summer. The committee in fact had no choice but to rely on the generous contributions of wealthy women, since they required no dues for membership and received no monetary support from the National Hughes Alliance or from the Republican National Committee.[25] The press and Democratic enemies translated the extensive contributions of wealthy Republican women—the only way the train could be financed—into tales of women campaigners wearing huge diamond rings and ball gowns from Paris, traveling with French poodles and hairdressers.[26] These images account for some of the hostility the campaigners faced and was one of the unanticipated reasons why the Hughes Train could not successfully reach out to all women and "unite them under the banner of Republicanism." Even though the women on the train were mostly professional, independent, and not wealthy, they never successfully repudiated the image of the "Billionaire Special."

They also failed to predict the hostility to their venture of many western women, who already enjoyed the right to vote. Since all the women who made the decisions, as well as most of the women on the campaign train, were from the East, they had difficulty establishing credibility among many women in the West.[27] While women on the train continued to insist that "it would be difficult to find a group of people with more widely differing views . . . " who were willing to "unite in one common interest," many western women remained skeptical that these "Easterners" had any insight into their lives.[28] For example, though the women campaigners had predicted that "woman suffrage" would be a divisive issue and had therefore decided to ignore it, they never anticipated that their mere presence in the West, as nonvoting women, would create such hostility. In Helena, Montana, the wife of Democratic Governor Sam V. Stewart remarked: "It is ridiculous for these women, who haven't a vote, to come all the way out here to tell women who can vote how to do it." In Portland three thousand women of the local Wilson Women's League registered disapproval of the "Eastern women's vote-getting invasion," referring to the campaigners as "impertinent" and "silly."[29]

The campaigners, however, had committed themselves to the strategy of silence on the suffrage issue, even though their candidate had recently come out in favor of a national suffrage amendment and President Wilson had yet to do so.[30] Though the vast majority of women on the train were personally in favor of woman suffrage, they continued to avoid the issue, attempting to show a solidarity for Hughes that went beyond his lukewarm support of one specific issue.[31] The women still hoped to win the support of both suffragists and antisuffragists for Hughes. On the one hand, they did not want to alienate potential "anti-suffrage" votes for Hughes; on the other hand, they were aware that many of the women in their audiences, even in nonsuffrage states, were decidedly in favor of suffrage. In front of a prosuffrage audience on October 7 in St. Paul, Minnesota, Maud Howe Elliott broke the "suffrage taboo" of the campaign train by declaring, "Now that I have told you about Mr. Hughes, I wish to add personally, as it were, that I am for suffrage from first to last." Her exclamation brought a steady round of applause.[32] Promoters of the train continued to stress, however, that the train was "in no sense a woman suffrage vehicle."[33] The object of the women's campaign, Davis declared, was to "get votes for a man [Hughes] and not for women."[34]

Early in the campaign, the *New York Herald* had optimistically reported that "many who have never cared for the 'votes for women' issue" have now joined together "on the broader lines of national politics."[35] But the suffrage issue would not go away. In California Rheta Childe Dorr declared that she was for Hughes because he supported suffrage. Robins also spoke publicly for suffrage in Colorado, on October 25.[36] Maud Howe Elliott remarked that "in the states where only one half the citizens have any political power," the question "is so acute and poignant that in general society the lovers of peace avoid mentioning suffrage."[37] But by trying to avoid the issue, the campaigners ended up angering both suffragists and "antis" in different parts of the country.

In addition, the campaigners angered many women by refusing to take a clear partisan stand, especially on issues of local importance. Elliott emphasized that it was the "unbroken rule" of the campaign that the women campaigners "were to take no part in local politics" and were "not allowed to speak for any of the local candidates."[38] But some of the women on the train could not resist speaking out on local affairs. When Elizabeth Freeman called upon the women of Montana to vote for Jeannette Rankin for Congress, many Montana woman voters were so angry that they demanded a public apology for this disruption.[39] The campaigners had hoped to avoid sticky local problems and elections, thereby dodging issues that would divide women.

Meanwhile the attacks of Democratic partisans continued, putting the Hughes campaigners on the defensive. They were even criticized from within for their inability to effectively fight back. Campaign worker Mrs. William Severin of Illinois complained that "there is too much non-partisanship on this train. These women ought to be straight Republicans."[40] But it was still more important to the campaigners to avoid alienating potential Progressive and independent or undecided votes for Hughes than it was to engage in a full-fledged partisan battle of words. At the outset of the campaign trip, Kellor had hoped to "nationalize the women of America—make them forget state, county, racial and sectional lines in a big national cause."[41] Clearly this was not happening, but the women were not about to change their strategy midstream.

The Hughes women campaigners still believed they could, through their strategy of political education on "national issues," overcome the tendency, as they perceived it, of women across the country to be most concerned with matters that directly affected their lives. In the fall of 1916, the two most pressing concerns in the lives of many women were, as Kellor later admitted, the "sentimental" one of keeping their husbands and sons out of any European war, and the "material" issue of general economic prosperity under the current Democratic administration.[42] The campaigners had hoped that by educating women on matters of national importance (which included informing people of the necessity of preparedness and the tenuousness of Wilson's economic plan) and by avoiding issues that might divide women, they could successfully "unite" Republican, Progressive, undecided, apolitical, and even a few Democratic women behind their candidate. Their strategy stressed the "higher goal" of electing a specific candidate for president over other concerns and assumed that American women in general could and would suspend some of their deeply held beliefs in order to help elect their candidate for the highest office in the nation. But while the campaigners were ready and willing to move from "local affairs to big politics," to turn "their eyes from the State House in Albany, [New York] to the White House," not all women were ready and willing to pursue that same strategy.[43]

NOTES

1. Maud Howe Elliott, "The Golden Special," Manuscripts Division, John Hay Library, Brown University, Providence, Rhode Island, 1.

2. Frances Kellor, *Women in National Politics* (New York: Women's Committee, National Hughes Alliance, 1916), 15.

3. Ibid., 5.

4. S. D. Lovell, *The Presidential Election of 1916*, 7–10, 174–75; Donald Bruce Johnson and Kirk Porter, eds., *National Party Platforms*, 194–207.

5. *New York Times*, July 2, 1916, 9:1, July 3, 1916, 5:5; Kellor, *Women in National Politics*, 6; Minutes of the July 7, 1916, meeting of the Women's Committee of the National Hughes Alliance, O'Shaughnessy Family Papers, box 5, Manuscripts Division, New York Public Library, New York [hereafter OFP].

6. *New York Times,* July 2, 1916, 9:1, July 3, 1916, 5:5.

7. Minutes of July 7, 1916, meeting, OFP.

8. "Constitution and By-Laws of the Women's Committee of the National Hughes Alliance," OFP; *New York Times,* July 2, 1916, 9:1; Kellor, *Women in National Politics,* 6.

9. *New York Times,* July 13, 1916, 20:4.

10. "Constitution and By-Laws of the Women's Committee."

11. Kellor, *Women in National Politics,* 17.

12. *New York Times,* July 8, 1916, 5:5; Kellor, *Women in National Politics,* 7.

13. Cornelia Bryce Pinchot to Edith O'Shaughnessy, July 5, 1916, OFP.

14. Minutes of July 7, 1916, meeting, OFP.

15. Kellor, *Women in National Politics,* 7.

16. *New York Times,* August 4, 1916, 5:6.

17. Kellor, *Women in National Politics,* 8.

18. *New York Times,* September 24, 1916, 7:3.

19. *New York Tribune,* October 2, 1916, 4:2; *New York Herald,* October 3, 1916, 3:1.

20. Elliott, "The Golden Special," 4.

21. The Republican and Democratic Parties in 1912 also encouraged women to participate in political work, though they continued to channel women's partisan activism into traditional women's auxiliaries. See Melanie Gustafson, "Partisan Women in the Progressive Era."

22. On Kellor and Davis, see Ellen Fitzpatrick, *Endless Crusade,* 75–77, 92, 147, 162. On Antin, see Edward James, et al., eds., *Notable American Women,* 1:57–58; and Oscar Handlin, Foreword to Mary Antin, *The Promised Land* (Princeton, NJ: Princeton University Press, 1969). On Robins, see Mary Dreier, *Margaret Dreier Robins,* 18–26. On Elliott, see Elliott, "The Golden Special," 1–5.

23. *Chicago Tribune,* October 10, 1916, 11:3.

24. Ibid. and many other examples of the "Billionaire Special," including Dreier, *Margaret Dreier Robins,* 130.

25. Frances Kellor, "Women in the Campaign," *Yale Review* 6 (January 1917): 238–40.

26. See for example *New York Times,* November 20, 1916, 8:1.

27. "Constitution and By-Laws of the Women's Committee," OFP.

28. Elliott, "The Golden Special," 6.

29. *New York Times,* October 12, 1916, 24:2, October 15, 1916, 6:3.

30. Lovell, *Presidential Election of 1916,* 73.

31. Many, though not all, of the women on the campaign train were already outspoken supporters of suffrage.

32. *New York Times,* October 8, 1916, 4:1.

33. Ibid., September 17, 1916, 5:2.

34. Ibid., October 4, 1916, 4:6.

35. *New York Herald,* October 8, 1916, magazine section, 5.

36. As Maud Howe Elliott later recalled, "several of the ladies were either indifferent to suffrage or down right opposed to it"; Elliott, "The Golden Special," 6.

37. Ibid., 92.

38. Ibid., 142.

39. *New York Herald,* October 13, 1916, 2:3.

40. Ibid., October 12, 1916, 2:3.

41. Ibid., October 3, 1916, 4:1.

42. Kellor, "Women in the Campaign," 233.

43. *New York Herald,* October 8, 1916, magazine section, 5.

CHAPTER NINE

CULTURE OR STRATEGY?
Women in New York State Parties, 1917–1930

ANNA L. HARVEY

Recent trends in historiography have made "gender" a popular frame of analysis for scholars interested in understanding various issues surrounding the relationship between women and politics in the United States. One such area of inquiry has concerned the admission of women to participation in partisan electoral politics after the passage of various statewide female suffrage laws and finally constitutional female suffrage in 1920. In particular many scholars have been interested in the question of why women did not gain more access to the party hierarchies upon receiving the vote, and many of these scholars have turned to gender as an answer.

While these scholars have used gender as an analytical concept in ways that differ from each other, the common thread in their arguments is an understanding of gender largely in terms of culture, or shared beliefs about what is valued by and acceptable to a given group. During the period when women were excluded from the suffrage, both women and men are thought to have developed distinctly gendered political cultures. Men developed the conduct of exclusively male partisan politics as a warlike enterprise, in which the goal was exclusively the capture of office and the division of the spoils of office among partisans. Women developed "nonpartisan" organizations that pursued the greater good of the community through moral persuasion rather than through the pursuit of office.[1]

When women were finally allowed to vote, so the argument goes, women came to electoral politics with a different understanding of politics than that held by men. Women did not believe in placing partisan loyalty above their understanding of what was best for the community, and men did not believe in

OFFICIAL BALLOT FOR THE PRIMARY ELECTION OF THE DEMOCRATIC PARTY

29 Election District
12 Assembly District

City of New York, New York County
APRIL 6, 1920

CANDIDATES FOR PARTY POSITIONS

DELEGATES AT LARGE TO NATIONAL CONVENTION (Vote for four)		STATE COMMITTEE (Vote for one)
1	ALFRED E. SMITH	5 CHARLES F. MURPHY
	ELIZABETH MARBURY	
	HARRIET MAY MILLS	
	LOUIS E. DESBECKER	

COUNTY COMMITTEE
(Vote for twenty)

ALTERNATES AT LARGE TO NATIONAL
CONVENTION (Vote for four)

2	EDWARD RIEGELMANN
	HELEN M. CONNOLLY
	WINFIELD A. HUPPUCH
	NETTIE M. HEWITT

	JOHN P. MURPHY
	GEORGE J. WEPPLER
	DANIEL ATKINSON
	CHAS. A. HORST
	JAMES T. MOONEY
	HUGH C. REILLY
	THOS. A. HAMMILL
	CHAS. B. McWADE
	FRANK J. BENNETT
	SUSIE SHERRY
6	MARY C. BYRNE
	ANNA WEPPLER
	ELIZABETH HALLORAN
	HELEN ORTON
	AMELIA O'CONNELL
	VERA MURPHY
	MICHAEL HALLORAN
	WILLIAM BAGGS
	HELEN MURPHY
	SAMUEL GORDON

DISTRICT DELEGATES TO NATIONAL
CONVENTION (Vote for two)

| 3 | LEWIS NIXON |
| | CHARLES F. MURPHY |

DISTRICT ALTERNATES TO NATIONAL
CONVENTION (Vote for two)

| 4 | MARY HAGGERTY |
| | ANNIE MONTGOMERY |

10. 1920 New York Democratic spring primary ballot, displaying for the first time the names of women nominated for positions in the party organization (New York Times, April 4, 1920).

pursuing the good of the community as a goal superior to that of winning elections. As a result women either shunned or did not advance far in male partisan politics and largely continued a tradition of female voluntary organizations, which operated outside of the context of partisan politics.[2]

This cultural understanding of gendered politics is directly at odds with an increasingly dominant trend in political science theory that sees the realm of electoral politics in particular as an arena of action defined by clear rules demarcating the players in the electoral "game," specifying both the rewards and costs of action by those players, and providing for procedures by which players may attain rewards at a minimal cost. These rules may be perceived by women as well as by men, and they are generally not open to interpretation. For instance electoral laws prescribe who may run for office, including both candidates and parties, what one is able to do once one attains office (namely make certain kinds of policy and distribute certain kinds of patronage), and how elections are to be conducted (including who may vote). Given these and other laws, at any particular time it is relatively easy to determine what both men and women will do to achieve their goals at a minimum cost.

Political scientists thus increasingly assume that those who seek office, for example candidates and party elites, are motivated primarily by winning office rather than pursuing policy. While party elites may have goals other than the simple seeking of office, they (or their nominees) must attain office first before they may pursue subsidiary goals. Because candidates and party elites are motivated by electoral concerns first and foremost, groups and organizations that seek policy change rather than elective office must provide electoral incentives if they are to have any hope of seeing their goals realized. The same logic holds if policy-seeking groups want positions in office-oriented organizations such as parties, as a means to further their pursuit of policy change. Party elites will be unwilling to cede control of their organizations to policy-seeking groups unless they are given a strong electoral reason to do so.[3]

The primary difference between the cultural and strategic theories of electoral politics lies in the divergent assumptions they make about the kinds of knowledge held and strategizing done by individuals. The cultural theory assumes that cultural beliefs will dominate the perception of the most efficient way to achieve one's goals: I may perceive that the most efficient way to realize my policy goals is to engage in electoral mobilization, but I refuse to do so because of a cultural norm against partisan electoral mobilization. The strategic theory assumes that strategy will dominate culture: no matter my cultural beliefs, I will see that given the rules of electoral politics, I must play the electoral game if I wish to have any leverage with those who actually make policy.

We need more discussion in both historiography and political science of the merits of these theories as theories. At the same time, we also need more testing of the alternative hypotheses that can be deduced from them. In particular if we are going to make any progress in explaining the experience of women in electoral politics, we need to discuss the criteria under which a cultural story as opposed to a strategic story would be true.

One way in which we can test these theories is to look at the variation over time in the grants of access made to women in the party organizations. In New York state, women in both major party organizations were relegated to the entirely segregated women's organizations that were created immediately after the passage of state female suffrage in November of 1917. These women's committees were not wholly separate from the male state party committees, as the latter had in all cases the authority to appoint and remove female partisans. But women simply did not sit on the men's committees, nor vice versa.[4]

Women in both parties sought access to the men's committees, however, for the latter retained all the decision making authority for both the men's and the women's committees. Under what conditions would male party leaders accede to women's demands?

If the hypothesis concerning women's distinct political culture is correct, then male political elites should have been least likely to grant women access to men's party committees when women were most different from men. Women would logically have been most "different" immediately upon attaining the vote, having spent so many years excluded from male-conducted partisan politics. As women gradually came to participate in male electoral politics, however, over time they should have lost some of the distinctive features of female-conducted politics and learned how to play the men's game; male partisan elites might have learned something about female politics as well. The culture hypothesis thus predicts that women should have seen grants of access to male committees grow over time.

If, however, the hypothesis concerning electoral incentives is correct, then women should have seen grants of access only so long as an independent women's organization posed an electoral threat to male party elites. Women were clearly policy seekers within both parties; throughout the 1920s female leaders in both parties, oftentimes in conjunction with independent women's organizations, pursued a policy agenda rather than or in addition to a purely electoral agenda.[5] Therefore these women would have had to provide party leaders with an electoral reason to cater to their organizational and policy demands. That electoral reason could not have been the result simply of a willingness of female voters to follow the cues of female electoral leaders, because the latter had no power to mobilize women's votes independently of the wishes of male partisan leaders. If female leaders threatened not to mobilize women's votes, or to mobilize those votes on behalf of another party's candidates, they could simply be replaced by male leaders.

Rather such an electoral incentive would have had to come externally, from an independent women's organization that supported the demands of female partisan leaders and that was also free from the organizational control of male leaders. Just such a women's organization, the National League of Women Voters, did in fact publicly support a policy of electoral retaliation upon its founding in 1920 and only later relinquished that policy privately in the early 1920s.[6] The league could therefore have been perceived as an electoral threat by male party leaders in the early 1920s but not after the 1924 elections, in which the league did not work for or against any candidates. The strategic hypothesis thus predicts that male party elites would have responded to the demands of women within the parties early in the 1920s but not later—exactly the opposite of what the cultural hypothesis predicts.

What actually occurred within the parties in New York state? The short answer is that in both parties, women were in fact granted access to male party committees shortly after they attained suffrage and for some years after that milestone. Those grants of access, however, largely ceased after 1925. By the end of the decade, some of those earlier grants were even beginning to be rescinded by male party elites.

This trend was evident in both major state party organizations. In the Republican Party, the state leadership in 1920 announced its support of legislation that would have made women eligible for appointment to newly created seats on the male state committees, if the parties so desired; but this bill did not make it through the state legislature.[7] In early 1922 the Republican governor again endorsed the general principle of granting women more access to party committees. Also in 1922 a bill was passed by the Republican-controlled state legislature calling for the election of at least two county committee members from election districts previously represented by only one seat on these committees; the stated intention of male party leaders was that women would fill these new seats.[8] And in August of 1922, in response to yet more prodding from the women in the party, the Republican State Committee voted to change the party rules governing county committee elections so that the doubling of county committee representation would in fact result in one woman being elected for every man elected to these committees.[9] Later that same year, the Republican State Convention endorsed the representation of women on the Republican State Committee.[10]

In 1923 the Republican State Executive Committee adopted resolutions calling for an equal number of men and women on the committee, asking the legislature to amend election law to provide for two state committee members from each of the larger senatorial districts rather than from the assembly districts and endorsing the principle of equal representation by sex from those districts.[11] Meeting in September the Republican State Committee also adopted the recommendations of its executive committee.[12]

In 1924 after several weeks of conferences, the Republican legislative leadership agreed on a bill to change the basis of representation on the state committees from the 150 Assembly to the 51 Senate districts, with two members elected from each of the latter.[13] However, this bill was killed in the Democrat-controlled Senate.[14] That year's Republican State Convention reaffirmed the endorsement by the male party elite of the principle of female representation on the state committees.[15]

From 1925 to the end of the decade, the Republican State Committee and Republican State Conventions made no new promises as to female representation on party committees. Republican legislators did act in 1925 to fulfill the many promises made by the party in earlier years to provide for women on the state committees; in that year the Republican-controlled legislature enacted a law permitting the parties to change the basis of representation for their state committees and allowing for sex-based representation if the parties so desired.[16] Early in the following year, the Republican State Committee acted on its own prior promises, moving to amend its internal rules so that of the two representatives elected from each Assembly district in the fall primaries to the state committee, one was required to be a woman.[17]

The combination of the new law, silent on sex-based balloting, and the party's sex-based rules, proved susceptible to legal challenge.[18] It was not until 1929 that a constitutionally permissible amendment to the state election law passed the legislature, empowering the state committees to "provide for equal representation of sexes from each unit," and adding, "When any rule provides for the equal representation of sexes from each unit, the designating petitions and primary ballots shall carry party positions separately by sexes."[19] During this period women served for only a brief time on the Republican State Committee, although it was apparently long enough to generate resentment among many of the male State Committee members, several of whom called at the close of 1927 for the county chairmen to run the affairs of the party.[20]

By 1930 then, Republican organization women could finally sit on the Republican State Committee, as had been promised to them as early as 1920 by the male state party elite. But also by 1930, the male Republican elite had found a way to in effect revoke that earlier grant of access. Male party leaders in Erie County had never acceded to the State Committee's directives that county state committee delegations be evenly split between men and women, and had kept these groups all male. When state party women attempted to rectify this situation in 1930, they invoked the state committee's rule, passed in 1926, that required all county committees to send one woman and one man from each Assembly district to sit on the state committee. The secretary of the Republican State Committee, however, flatly denied the existence of such a rule, forcing the women to contest the county organization's nominations in the fall primaries.[21] Moreover backtracking by the male state elite now left the door open for other counties to again send only male representatives to the state committee.

But after another party reorganization at the close of 1930, this issue was essentially rendered moot. Amidst growing complaints from male state committeemen that the newly doubled state committee (now 316 members) was too large to transact party business, the Republican state chairman announced the creation of an even newer committee to manage the affairs of the party. This new state executive committee was intended, said the chairman, to function much as had the old state committee during the years prior to the enfranchisement of women. The new committee was appointed by the state chairman and consisted of nineteen men and only five women.[22] The long struggle of Republican organization women to gain access to the elected state committee appeared now to be irrelevant.

A similar pattern may be seen with respect to New York Republicans' selection of delegates to their own state conventions. The percentages of women who were delegates and alternates at the conventions grew from a combined 20 percent in 1918 to 21 percent female delegates and 37 percent female alternates in 1924, but then fell to 17 percent female delegates and 32 percent female alternates by 1932.[23]

In the Democratic Party a similar pattern in grants of access occurred. In 1920 male Democratic leaders announced their support of legislation permitting women to serve on both parties' state committees.[24] And after the passage of the 1922 bill doubling county committees, the Democratic State Committee enacted a rule making compulsory the selection of a woman for every man serving on the county committees and calling for the appointment of vice chairwomen of those committees.[25]

The following year the Democratic State Committee adopted a resolution asking the legislature to provide for the election of two rather than one state committee member from each Assembly district, "in order that if the electorate so desire the representative from each district may consist of one man and one woman."[26] In 1924 the Democratic State Committee again endorsed legislation doubling the number of seats from each Assembly district on the parties' state committees, with the expressed intent that the new seats be filled by women.[27] After a bill permitting such representation became law in 1925, the

Democratic State Committee voted to double itself by electing two members from each of the state's 150 Assembly districts, with a statement that it was "the sense of the committee" that a man and a woman should be elected from each district.[28]

As noted above, however, the representation of women on the Democratic State Committee would not be legal until 1930. In the meantime Democratic women saw no other grants of representation by the male state party elite. In fact at the 1926 Democratic State Convention, where women sat for the first time on the state committee, the state chairman sought to remove the leader of the state party's women's organization as first vice chairman of the state committee in favor of a man, the women's leader holding that post by "courtesy" only.[29]

The male state Democratic elite also displayed a willingness to grant women partial access to national convention delegations during the early 1920s, but not later. In 1920 women were given two out of four positions available for New York State delegates-at-large to the Democratic National Convention.[30] In 1924, in response to a Democratic National Committee request, the state party elite made a 50/50 male-female split in their at-large delegation to the Democratic National Convention a matter of party policy.[31]

However, by 1932 the Democratic State Committee was prepared to renege on the even split. In March of 1932, male Democratic state leaders decided to nominate only four women out of sixteen delegates-at-large to the impending national convention. This action was taken despite the repetition by the Democratic National Committee in its convention call advising the equal division of delegates-at-large between men and women.[32]

If the cultural story concerning the experience of women in the parties were correct, then we would logically expect women to have received access to men's party committees only after sufficient time had passed to allow women to relinquish their previously held gender norms against participation in partisan electoral politics, or against adherence to party loyalties. But this did not occur: women received the bulk of their grants of access to the New York State men's party committees in the years between 1920 and 1925. Those years demarcate relatively well the period during which the National League of Women Voters could have been seen by party elites as an electoral threat, a threat to be feared if male party leaders did not accede to the demands made by women within the party organizations. Once the League could safely be dismissed as an electoral threat, then party leaders no longer had incentives to cater to the demands of women within the party organizations. Regardless of their cultural beliefs about gender, party elites appear to have responded to women's strategic intra-party search for policy benefits with strategic moves of their own.

NOTES

1. See for example Paula Baker, "The Domestication of Politics,"; and Michael McGerr, "Political Style and Women's Power."

2. See for example Kristi Andersen, *After Suffrage;* and Maureen A. Flanagan, "Chicago Women and Party Politics."

3. For an overview of strategic theories of electoral politics, see Ken Shepsle and Mark Bonchek, *Analyzing Politics.*

4. See Anna L. Harvey, *Votes without Leverage,* chap. 5.

5. Ibid.

6. Ibid., chap. 4.

7. "Mack Senate Boom Started by Women," *New York Times,* February 8, 1920, p. 12; "Puts Women on Committees," ibid., February 23, 1920, p. 15; "Two Women Urged on 'Big Four' Slate," ibid., February 24, 1920, p. 1.

8. "Legislature Opens Session with Rush," *New York Times,* January 5, 1922, p. 4; "Get Bill for Party Committee Women," ibid., January 26, 1922, p. 19; "Report Will Favor Women," ibid., February 8, 1922, p. 19.

9. "County Committees to Be Half Women," *New York Times,* August 6, 1922, p. 10.

10. "Platform Pleases Republican Women," *New York Times,* September 29, 1922, p. 2.

11. "Women Seek Places in State Committee," *New York Times,* June 10, 1923, II p. 1; "Republican Women To Press Demands," ibid., June 14, 1923, p. 10; "State Republicans Dodge Dry Question," ibid., June 15, 1923, p. 1.

12. "Lehman Named by Republicans, Too; Smith Is Assailed," *New York Times,* September 30, 1923, p. 2.

13. "Equality Planned on State Committees," *New York Times,* February 14, 1924, p. 19.

14. "Stand by Film Censorship," *New York Times,* February 29, 1924, p. 19; "Mrs. Sabin Replies to Mrs. Blair's Charge," ibid., June 22, 1924, p. 24.

15. "Women Play a Big Part," *New York Times,* September 24, 1924, p. 2; "Anti-Klan Forces Win by One Vote," ibid., September 25, 1924, p. 1; "Roosevelt Nominated for Governor," ibid., September 26, 1924, p. 1.

16. "Lowman to Control Party in Senate," *New York Times,* January 25, 1925, p. 17; "Finds Leaders Friendly," ibid., January 26, 1925, p. 2; "Women Press Leaders for Equality Bill," ibid., February 10, 1925, p. 25; "Assembly Passes Measure Affecting Women Politicians," ibid., March 26, 1925, p. 2.

17. "Smith Sticks to Retirement Plan; Says 'It Must Be'," *New York Times,* January 16, 1926, p. 1; "State Republicans Meet Here in Fall; Wet Victory Seen," ibid., May 22, 1926, p. 1.

18. "Test on Women Members," *New York Times,* September 26, 1926, p. 18; "Legislature Delays Adjourning a Week," ibid., March 8, 1928, p. 3.

19. *New York Times,* April 13, 1929, p. 6 ; "Up-State Women in Fight for Place," ibid., August 24, 1930, 3:5.

20. "Republican Chiefs in Up-State Revolt," *New York Times,* December 18, 1927, p. 26.

21. "Up-State Women in Fight for Place," *New York Times,* August 24, 1930, 3:5; "Women Take Active Part," ibid., September 14, 1930, 3:5.

22. "24 Named by Macy to Lead State Party," *New York Times,* December 21, 1930, p. 1.

23. "Want Roosevelt to Lead in State," *New York Times,* July 18, 1918, p. 9; Marguerite Fisher, "Women in the Political Parties," 92–93.

24. "Mack Senate Boom Started by Women," *New York Times,* February 8, 1920, p. 12.

25. "Anti-Hearst Women Will Organize City," *New York Times,* June 28, 1922, p. 19.

26. "Lehman Is Named for Appeals Court," *New York Times,* September 29, 1923, p. 3.

27. "Women Democrats Lose Equality Point," *New York Times,* September 26, 1924, p. 3.

28. "Smith Sticks to Retirement Plan; Says 'It Must Be'," *New York Times,* January 16, 1926, p. 1.

29. "Women Fight for Mrs. O'Day," *New York Times,* September 27, 1926, p. 3; "Democrats Re-Elect Committee Officers," ibid., September 28, 1926, p. 14.

30. "Democratic Women Win Two Places on Party 'Big Four'," *New York Times,* February 26, 1920, p. 1; "State Democrats Declare Boldly for Dry Repeal," ibid., February 27, 1920, p. 1.

31. Eleanor Roosevelt, in "Democratic Women Win," *New York Times,* April 16, 1924, p. 2.

32. "Democrats to Pick 16 for Convention," *New York Times,* March 5, 1932, p. 2.

CHAPTER TEN

DEFYING THE PARTY WHIP
Mary Garrett Hay and the Republican Party, 1917–1920

ELISABETH ISRAELS PERRY

In 1920 feminist writer Crystal Eastman speculated that on the day the woman suffrage amendment was ratified, men would say, "Thank God, this everlasting woman's fight is over!" In contrast women would say, "Now at last we can begin!"[1] But how? Eastman probably assumed that a clear path would lead women toward political empowerment. In reality women were unsure how to proceed. Should they join political parties? No, some said; women should first learn how parties worked, meanwhile continuing to pursue nonpartisan agendas through their powerful voluntary associations. In response to such arguments, others warned that as long as women held aloof from partisanship, they would remain politically inconsequential.

Disagreeing among themselves was not the only obstacle political women faced after suffrage. Seeking empowerment within political parties proved well-nigh impossible. After suffrage the major parties courted women's votes, especially in the early years after suffrage, when a "woman's voting bloc" appeared real. Party leaders also showed some interest in integrating women into their power structures. They formed "women's divisions" or created committees of equal numbers of committeewomen and committeemen. But these institutions, which kept women in auxiliary roles, gave them little room for the exercise of independent judgment or leadership.[2]

Mary Garrett Hay's experience with the Republican Party dramatically illustrates these two salient aspects of women's political lives after suffrage, their debates among themselves over how to function politically, and their struggles to play effective roles within the male-dominated political hierarchies. Having won the vote, women with close ties to the Republican Party found themselves

11. Mary Garrett Hay, wearing her trademark GOP elephant pendant (Mary Garrett Hay Scrapbook, Manuscripts and Archives Division, New York Public Library; Astor, Lenox, and Tilden Foundations).

deeply torn between partisan and nonpartisan loyalties. When Hay became leader of a group that chose loyalty to women's agendas over submission to party dictates, they lost the political status they had achieved in state and national party circles. Their experience illuminates the complex challenges and numerous hazards women faced in their quest for full citizenship after suffrage.

On June 10, 1920, the following exchange took place in the corridor of a hotel near the Republican Party national convention. A man catching sight of Mary Garrett Hay congratulated her. "What for?" she asked. "For placing your sex on an equal footing," he replied. "Humph," she sniffed. "I haven't. They aren't." And off she went.[5] Indeed by summer 1920, despite her own and others' efforts, women were not "on an equal footing," not in the national Republican Party nor in any other party. Why did Hay's interlocutor think she had succeeded, and how did Hay already know she had failed?

The answers lie in New York politics of the previous year. When New York women won the vote in 1917, they capped a long tradition of political activism in the state. Although their political tradition was primarily nonpartisan, some had already joined political parties, most notably the Progressive Party in 1912, and many had campaigned for and against political party candidates.[4] After suffrage their opportunities for partisan activity increased. One woman who took advantage of new party posts was Mary Garrett Hay, leader of the political wing of New York City suffragists. Born in 1857 she had grown up in an Indiana doctor's family long identified with Republican politics and become a suffragist through temperance work. After moving to New York in 1895, she continued to pursue nonpartisan causes, serving as president of the New York State Federation of Women's Clubs from 1910 to 1912 and then as head of the New York City Woman Suffrage Party.

Throughout the second decade of the century, Hay cemented a relationship with the Republican Party of New York, attending its state conventions annually and every year asking the platform committee to approve the woman suffrage amendment to the U.S. Constitution. In 1917 New York State women won the vote. The following year a secret conference of party leaders chose Hay over the president of Columbia University, Nicholas Murray Butler, to chair the platform committee. At last she was in a position to get the committee to endorse the amendment, which it did. That same year Hay began to rise in Republican national politics. Thanks to fellow Indianan Will H. Hays, Republican national committee chair and longtime woman suffrage supporter, she won a seat on the Republican Women's National Executive Committee. In 1919, after becoming this committee's chair, she worked closely with Hays to equalize women's roles in the national party.[5]

Soon, however, Hay found that her loyalty to women's causes clashed with her loyalty to the party. Late in 1919 Republican James W. Wadsworth, Jr., announced that he would run for reelection. A U.S. Senator from New York since 1914, Wadsworth had taken a "states' rights" stand against Prohibition, arguing that local liquor options should prevail; on similar grounds he opposed woman suffrage, claiming that the states alone should determine the franchise. In mid-1917 his wife Alice Hay Wadsworth became head of the National Association Opposed to Woman Suffrage, a group that identified woman suffrage and other feminist causes with "Bolshevism."[6] By the time Wadsworth announced his campaign, New York suffragists considered him their inveterate enemy.

Mary Hay spearheaded the movement to deny him the party's renomination. Her leadership in the movement was not surprising. She had been carving out an exemplary role as "new woman citizen." Considered an able leader of women who could also "cooperate with men in politics," she was being talked about as a future officeholder. But she had long been hesitating before the partisan threshold, in statements over the previous two years expressing a continuing loyalty to women as nonpartisans and ambivalence about women's readiness for partisan roles. When delivering a suffrage victory speech to women's club members in November 1917, for example, she begged former suffragists to remain nonpartisan until they had learned how to be voters: "Oh, women, let me urge you while you may believe in this party or that party, . . . first get on your feet, grasp the situation, study the condition, study what parties stand for, study what candidates stand for and let us as women not be partisan but stand for the man or the woman that stands for the *right* (applause)" [emphasis added]. She also discouraged women from running for office. "Don't let us have our heads turned," she warned. She told the story of being in Albany for the counting of soldiers' ballots when the newspapers announced that three suffragists were going to run for Congress. All three women wired her, "Don't believe it, Miss Hay, we are going to be non-partisan . . . the reason we wanted the ballot was to do something constructive and worth while in this glorious old state." To Mary Hay "politics," defined as running for office, was neither "constructive" nor "worth while."[7]

The following summer she still clung to traditional views of women's proper political place. In 1918, after her small triumph over Nicholas Murray Butler, friends of Republican Governor Charles S. Whitman asked her whether women "wanted representation on the state ticket." Hay said that, as far as she knew, "they did not."[8] After the Republican victory in 1920, in response to talk that president-elect Warren Harding might appoint a woman to head a new Welfare Department, Hay warned women not to take such political "plums," as they would only prove burdensome to the woman who accepted them.[9] Hay hesitated to exercise political power herself. After Wadsworth announced his reelection campaign, she predicted that a women's voting bloc would defeat him. But when asked if she planned to offer an alternative candidate, she said it was not the "business of women voters to select the Republican candidate. The task is for the *men in charge* of Republican affairs. They should see to it at an early day" [emphasis added].[10]

State suffrage party leaders followed Hay's signals. They too asked members not to leap into party politics. Early in 1918 an upstate suffragist wrote to suffrage headquarters in Utica reporting that some of the "newly enfranchised women here are worried because, if they refrain from joining any of the political parties (the advice given from suffrage headquarters), they will not be able to take any part in the party caucus." She then asked, "Could you supply me with arguments to uphold the Headquarter instructions?"[11] By April 1918 headquarters had revoked these "instructions," but there was still confusion. At the end of May less than 50 percent of New York's registered women had enrolled in a political party, a situation that critics later blamed on Molly Hay.[12]

Senator Wadsworth's reelection campaign brought to a head the issue of how women should reconcile partisan and nonpartisan agendas. When he won his party's renomination, the head of the New York State League of Women Voters, Caroline Slade, took action. Calling upon her network of suffragists, she organized a meeting of women that raised $5,000 to support a "Non-Partisan Senatorial Committee." Mary Garrett Hay then persuaded Ella Boole, president of the New York State Woman's Christian Temperance Union, to run against Wadsworth in the primary. These actions did not endear Hay to Republican Party leaders. Three groups of them retaliated against her: national party men, state party men, and some state party women more anxious than Hay was to act like party regulars.

The first signs of trouble came in May 1920. Hay received word that if she continued to oppose Wadsworth she would lose her "delegate-at-large" status to the Republican National Convention in June. "Being a new voter," she said ingenuously, "I can not see how my opposition to the candidacy or election of a United States Senator can have anything to do with being a delegate to the Republican National Convention."[13] She went to Chicago, almost immediately discovering herself marginalized by party leaders. Forging ahead regardless, she launched the revolutionary request that the party's executive committee be doubled and that only women be appointed to the newly opened seats. Will Hays, her friend and party chair, tried to push her request along, but Republican men either charged that Hay's plan would create a "sex division" in the party or joked that the nation might as well elect two presidents, one for men and one for women. In the end twelve committeemen gallantly ceded their seats to women, but Hay remained outraged. "Men should be ashamed of the representation given women," she said. "They will learn, however, that they can not toss a few crumbs to the women and then sit down to the feast table." This threat would soon prove idle.[14]

By the end of the convention, the executive committee had forced Mary Hay out of the chair of the Women's Executive Committee. She put a positive construction upon her resignation, saying that Will Hays had given her the post only as a "temporary" measure in order to work out a "permanent model of organization by means of which to relate the woman voter to the Republican Party." She also said that her top priorities now were to work for the ratification of the federal suffrage amendment and Wadsworth's defeat. She took care not to attack men as such, insisting that "The men don't mean to shut us out. They just do not think about us."[15]

Hay then returned to New York, only to find that the state party executive committee had dropped her. Now she was furious. Having reached a turning point, she began to express new attitudes toward women running for office. She was opposed to a "Woman's Party," she said, but now she thought her followers should help younger women "take their right places in politics" and support "good" women running for office, regardless of party affiliation.[16] In statements bordering on the militant, the once "cooperative" Mary Hay now proclaimed, "I rebel" against the "crack of the party whip." How dare her party challenge her opposition to a man who was working against woman suffrage! Women aren't making a "sex war," she riposted, men are, by keeping the party a "man's party." In Saratoga for the state convention, she complained that the men held secret conferences and then called meetings at which they told women what to do. She would not stand for it![17]

Such statements merely intensified the backlash against her. Editorials pointed out that suffragists themselves had opposed "sex in politics" and that men and women should participate equally "on the basis of worth and merit." The party's inner councils exclude not just Miss Hay but millions of others, the *Knickerbocker Press* observed, because they had not worked their way up from the bottom or proved their abilities.[18] Finally "stand-pat" Republican women went "after her head." Grace Vanamee and Rosalie Loew Whitney, both on the Republican Women's State Executive Committee, observed first that Hay could have fought the endorsement of Wadsworth's candidacy from the floor and second that they had been on the resolutions committee and had worked with the men as equals. They also pointed out that a secret conference is not necessarily corrupt; Miss Hay may have been excluded, but so were many men. Moreover in 1918 a "secret conference" had chosen Hay rather than Butler as chair of the state party platform committee; they recalled "no animadversions by Miss Hay following that occasion."[19]

In the 1920 election, Hay's group fared poorly. After losing in the primary, Ella Boole ran in the main contest on the Prohibition ticket, winning four counties and 153,000 votes. This was an impressive total for a novice woman candidate running against a male incumbent, and although Wadsworth won reelection, he was 600,000 votes short of Warren Harding's total New York vote.[20] These were minor consolations, however. The suffragists' opposition to a party standard bearer had severe political consequences. By 1921 neither Republican nor Democratic state party had advanced female candidates for office, and when a measure came up in the legislature to get equal representation of women on all state political committees, the men in both parties killed it.[21]

Mary Hay's approach toward realizing women's political dreams after suffrage was now discredited. She had tried to balance partisan and nonpartisan loyalties, but when her party supported a man she detested, she could not keep them level. At first she had deferred to the men in power, thinking they would cooperate with her goals; when they did not and she defied them, she lost everything. She had also shown herself deeply ambivalent about the prospect of women exercising direct political power. By the time she started to change her mind on this issue, she had suffered too many defeats to recapture the initiative.

Some of her critics were particularly severe with her on this score. In a privately circulated essay, Frances Kellor, sociologist, author, and Progressive Party activist, condemned former suffragists for having "disinherited women by regulations forbidding them to engage in political activities. 'Get the vote first' was the order," Kellor wrote, but by the time they had gotten it, they had neither training nor experience in public affairs. Kellor went on to accuse former suffragists, whom she described as tired, disillusioned, and "egotistical through use of power," of having clung to a "non-partisan doctrine in the face of a victory in which the only fruit could be partisanship."[22] This indictment, while never naming Mary Garrett Hay, so accurately described Hay as to leave little doubt that she was its prime target.

Still a revered figure among nonpartisans, Hay held presidencies of the city's League of Women Voters and the Women's City Club of New York, but the former eased her out in 1923 and she retired from the latter in 1924. Senator Wadsworth ran again in 1926. By then his chances for reelection had diminished. Women prohibitionists split the Republican vote when they gave their support to State Senator Franklin Cristman, an independent "dry." Democratic State Senator Robert F. Wagner, Sr., a "wet" and close associate of Governor Alfred E. Smith, took advantage of rising ethnic support from the cities and won. Republican Party pundits blamed Wadsworth's loss to Wagner solely on the actions of the "fanatic dry's."[23]

Had Wadsworth's candidacy not been an issue, would the Republican Party have acceded to Hay's demands for equal political space with men? Probably not. The "men in charge" in 1920 were just as unable to visualize new ways for women to function in politics as were the suffragists of Hay's generation. Men like Will Hays and the twelve gallant men on the national Republican Executive Committee who had ceded seats to women were sympathetic but unwilling to do much more. The rest of the party men did not like Miss Hay's "bullying" them, and they could not understand what motivated her when she did so.

A letter to Wadsworth from Nicholas Butler, Hay's rival for the state Republican Platform Committee chair in 1918, illustrates this point. Writing in January 1920, Butler expressed support for Wadsworth's reelection, predicting that "the opposition of a certain group here, however bitter and well organized, will prove ineffective," as voters will not "punish a public officer for a standing on a question that has been settled, not to his liking, but to theirs." He went on, "If these people had been disappointed in their hopes, the situation would be quite different, but they have had their way, and you did not get yours."[24] Although he never named the "certain group" to which his letter referred, surely he meant the suffragists who had opposed Wadsworth's stand against Prohibition.

Butler's letter illustrates the accuracy of Crystal Eastman's construction of divergent reactions of men and women to the suffrage victory. For Butler, since the "everlasting fight" was over, suffragists had no reason to continue opposing a man who had lost. That Wadsworth was continuing to fight the federal suffrage amendment did not seem relevant. Butler's letter reveals the depth of the chasm that remained to be crossed between the male and female political cultures of the early postsuffrage era.

New York women would experience few political joys in the immediate years after suffrage. They could not even take credit for Wadsworth's 1926 defeat. Still, at least one person believed women had played some role in that defeat. The day after the election, this person sent him an anonymous telegram boasting, "THE WOMEN OF NEW YORK STATE DID NOT FORGET."[25] Preserved in Wadsworth's papers at the Library of Congress, the telegram reveals that although consigned to the political margins in the 1920s, at least some women still believed in the power of their ballot.

NOTES

1. From "Now We Can Begin," *The Liberator* (December 1920), rept. in *Crystal Eastman on Women & Revolution*, ed. Blanche Wiesen Cook (Oxford: Oxford University Press, 1978), 53.

2. Many scholars have addressed these dilemmas of postsuffrage political women; see Kristi Andersen, *After Suffrage*; Felice Gordon, *After Winning*; Nancy Cott, *The Grounding of Modern Feminism*; William H. Chafe, *The American Woman*; Estelle Freedman, "Separatism as Strategy"; and J. Stanley Lemons, *The Woman Citizen*.

3. "Morsels of Favor Passed Out by G.O.P. Dissatisfying Women," *Chicago Evening Mail*, June 10, 1920.

4. See S. Sara Monoson, "The Lady and the Tiger" and Melanie Gustafson, "Partisan Women in the Progressive Era."

5. For biographical information on Mary Garrett Hay, see Edward James *et al.*, *Notable American Women*, vol. 2, "Mary Garrett Hay"; Grace Julian Clarke, "Says Club Women Are Equal to All Demands," *Indianapolis Star*, September 19, 1920; Fay Stevenson, "New York League of Women Voters Pays High Tribute to Old Leader, Mary Garrett Hay, Who Retires," *New York Evening World*, March 13, 1923; and "Miss Hay Tells of Experiences in Long Career," *Indianapolis Star*, June 2, 1925, all preserved in the wonderfully entitled Mary Garrett Hay scrapbook, "Some Incidents in the Life of Mary Garrett Hay, A Wonderful Boss and a Gallant Fighter," Rare Books & Manuscripts Division, New York Public Library, New York (hereafter Hay scrapbook). The state Republican Party Platform Committee had fifty-one members; only two besides Hay were women: Mary Wood and Mary Weitmer Schmiedendorf. See also Will Hays, *The Memoirs of Will H. Hays* (New York: Doubleday, 1955), 257–61.

6. The following oral histories in the Columbia University Oral History Collection provide information on this period in Wadsworth's career: that of Wadsworth himself, 344–56; "William A. Prendergast," 236–37; "John Lord O'Brian," 65–66, 112–13, 325–27; "Paul Windels," 174–78; "Alice Paul," 135–37, 443; "Robert F. Wagner, Jr.," 45–46; and "Ella A. Boole," 22–24. For his views on Prohibition, see his letter to Nicholas Murray Butler, February 14, 1926, Butler Papers, Columbia University, New York. Wadsworth's papers can be found in the Library of Congress.

7. A typescript of this speech, delivered to the New York State Federation of Women's Clubs in Albany, can be found in Hay scrapbook.

8. "She Wins Place, Beating Butler," *New York Globe*, July 18, 1918.

9. "Harding Wants Woman in Cabinet; Mary Garrett Hay Makes Conditions," *New York Evening Mail*, December 16, 1920.

10. "Republican Chief Shy at Wadsworth," *New York Sun*, November 23, 1919.

11. Frances E. (Mrs. A. E.) Rhodes (of Clark Mills, NY), to Glendolen (Mrs. Samuel J.) Bens, New York State Suffrage Party leader in Utica, NY, January 17, 1918, New York Woman Suffrage Collection, New York Public Library, New York.

12. *New York Times*, April 2, 1918, announced the lifting of the ban against women joining parties.

13. "Republican State Convention May 1920, Statement of Mary Garrett Hay," Hay

scrapbook. She also protested that her own state Republican Party was sending women to Chicago "merely as alternates" and not as delegates.

14. See "Miss Hay Confers on Women Voters," *Chicago Tribune,* June 3, 1920; and "Leader of GOP Women's Division to Leave Office after Convention," June 5, 1920, and "Morsels of Favor Passed Out by G.O.P. Dissatisfying Women," June 10, 1920, both from the *Chicago Evening Mail,* all in the Hay Scrapbook. The Republican National Committee finally acceded to Hay's original demand for 50 percent representation in 1924, following the Democratic National Committee, which had made that change in 1920.

15. Mary Hay public statement (no title), June 1, 1920; articles from early June 1920 in the *Chicago News, New York Sun, New York Herald,* and Gladys Denny Shultz article, *Des Moines Register,* July 16, 1920, all in Hay scrapbook.

16. Statement, "Present Responsibility of Women as Citizens," August 1920, Hay scrapbook. In the national elections of 1920, Carrie Chapman Catt also endorsed individual candidates. Local leagues found themselves doing the same, arguing that they were not endorsing parties but individuals.

17. Numerous newspaper articles commented on these events in the *New York Tribune, New York Times,* and *New York World* of July 24, and 27, 1920.

18. "Miss Hay's Position," *Knickerbocker Press,* July 29, 1920.

19. See Emma H. De Zouche, "Fight to Defeat Wadsworth . . . ," Ethel Eyre Dreier Papers, Sophia Smith Collection, Smith College, Northampton, MA; and "Women Delegates at Saratoga," [New York] *Evening Post,* August 26, 1920. A "Women Voters Anti-Suffrage Party" also took out its animus upon Hay, issuing a flyer, "Watch the Woman Boss in Action," that charged Hay with starting "sex warfare" in the state (Hay scrapbook).

20. Boole claimed this was the largest vote any woman running for public office had received. Although she never ran for office again, she became national and then world WCTU president. See "Ella A. Boole," 22–24, Columbia University Oral History Collection.

21. *New York Telegram,* September 5, 1921.

22. Frances Kellor, "Cloisters in American Politics," carbon of draft in "Women in Politics" fol., box 3, Ethel Eyre Dreier Papers. Dreier, a nonpartisan herself and sister-in-law of Mary Dreier, Kellor's lifelong companion, underlined and queried many sections of this article. On Kellor and the Dreiers, see Ellen Fitzpatrick, *Endless Crusade.*

23. Buffalo lawyer John Lord O'Brian did not agree, pointing out that Wadsworth had alienated not one but two groups of voters, suffragists and prohibitionists; "John Lord O'Brian," Columbia University Oral History Collection. Wadsworth's career was far from over; he returned to Washington as a congressman, serving in the House for more than two decades. After World War II he worked with a younger generation of League of Women Voters leaders on an Equal Rights Amendment, albeit one that preserved a recognition of the social importance of biological differences between the sexes. In the early 1950s, when Wadsworth recorded his oral memoirs for Columbia University, he blamed his 1926 defeat only on the "dry's."

24. Butler to Wadsworth, Jr., January 15, 1920, Butler Papers, Columbia University Rare Books and Manuscripts Library, New York. At the letter's end, Butler advised Wadsworth, as a "practical matter," to form a "Woman's Committee" made up "not wholly of women who

opposed the Suffrage Amendment, but of women drawn from all types and classes of thought." This plan, he thought, would "to some extent blanket the fire on the other side." Unfortunately no reply is preserved in Butler's collection.

25. Folder, "Senate campaign of 1926," James W. Wadsworth, Jr., Papers, Library of Congress. Although Wadsworth threw away many documents—the collection has a distinctly cleaned-up look—he, or someone else, kept this telegram. There is little else in the folder.

12. *Emily Newell Blair: Vice Chairman, Democratic National Committee, 1922–28 (Schlesinger Library, Radcliffe College)*

CHAPTER ELEVEN

EVOLUTION OF A PARTISAN

Emily Newell Blair and the Democratic Party, 1920–1932

KATHRYN ANDERSON

When Franklin D. Roosevelt appointed Emily Newell Blair to an administrative position in the National Recovery Administration in 1935, a magazine editor estimated that her name was familiar to six million women.[1] Born and wed into political families, she rooted her activism in clubwomen's social reform activities in southwest Missouri, then flourished in state and national suffrage movements. Concerned that politicians might subvert women's efforts to achieve political equality, Blair accepted Democratic Party leaders' invitation in 1921 to develop strategies for attracting and involving new women voters in the wake of a Republican victory. While forging new roles for women within partisan politics, she addressed broader questions of political equality in nearly forty essays published from 1920 to 1932. They document the evolution of her thinking from confidence that women would change politics to consciousness of men's resistance and the difficulty of organizing women in their own interests.

Historic tensions in Missouri's Democratic Party erupted in 1919 with a schism between President Woodrow Wilson's supporters and those of Senator James A. Reed, an outspoken opponent of Wilson's war aims and the League of Nations. In a highly unusual move, Wilson Democrats censured Reed and denied him delegate status at the 1920 national convention. Reed staged a comeback to retain his Senate seat in 1922, with support from Thomas J. Pendergast's Kansas City machine.[2] Missouri suffragists joining the Democratic Party typically supported Wilson and opposed Reed, a vociferous antagonist to woman suffrage and other progressive measures, notably child labor legislation and the Sheppard-Towner bill.

During World War I Blair developed publicity for the Women's Division of the Council of National Defense (CND), headed by National American Woman Suffrage Association leader Anna Howard Shaw, an experience that intensified her support for Wilson and her antipathy toward Reed. As she evolved from suffragist to Democratic partisan, she cultivated a national constituency as the Pendergast machine's ascendance after 1924 diminished her role in Missouri.

Although one of the founders of the Missouri League of Women Voters (LWV), Blair encouraged women to join a political party rather than remain independent voters: "The sort of person who finds it easier to wear a label than to wait, who prefers to control rather than to make decisions, who wants to function rather than to count, will naturally become a partisan."[3] Moreover she urged women to get involved at the precinct level, because electing delegates committed to your issues made more sense strategically than lobbying delegates committed to others.

Contemplating the Nineteenth Amendment's significance a few months before ratification, Blair reasoned that the woman voter was likely to vote as an individual, even though she would gain the right to do so as a group: "She is not going to vote as one, any more than she acts as one, or loves as one, or thinks as one." Similarly she expected women to choose parties based on region, family, and sentiment, much as men did, rather than form a woman's bloc. A principled choice would be difficult, she explained to prospective voters, for "between the progressive Republicans and the liberal Democrats there did not seem much rational disagreement."[4]

Blair did not commit fully to the Democratic Party until 1920, making her rise to national committeewoman in 1921 seem meteoric. She attended the 1916 Democratic convention in St. Louis as a suffragist, demonstrating for a plank in the Democratic platform. As a member of the League of Women Voters delegation in 1920, she attended both conventions but presented the "Women in Industry" plank only at the Democratic convention. She attended the Missouri State Democratic Convention in 1920 as a delegate, but later described her participation as an accident. Others clearly perceived her as a Democrat. The Carthage Federation of Women's Clubs endorsed Blair as the Democratic candidate for school board, when state legislation in 1918 permitted women to serve (she withdrew before the primary).

Blair claimed as late as 1920 that she sought to define a position outside both parties. When Ruth Hanna McCormick invited her to help formulate social reform programs to attract women to the Republican Party, Blair found the thought of working together appealing. She had "a wild idea that the Democrats might try to meet it, and we would have both parties falling over themselves in an effort to win the woman vote."[5] Although she eventually committed to the party of her father and husband, a man recommending her for national committeewoman described her as "a Democrat from principle and conviction rather than environment and tradition."[6]

Ironically some party regulars questioned her loyalty as a Democrat because of her affiliation with the LWV. However, opposing Senator Reed enhanced her credibility among those who equated political effectiveness with combativeness. She confronted Reed in 1918 over the meaning of his statements against the Nineteenth Amendment on the Senate floor. His remarks had the kind of ambiguity politicians employ to make insinuations and then deny responsibility for them. Blair and her journalist colleagues understood them as an insult to women and woman suffrage. When her private correspondence condemning Reed's remarks became public, she became firmly established in the anti-Reed camp. As the conflict resurfaced in subsequent intraparty struggles, it enhanced her visibility.

Blair's opposition to Missouri's most powerful Democrat renders her election in 1921 as national committeewoman and reelection in 1924 all the more remarkable. When Mrs. Burris Jenkins resigned in February of 1921, several of Blair's former suffrage colleagues began early to ensure that women would choose Jenkins's successor and that the choice would be Emily Newell Blair. Some male leaders thought the state committee, composed of both men and women, should choose representatives to the national committee. George White, chairman of the Democratic National Committee (DNC), ruled that women could choose their own representative and submit their selection to the committee for ratification.[7] Reed supporters countered Blair's nomination with their own candidate but lacked the strength to halt the groundswell for Blair. When they tried to erect a financial barrier by suggesting that the woman elected should contribute $1,000 to the national committee, Blair's supporters responded with a commitment to raise the money.

Missouri women, confident in Blair's leadership, elected her national committeewoman. A national constituency, established through suffrage and the LWV, a series of articles in *Ladies Home Journal* on women and the war, in *Green Book* on women and politics, and her acclaimed "Interpretative Report" of the CND, positioned her for election to the executive committee of the DNC. For Cordell Hull and other Wilson supporters, Blair had much to commend her, especially her public opposition to Reed. Her reputation as an effective speaker and writer gave her unique access to the press. Women trusted her, and most men, with the exception of Reed, found her agreeable.

As "vice-chairman" of the DNC, she understood the contradictions in her role. Women expected her to open doors to full political equality. Men wanted her to attract independent voters and motivate Democratic women to become active workers. In one of her first major addresses, she vowed to "begin where the argument over woman suffrage ends," articulating the challenges ahead:

> To make party organization profit by all that women can bring to it, to enable women to make that contribution in their own way, to make women effective and at the same time to see that women are not segregated into a small auxiliary group used to do all the details and drudgery of politics without having a voice in the decisions that determine party policies.[8]

Later her concern shifted to how women might ensure a voice in party platforms and strategic decisions.

From 1920 to 1924 Blair engaged her partisan roles enthusiastically. She expected women and men to be different kinds of partisans because they performed different social roles, but she neither expected nor desired a woman's bloc. She represented women who had struggled for suffrage to eliminate, not repeat, "the injustice of the sex line," but warned that they "will not be satisfied to have the woman vote swallowed bodily by the political parties without making any impress on results."[9] She struggled with the tension between dropping the sex line and creating a space for women in politics throughout her tenure on the DNC.

Blair's ideas of a new partisanship were rooted in her involvement with LWV efforts in 1920 to achieve consensus on issues (maternity and infant care, citizenship, child labor, equal wages, and education), then assign partisan women to speak for them at their respective national conventions. Blair understood that determining issues and setting the terms of debate might outweigh winning a particular point, reflecting a sophisticated analysis of power in the political process. For example women agreed on the need for legislation benefiting women and children regardless of party affiliation, even though they might disagree about which particular bills might achieve the most desirable results. Most importantly, she argued, "legislation affecting women and children will command more interest in the halls of Government since women have the vote, than it has ever done before."[10]

Years of leadership in women's groups gave Blair a sense of how women might engage in partisan politics, even in an inhospitable political culture. She sought familiar ground where women might develop confidence in their political skills and weigh the impact of political issues on daily life. She gathered national committeewomen and presented her plan in April 1922, two months after assuming her position. While many states, including Missouri, had passed legislation known as "50–50 plans," granting women and men equal representation on party committees, others had no provision for women in regular party organizations. To provide continuity Blair created a national organizational structure of Democratic women's clubs to complement women's work within party committees. She offered a detailed organizational plan, complete with by-laws and suggested topics for study and discussion, for meetings designed to give women an equal place in the Democratic Party, while recognizing lines society had drawn between the sexes.[11]

Autonomous clubs would create opportunities to expand women's small circles, gain information, and share ideas about political issues. Blair targeted uncommitted voters but expected benefits for all: "these clubs will do more than any other one thing to confirm our women in their democratic faith, to stabilize them in their party affiliations, and to make them feel themselves an integral and essential part of our party organization."[12] Her office organized one thousand clubs by the 1922 election, with priority given to highly contested states, and nearly three thousand by the 1924 elections. In 1923 she helped found the Women's National Democratic Club in Washington, D.C., to provide a social context in which Democrats might discuss, even reconcile, their differences. She served one year as president in 1928, after resigning from the DNC, and continued to advocate clubs as crucial vehicles for women's participation.

Blair realized that creating a special place for women conflicted with the idea of political equality and eliminating the sex line in politics: "they should run and be elected to political committees as individuals and not as men or as women." She also knew that "men held the citadel. The only way women could get in was by making a place for women."[13] In 1940 Blair remembered clubs as a more important element in party strategy than did her successors, Nellie Tayloe Ross and Molly Dewson.[14] Harriet Taylor Upton, "vice-chairman" of the Republican National Committee, agreed on the importance of women's clubs in 1922. Indeed Blair used the proliferation of Republican women's clubs to argue that Democratic national committeemen should support Democratic women's clubs in their states.

At every opportunity Blair characterized the Democratic Party as more responsive to women's needs and interests. Democrats had incorporated more LWV proposals into their platform in 1920. They also resolved to elect women to the national committee on the same terms and with the same authority as men, four years before the Republican National Committee. "This hospitable spirit manifested by the Democratic party to women is in glaring contrast to the grudging reluctance of the Republican organization to give women anything more than the ancient opportunity of unrecognized service," she wrote. The fact that women on the Republican National Committee were appointed, not elected, suggested a role more social than political, a charge Upton hastened to disclaim. Blair claimed that "the Democratic party makes it possible for women to build into it their own ideas and ideals," but later conceded that Democrats may have been more responsive because they were out of power.[15]

Women participated as full voting members in a national party for the first time at the DNC's meeting to finalize a convention site in January 1924. Blair urged women to get involved early and participate fully in the 1924 conventions. She expected fierce political jockeying but honestly thought women who worked hard enough would find a place.[16] They seemed to win the debate over whether to "suggest" or "recommend" that states send eight delegates-at-large, four women and four men, each with one-half vote. The vote was a small victory for Blair, who hoped it would help overcome the psychological barrier to women at the conventions.[17] However, the decision to stop paying railroad fares and hotel bills for national committee members diminished the position that women had finally achieved.[18]

Women delegates paid attention to the nuances of position and status in 1924. They rejected recycled 1920 badges labeled "Associate National Committeewoman," insisting on recognition as full-fledged members of the convention. They resisted expectations that they would yield patronage rights or tickets to male delegates. They sought committee positions but were disappointed to see few women selected, not even to the relatively uncontroversial credentials committee; no woman served as chair. They invited men to preconvention meetings for women delegates, to avoid legitimizing any exclusive gatherings men might have in mind. Personally Blair realized that recognition did not equal power only after expending considerable energy to upgrade her position on the DNC from resident committeewoman to "vice-chairman" to "first vice-chairman."

Blair's biggest disappointment in 1924 was that Democratic women could not make social and economic issues generated by women's organizations bigger priorities in the party platform. A women's committee chaired by Eleanor Roosevelt held hearings for days, but its recommendations received a cursory response as the convention focused on Prohibition, League of Nations, and anti-Klan planks.

When Senator Reed won reelection in 1922, he vowed (and failed) to have Blair removed from her post in Washington, D.C. In 1924 Kansas City and St. Louis delegations tried at the last minute to deny Blair's reelection to the National Committee, but women foiled the attempt. She had not decided whether to seek reelection as vice chair of the executive committee, when rumors surfaced that organizations in New York and Chicago planned to unseat her. Missouri women, who constituted the second largest delegation at the convention behind New York, rallied to Blair's defense, as did women throughout the nation. Despite deep divisions in the party and prospects for a difficult campaign, Blair stayed on to finish what she had started, "the inclusion of women in politics."

The 1924 convention and campaign gave Blair a more realistic understanding of politics and the nature of political power. Still convinced that she could work more effectively for good government inside the party than outside, she admitted that in spite of the high-sounding title, hers was merely a "nominal position." Party chairmen Hull and Shaver made every effort to include her, but men who controlled state and local organizations offered "dinners and compliments," not "participation in their councils."[19]

A specific experience helped Blair realize the limitations of her political power. To avoid the appearance of excluding women, party leaders invited her to attend a late night caucus in chairman Cordell Hull's room to break a deadlock between McAdoo and Smith. Blair had no illusions that she contributed anything for, compared to the men in the room, she lacked experience and commanded no faction of voters. She felt like "stage furniture and nothing more" but had no expectation that women would unite behind a specific candidate.[20]

Blair saw little evidence that organized women had achieved political power. Clubwomen were too removed from political issues and even the LWV, still using suffrage tactics, focused on good government rather than organizing women as voters. Their leaders had succeeded because they spoke to compelling social issues, not because they led women. To explain her continued hopefulness and allegiance to the party, she pointed to individual women who had gained power. Governors Nellie Tayloe Ross and "Ma" Ferguson were not leaders of women, but their sex had not been a serious handicap to their elections. Mabel Walker Willebrandt and Florence Allen had become assistant attorney general and judge, respectively, because of their professional excellence.[21]

After a devastating defeat at the polls in 1924, the DNC streamlined its headquarters and destroyed Women's Division files, the result of two years of hard work. Blair appealed for party support to continue organizing women through the Women's National Democratic Club, spending a few weeks there each winter, but she was not proud of her second term.[22] Still nominally "vice-chairman" of the DNC, she returned to Missouri and her writing. With no tradition of female pundits, she expressed a range of views in her monthly *Good Housekeeping* column from 1926 to 1934, while recommending books to her readers. She continued writing on women and politics, informing a *Harper's* audience that men always had been perfect gentlemen but either ignored her or refused her "a place on the firing line." Men and women had learned to organize themselves differently, she concluded, with men relishing sporadic bouts of competition and political fights, like sporting events, and women preferring the long-term planning and routine programs they knew in their clubs. She wondered whether women would learn to fight (and like it) or succeed in transforming politics into a club.[23]

In 1927 Blair distanced herself from party leadership, even as she continued to advocate partisanship, reasserting the wisdom of "boring from within" over trying to influence public opinion outside of established party structures. Although she had considerable experience with machines resistant to women and reformers, her broader experience convinced her that partisan affiliation was not futile. Women needed to prepare for a long struggle and be willing to accept defeat.[24]

These were strong words from a woman who had decided to resign from national political office. Her writing career was blossoming. Chances of reelection as national committeewoman were slim, with Reed and Pendergast now firmly in control of the Missouri Democratic Party. Jasper County Democrats still supported Blair as a delegate to the state Democratic Convention in 1928, but she declined their nomination because she expected delegates to be instructed to vote for Reed, and she "could not conscientiously vote for his nomination as a candidate on the Democratic ticket for president, under any consideration whatever."[25] The realization that she was no longer an insider came abruptly, when she learned about new officers of the DNC from the daily news. Smith supporters still invited her to campaign in Missouri and elsewhere, because they recognized her value as an advocate for tolerance on issues of prohibition and religion. Blair liked Smith's economic ideas, although she understood why his style rankled midwesterners. She agreed to campaign, in spite of fears that supporting Smith might alienate friends (southwest Missouri was largely dry) and more importantly readers, which could threaten her regular column.[26]

Her essays in 1928 continued to advocate partisanship for women, as she became a political analyst on topics such as the importance of challenging corruption, improving modern campaign methods, substituting a statement of principles for party platforms, and better child welfare legislation. In an unsigned article for *Century*, Blair urged Democrats to develop long-range strategies for gaining strength in Congress and perhaps even the presidency. Someone may have thought Democrats would take such advice more seriously from an anonymous source than from a woman.[27]

Blair saw some signs of progress for individual women. Politicians who once had "endured" her eventually sought her counsel.[28] Compared to the feminine women that suffragists had featured to disarm men, women emerging in political Washington had a different look: "their faces and tongues gave notice to the world that they had ideas." Men's attitudes toward women in politics were changing, according to Blair: "They might not care to have someone around they would fear but they wanted to fight with some one whom the others would fear. . . . and women's chins came into their own."[29]

Yet in 1929 Blair was discouraged to see skilled political women capable of representing the social reform interests of voluntary women's organizations replaced by women more amenable to male political agendas. She pondered the difficulty as well as the necessity of organizing women as women. Sex consciousness in politics was inevitable; women might think of themselves as Democrats, but leaders and voters saw them as women.[30] Dropping the "sex line" was a mistake for feminism. It meant that men could retain control without paying much attention to women.[31] Increasingly she argued for a woman's bloc, recalling men's initial fears as evidence of its potential power. Still a Democrat, she envisioned women supporting each other for party positions and challenging men on issues important to women with the votes to back them.[32]

Blair displayed uncanny foresight in 1922, when she predicted that "historians will find it difficult to say how women have changed the laws, and government. Nevertheless woman's participation in government will have had an effect."[33] Surprised at the level of men's resistance, she came to believe that greater gender consciousness was the key to political equality rather than "dropping the sex line." She could not imagine the long-term impact of her efforts to create a comfortable transition for women from voluntary reform organizations to partisan politics. Pamphlets framing political issues in terms of ordinary life, political education workshops, and clubs all made politics more accessible to women at the same time that they brought issues and strategies from women's reform activities into the process. This was Blair's contribution to what Kristi Andersen calls a critical period for negotiating boundaries between gender and citizenship in the 1920s.[34]

NOTES

1. Clipping, February 19, 1935, Emily Newell Blair Family Papers, Western Reserve Historical Society (hereafter Blair Papers).

2. See Richard S. Kirkendall, *A History of Missouri;* and Franklin D. Mitchell, *Embattled Democracy.*

3. Emily Newell Blair, "The Woman Vote," *Green Book* 24 (November 1920): 22.

4. Emily Newell Blair " 'I Nominate—,' " *Green Book* 23 (June 1920): 81.

5. Emily Newell Blair, "Gamma's Story," Schlesinger Library, Radcliffe College (hereafter SL), 134.

6. Letter, Ellis Meredith to Edward F. Goltra, 10/20/21, box 16, f: 2, Goltra Papers, Missouri Historical Society (hereafter Goltra Papers).

7. See letters to Goltra from Jenkins, Laura S. Brown, Mary Semple Scott, and Rachel Tingle, from February to October 1921, Goltra Papers.

8. Emily Newell Blair, "What Women May Do with the Ballot," 20, typescript of speech to Philadelphia-Democratic Women's Luncheon Club, August 28, 1922, Woman's National Democratic Club (WNDC) Archive, Washington, DC.

9. Blair, "The Woman Vote," 23.

10. Blair, "What Women May Do with the Ballot," 4–5.

11. Emily Newell Blair, "Democratic Women's Clubs: Organization Plan," pamphlet, 1923; "How the Democratic Party Has Organized Women," 89, pamphlet, both in WNDC Archive.

12. "Democratic Women's Clubs," *Bulletin,* no. 1, n.d. [probably 1922], box I-14, f: DNC 20–24, League of Women Voters papers, Library of Congress.

13. Emily Newell Blair, "Women in the Political Parties," *Annals of the American Academy* 143 (May 1929): 219.

14. Emily Newell Blair, Nellie Tayloe Ross, and Mary Dewson, "Advance of Democratic Women," pamphlet, n.d. [probably 1940], DNC, Women's Division, SL.

15. Blair, "Gamma's Story," 158; and "How the Democratic Party Has Organized Women," 90.

16. Emily Newell Blair, "On to the Conventions," *Woman Citizen* 8 (April 19, 1924): 20–21.

17. Blair, "Gamma's Story," 188–89.

18. Clipping, 1/17/24, Blair Papers.

19. Blair, "Gamma's Story," 190–91, 200–202, 205, 208.

20. Blair, "Are Women a Failure in Politics?" *Harper's Magazine,* 151 (October 1925): 521.

21. Ibid., 516; Blair, "Are Women Counting in Politics?" *Saturday Evening Post* (July 18, 1925): 78.

22. Blair, "Gamma's Story," 215.

23. Emily Newell Blair, "Men in Politics," *Harper's Magazine* 152 (May 1926): 709.

24. Emily Newell Blair, "Boring from Within," *Woman Citizen* 12 (July 1927): 49–50.

25. Emily Newell Blair, handwritten speech notes, 1928, Blair Papers.

26. Blair, "Gamma's Story," 223–24.

27. Emily Newell Blair, "A New Role for the Donkey," *Century* 116 (May 1928): 68–75.

28. Emily Newell Blair, "Women in the Political Parties," 220.

29. Emily Newell Blair, "New Styles in Feminine Beauty," *Outlook and Independent,* 152 (June 26 1929): 330.

30. Blair, "Women in the Political Parties," 221.

31. Emily Newell Blair, "Why I am Discouraged about Women in Politics," *Woman's Journal* 16 (January 1931): 22.

32. Emily Newell Blair, "Putting Women into Politics," *Woman's Journal* 16 (March 1931): 29.

33. Blair, "What Women May Do With the Ballot," 6.

34. See Kristi Andersen, *After Suffrage.*

13. 1924 Campaign photo of Miriam A. Ferguson dressed as a farm wife, with her bonnet and her mule (The Institute of Texan Cultures, The San Antonio Light Collection).

CHAPTER TWELVE

"ME FOR MA"

Miriam Ferguson and Texas Politics in the 1920s and 1930s

NANCY BECK YOUNG

Miriam Amanda "Ma" Ferguson served twice as governor of Texas. Many contemporaries criticized her lack of independence from her husband, James Edward Ferguson, who had been barred from state office, but her political accomplishments deserve fresh attention. Ambiguity colored her public life. On the one hand, she seemed a mouthpiece for her husband. Yet the same evidence suggests she understood the importance of political cooperation with men, especially since males dominated state affairs. Ferguson's strategy was never to associate her work with suffrage politics. Her use of an alternative means to political power caused discomfort among women who looked at suffrage and women's issues as the appropriate path. Instead Ma Ferguson used the "culture" associated with women, especially rural Texas women, to prove her fitness to hold office and her ability to cooperate with men.

The intriguing blend of her strengths and weaknesses provides scholars the opportunity to examine her career, male politics, and the level of cooperation between women and men in state affairs from a new perspective. Despite the still controversial nature of female political participation, the peculiarities of the Ferguson family's political past had a greater influence on her career—her gender proved much less important than the way in which Texans viewed her family. She made herself appealing to the majority of Texans, both men and women, by adopting rural female mores. Her defeats resulted not because she was female, but because she incorporated her husband's style of corrupt politics into her administration. Ambivalence about her gender proved less important than ambivalence about Jim Ferguson's public morals, since she presented herself as a traditional woman not a new woman. The question of how Texas voters would respond to a woman who sought political power independent of a husband remained open, however.

Born to Joseph and Eliza Wallace, Miriam Amanda grew up in rural luxury in Bell County, Texas. While she had known of James Edward Ferguson, a first cousin on her mother's side, since childhood, she saw little attraction in the man who proposed to be her suitor. After much effort and his election as Belton's city attorney, Jim Ferguson finally persuaded Miriam Wallace to marry him on December 31, 1899. The new couple settled in Belton, where he worked as a lawyer and a banker. State politics became increasingly important to the young man, who had been a devout follower of late nineteenth-century agrarian protests. Daughters Ouida Wallace and Ruby Dorrace were born in 1900 and 1903, after which the Fergusons moved to Temple, where he controlled a large bank.[1]

Jim Ferguson announced his support for measures benefiting tenant farmers when he ran for governor in 1914, a contest in which he avoided precise comment on the most divisive issue in state politics—prohibition. The strategy worked and Ferguson gained election. When the Fergusons arrived in Austin, Miriam complained that the governor's salary and the mansion budget were not sufficient to run a household. Her husband's "war" with the University of Texas over appropriations and appointments to the university's governing body determined her political future. Evidence revealed that he had accepted a bribe from brewery interests. The imbroglio reached a climax in the summer of 1917, and the Texas legislature impeached Ferguson. He resigned days before the Senate voted for his removal and barred him from future elective office.[2]

Ferguson believed he could sustain his political career as long as he retained support from rural Texans. Yet he failed in his 1918 reelection bid, his 1920 presidential race, and his 1922 Senate race. In 1924 his efforts to gain a place on the Democratic ticket for governor proved futile. He finally realized that he had little chance of returning to political power in his own right, and he considered a new strategy for controlling if not holding political office. One month before the June 1924 primary, Jim Ferguson told a friend that "I am going into the woman business with renewed vigor."[3]

Miriam Ferguson's 1924 candidacy splintered a divided Democratic Party. For most of the twentieth century, issues such as prohibition and suffrage attracted progressive Democrats, while conservative Democrats opposed these and other proactive government measures. When the second Ku Klux Klan became a political force, it introduced other cleavages into the political system. The personality and history of Jim Ferguson proved equally divisive. With several different forces tearing at the political and social fabric of the state, turmoil shaped the 1924 gubernatorial election. Ferguson's 1924 candidacy presented progressive Democrats with a dilemma. Felix Robertson, her major opponent, was a member of the Ku Klux Klan. Despite the candidate's gender, few politically savvy women believed Miriam Ferguson would be her own person once in office; instead progressives viewed her as a replacement for the governor they had forced out of office in 1917. They faced a tough choice between candidates with high negatives.[4]

After she gained a spot in the run-off against Robertson, some Ferguson opponents looked for ways to disqualify her candidacy. These men understood that the right to vote was different from the right to hold office. G. C. Groce, a Waxahachie attorney, suggested to Martin McNulty Crane that the crafting of the state constitution before the adoption of suffrage and the exclusive use of male pronouns for the gubernatorial officeholder rendered her ineligible. The argument suggested two themes that commingled throughout the Ferguson era—general opposition to women in politics and specific opposition to the Fergusons. Many who fell into the latter group had supported suffrage. In other words defeat of Ferguson proved more crucial than paving the way for more acceptable female candidates. Other progressives feared the Klan more, and the argument against female eligibility was dropped. Crane believed that Jim Ferguson as an influence on Miriam Ferguson posed less of a threat to the state than the antiprohibitionist and Ku Klux Klan ties that Felix Robertson maintained.[5]

Another Democrat willing to accept Ferguson over Robertson found biblical evidence to support Miriam Ferguson's candidacy: "The Book of Judges in the Bible is a history of the Jewish race when governed by judges. As you know, a judge as referred to in this Book was the same office as the President of the United States, yet one of the most learned judges, Debora, a woman, was a successful and renowned judge."[6] Recognizing the discomfort women in politics produced, Ferguson supporters employed the rhetorical strategy of referring to the Bible, which for Texans in the 1920s was part of their natural idiom.

The 1924 contest presented opposite styles regarding the issue of gender and women's political participation. Miriam Ferguson had publicly opposed the vote for women at the 1916 Democratic National Convention. As a candidate in 1924, however, she explained, "'I never fought for woman suffrage, but they made it law; they gave us the ballot, and I see no reason why we shouldn't exercise our right.'" Furthermore she seemed less than eager in the role of campaigner. She had little regard for the reporters who crowded her Temple home or the questions they posed. Her platform represented a modified version of Jim Ferguson's past political goals. The rhetoric about the power of the state university was less harsh, but the focus remained on rural education. Herself an opponent of strong drink, Miriam Ferguson endorsed Prohibition as the law. She also spoke against the Klan and excess state spending, while endorsing her version of prison reform and better roads. Ferguson explained her most important goal: " 'my husband and I are not seeking revenge. We are asking for the name of our children to be cleared.' "[7]

The contest became one in which image contrasted sharply with reality. When the antisuffragist became a candidate, she crafted an image for herself that deviated sharply from that of the pampered woman she was. She grudgingly accepted the down-home nickname "Ma," which resulted from her husband's public references to her and the work of a newspaper copy editor, who shortened her name, Miriam Amanda, to initials. Texans enjoyed the theater of a Ferguson campaign in any event, and this appellation added one more scene to the play. Furthermore her trademark campaign photo, taken on her parents' old farm, depicted her wearing a bonnet, the clothing accessory common to laboring rural women but in fact anathema to the candidate, who preferred more stylish dress. Taken together her nickname and her political persona negated the fears some Texans harbored about female political power.[8]

The 1924 contest attracted national attention along with increased Republican competitiveness. Miriam Ferguson bested Robertson in the run-off but still faced Dr. George Butte in the November general election. The nascent GOP hoped for its first gubernatorial victory in the one-party state. Butte made Ferguson's battle with the University of Texas the theme of his race. Some Democratic Party stalwarts even considered the unthinkable—a vote for the Republican Party in the fall. Despite her representation as the ideal woman, these Democrats still found Miriam Ferguson lacking the "purity of public faith" required of the governor.[9]

As the general election neared, Crane worked with the political couple to ensure that they retained the allegiance of progressive Democrats. The political climate became tempestuous when Jim Ferguson discussed using his wife's pending election to reinstate his political rights. Hints from the Ferguson camp that their candidate had single-handedly eliminated the Klan angered progressives and threatened the outcome of the election. Crane's criticism of Jim Ferguson's statements, however, combined with his continued support of Miriam Ferguson, helped calm the situation. Miriam Ferguson won handily, but Butte's totals, three times that of previous GOP contenders, indicated the skepticism many had for Ferguson.[10] The corruption and unsavory tactics exhibited within the 1924 campaign followed the norm for male politics in the period and predicted the operating procedure for her administration.

The Ferguson victory brought attention both from within and outside the state. Fred Acree once wrote to the "Hon. James E. Ferguson and wife," declaring that "it is a very unique distinction for each of you to have been Governor of this great State of Texas." A correspondent for the *Dearborn Independent* addressed the question of which Ferguson was the real governor, while the *New York Times Magazine* proclaimed "two governors rule Texas." The two Fergusons "demonstrated amply to the world that there is as much masculine backbone in one half of the Administration as there is feminine kindliness in the other half." He usually greeted visitors, while she signed papers. Division of power between the couple colored much of the administration.[11]

Ma Ferguson compared her new responsibilities to the management of a family. Despite her election as governor, her husband still handled a share of the state's business. He corresponded with political supporters about road markers, political appointments, and clemency matters. In May 1925 Jim Ferguson, using the governor's letterhead, told one office seeker that the job would go to one of "those hungry lawyers down here that are exceedingly anxious to extinguish themselves upon the altar of their country." H. F. Kirby, the county judge in Limestone County, wrote to Jim Ferguson asking for a complete pardon for a local citizen who wished to vote for Ma Ferguson in her 1926 reelection contest. Jim Ferguson noted in his own handwriting that the request was granted. The former governor also negotiated matters of federal-state relations with the national government. Furthermore Jim Ferguson handled the public addresses in his wife's various contests for public office. He even told some newspaper reporters that he was the real governor. A staff member recalled years later that Jim Ferguson's informal control was the only explanation for Miriam Ferguson's victory: " 'If the people hadn't thought that Ferguson would be the governor *himself,* they never would have elected Mrs. Ferguson.' "[12]

The issue of Fergusonism doomed Miriam Ferguson's first term to a focus on scandal and corruption. The first major difficulty revolved around Jim Ferguson's political status. The legislature, in granting Jim Ferguson the restoration of his political rights, helped spark a long-running political controversy between the Fergusons and Dan Moody, the attorney general, who found the measure unconstitutional. Financial difficulties dating as far back as Jim Ferguson's 1917 impeachment plagued the family in 1924 and contributed to their lax comportment in the executive mansion. To compensate he accepted several legal appointments after her election. One carried a yearly retainer of $10,000. These advisory positions created ethical questions, since legislative policy was involved. Furthermore suggestions that the couple would not grant interviews without payment brought negative press. The *Ferguson Forum,* a partisan tract used for the family's political efforts, proved to be a financial boon for the couple. Jim Ferguson encouraged government employees to subscribe, along with all highway contractors wanting business with the state. Jim Ferguson also handled most highway matters for Miriam Ferguson's administration. He attended meetings of the State Highway Commission and ensured that his friends received lucrative contracts for road work. In addition to Jim Ferguson's bribes via highway contracts, their elder daughter, Ouida Nalle, used positions with the American Surety Company and the Capitol Insurance Agency for the family's profit. Rumors circulated that the Ferguson family even made money off the state textbook adoption process, via Jim Ferguson's role as clerk for the State Textbook Commission.[13]

Miriam Ferguson described her grant of "mercy" to the "poor unfortunates who were in the state penitentiary" as one of the major accomplishments of her first term; her husband believed in leniency for Prohibition violators. She advocated a pardons board to advise her on clemency matters. Visits to state prisons convinced the Fergusons of wrongful treatment of prisoners. As a result they became more sympathetic to pardon seekers. In her first term Ferguson granted 3,595 pardons compared with none for her predecessor, who opposed such decisions. Jim Ferguson often persuaded pardon supplicants to engage his legal services in order to expedite their release, suggesting that those inmates who employed the former governor were much more likely to receive favorable consideration from his wife.[14]

Women's groups had little regard for Ferguson's difficulties. Kate G. Winston, a Texas official with the National Woman's Party, declared that " 'this is not a case of a woman failing, in public office. Mrs. Ferguson was elected as a figurehead and she has served as a figurehead.' " Gender certainly did not inhibit Miriam Ferguson's detractors from ridiculing her record. An anonymous author composed a bit of doggerel under the title "Ma Ferguson's Prayer," which lambasted the governor for her pardon policy and corruption within the highway department:

> Thou knowest, Oh Lord, that I have been true,
> To my husband, Jim, all the way through,
> I've turned out crooks from the Huntsville pen,
> Such as murderers, thieves and hold-up men,
> But each had the cash to show,
> He deserved a pardon, so I let him go.[15]

Talk of impeachment filled the halls of government in Austin, but Ferguson, remembering her husband's fate in 1917, refused to call a special legislative session. Nevertheless Attorney General Dan Moody investigated charges of corruption within the Highway Department. Allegations against Ferguson included charges that she permitted her husband to conduct the state's business, that she sanctioned corruption within the Highway Department, and that she granted pardons far in excess of those meriting clemency. The political family survived these charges and a Travis County Grand Jury investigation that had studied the highway funding issue.[16]

When it came to her candidacy for reelection as governor, her gender did not necessarily bring women to her defense. In fact her attitude toward criminals angered women activists, who advocated fair but strict treatment of prisoners. Most troublesome were frequent rumors about the sale of pardons. Defeated for reelection in 1926, Miriam Ferguson contented herself to return home to her garden. Her husband, however, was not through with politics, and he encouraged her to run again in 1930, a race she lost to Ross Sterling, a businessman who helped found what became Humble Oil. The year 1932 brought a rematch with Sterling.[17]

The financial condition of the state helped the Fergusons' cause, since they seemed more sympathetic to Depression sufferers than the wealthy incumbent. Ferguson's 1932 campaign platform promised relief from foreclosures, other measures ameliorating the depressed economy, and "the Ferguson usual and successful operation of the state prison system." The contest, marked by fraudulent votes on both sides, wound up in court. Miriam Ferguson prevailed and went on to win the general election against Orville Bullington, the GOP contender.[18]

The second Miriam Ferguson administration paralleled the first, especially with regard to Jim Ferguson's unofficial power, scandals, and suggestions of official misconduct. She reinstated her generous pardon policy. The pardons secretary recounted tales of storing money in a governor's office vault. The war with the University of Texas flared up during her second term, when Miriam Ferguson rejected a list of proposed nominees for the university's board of regents. But the Depression, not Fergusonism, marked Miriam's second term. To handle the crisis, she reduced state expenditures. The collapse of the nation's banking system provided a strong test of her leadership. After studying the problem in other states and consulting with federal officials, the governor, on her husband's advice, declared a bank holiday. The move was risky, since she had no authority for her declaration, but combined with the federal bank holiday declared just days later, it ensured the protection of what remained of the Texas banking community.[19]

In 1933 leading state newspapers found few substantive legislative accomplishments to report, and at the end of her second term newspapers still recognized the dual nature of her tenure in office. Indeed Miriam Ferguson's two terms as governor provided little in the way of direct advancement of women's issues and rights within the Lone Star State. Beyond a few female appointments, Ma Ferguson paid little attention to issues advocated by politically active women, such as child labor laws and legitimate prison reform.[20]

Her election as governor, then, reads more like an aberration in the study of women's political advancement in Texas. Instead of yielding significant lessons about female political power in the postsuffrage decade, a study of the Ferguson political marriage shows the complexity of relying on any one construct for understanding past events. The way in which Ferguson came to power and the way in which she ran, or permitted her husband to run, the state's affairs reflects much of the ambiguity about women in Texas public life and about the Ferguson family in the 1920s and 1930s. Texas voters accepted Miriam Ferguson as governor only because they knew Jim Ferguson would have control of state affairs. Those same voters would not accept Minnie Fisher Cunningham, a woman with a sterling record of political accomplishment with the suffrage fight, when she ran for the United States Senate in 1928. Another important result from the Ferguson experiment remains the lesson that women who sought political office still needed male votes. Female politicians and political activists therefore learned that advocacy of women's issues alone was not sufficient to assure victory. In the end, whatever the analytical yardstick, be it feminism or political ethics or governmental leadership, Miriam Ferguson's administrations contained little of substance. She had few political deal-making skills, and she seemed content to let her husband work his brand of political entrepreneurship for the benefit of the family's coffers instead of the citizens of the state.

NOTES

1. May Nelson Paulissen and Carl McQueary, *Miriam,* 1–31, 34–38; Miriam Ferguson and James Ferguson Vertical Files and Scrapbooks, Center for American History, University of Texas at Austin (hereafter CAH).

2. Lewis L. Gould, *Progressives and Prohibitionists,* 120–49, 185–221; Paulissen and McQueary, *Miriam,* 52–53, 57–58, 65.

3. James E. Ferguson (JEF) to John Bickett, Jr., 6/13/24, in "file 6," box 3P45, James Edward Ferguson Collection (hereafter FC), CAH.

4. Norman D. Brown, *Hood, Bonnet and Little Brown Jug,* 211–52.

5. G. C. Groce to Martin McNulty Crane, 7/31/24, in "January 1924–July 1924"; Crane to W. L. Baird, 8/6/24; Crane to Groce, 8/1/24 [two letters from that date]; Crane to L. W. Stephens, 8/1/24; Stephens to Crane, 8/7/24; R. L. Paschal to Crane, 8/3/24, all in "1–9 August 1924," all in box 3N106, Martin McNulty Crane Papers (hereafter CP), CAH.

6. S. C. Padelford to Crane, 8/2/24, in "1–9 August 1924," box 3N106, CP, CAH.

7. Brown, *Hood, Bonnet and Little Brown Jug,* 219, 225; Gould, *Progressives and Prohibitionists,* 174; Paulissen and McQueary, *Miriam,* 97 (first quote), 98, 103 (second quote).

8. Brown, *Hood, Bonnet and Little Brown Jug,* 227–28; Paulissen and McQueary, *Miriam,* 99–100; Shelley Sallee, " 'The Woman of It.' "

9. *New York Times,* August 21, 1924; Brown, *Hood, Bonnet and Little Brown Jug,* 238; S. W. Fisher to the editor of the *Statesman,* 8/16/24, in "January 1924–July 1924," box 3N106, CP, CAH.

10. JEF to Crane, 9/30/24, in "September 1924–December 1924"; Crane to JEF, 8/25/24, in "10–30 August 1924"; Crane to JEF, 10/1/24, JEF to Crane, 10/15/24, and Crane to JEF, 10/16/24, all in "September 1924-December 1924"; all in box 3N106, CP, CAH; Brown, *Hood, Bonnet and Little Brown Jug,* 250.

11. Fred Acree to Fergusons, 3/6/31, in "James E. and Miriam Ferguson, 1913–16, 1924, 1926, 1928–34, and undated," box 2A119, Fred Acree Papers (hereafter AP), CAH; Max Bentley, "Who is Governor of Texas?" *Dearborn Independent,* February 27, 1926; Owen P. White, "Two Governors Rule in Texas," *New York Times Magazine,* April 5, 1925; French Strother, "The Governors Ferguson, of Texas," *World's Work* (September 1925): 489–93.

12. Paulissen and McQueary, *Miriam,* 126; JEF to Acree, 3/30/26 and Acree to JEF, 11/10/33, both in "James E. and Miriam Ferguson, 1913–16, 1924, 1926, 1928–34, and undated," box 2A119, AP, CAH; JEF to J. B. Hubbard, 5/14/25, in "file 6," box 3P45, FC, CAH; Jessie Ziegler to Dearest Family, 10/7/32 and H. F. Kirby to JEF, 3/5/26, both in "file 8," box 3N141, and Ziegler to Eppie, 5/5/33, in "file 1," box 3N142, all in Jessie Ziegler Papers (hereafter ZP), CAH; JEF to Crane, 10/17/24, in "September 1924–December 1924," box 3N106, CP, CAH; *San Antonio Express,* November 28, 1925; Brown, *Hood, Bonnet and Little Brown Jug,* 269 (quote).

13. Brown, *Hood, Bonnet and Little Brown Jug,* 266–68, 274–80, 284–85; Paulissen and McQueary, *Miriam,* 137, 140–47; *Houston Chronicle,* February 9, 1926.

14. *San Antonio Express,* January 20, 1926; Paulissen and McQueary, *Miriam,* 150–66.

15. Winston, quoted in "A Texas Twister Brewing for 'Ma' Ferguson," *Literary Digest* 87 (December 12, 1925); "Ma Ferguson's Prayer," n.d., in "Politics—General—1922–23–24–25," box 2J351, Will C. Hogg Papers (hereafter HP), CAH.

16. Proceedings of a Court of Inquiry, Conducted by Henry Houston Jones, 9/17/25, 9/23/25, in "Politics—General—1922–23–24–25," box 2J351, HP, CAH; Robert M. Field, "Will 'Ma' Ferguson be Impeached?" *Texas Outlook,* December 9, 1925; *San Antonio Express,* October 18, 1925; Brown, *Hood, Bonnet and Little Brown Jug,* 285–96; Paulissen and McQueary, *Miriam,* 140–47; Miriam Ferguson Vertical File, CAH; *Dallas News,* November 25, 1925.

17. Jno. to Ziegler, Wednesday, in "File 5," box 3N141, ZP, CAH; *Austin American Statesman,* February 28, 1926; Brown, *Hood, Bonnet and Little Brown Jug,* 297–339; Paulissen and McQueary, *Miriam,* 37–39, 167–86.

18. *Ferguson Forum,* April 7, 1932; see for example Ziegler to Dearest Folks, 9/1/32 and Ziegler to Dearest Family, 10/7/32, both in "file 8," all in box 3N141, ZP, CAH; *Dallas News,* September 2, 13, 21, and 24, 1932.

19. Jessie Ziegler to Dearest, 1/17/33, in "file 1," box 3N142, ZP, CAH; Paulissen and McQueary, *Miriam,* 161, 193, 196, 198, 201–7; *Dallas News,* January 19, 1933; Paulissen and McQueary, *Miriam,* 200–201.

20. *Dallas News,* June 1, 1933, January 14, 1935, January 21, 1925, and September 9, 1933; Miriam Ferguson Vertical File, CAH; Paulissen and McQueary, *Miriam,* 133, 160.

14. Florence Prag Kahn, acting Speaker, House of Representatives, Washington, D.C., 1926 (Western Jewish History Center, Judah L. Magnes Museum).

CHAPTER THIRTEEN

"THERE IS NO SEX IN CITIZENSHIP"

The Career of Congresswoman Florence Prag Kahn

GLENNA MATTHEWS

When former Republican Congresswoman Florence Prag Kahn died in 1948, Governor Earl Warren announced that California had lost one of its "great citizens." The first Jewish woman to serve in Congress, she had replaced her deceased husband Julius Kahn in the House in 1925 after winning a special election in San Francisco's Fourth Congressional District; she went on to win reelection five times. Only the Roosevelt landslide of 1936 sent her back home to San Francisco permanently. Obituaries referred to her "dazzling wit," "indomitable spirit," "fabulous intellect," and "occasionally frightening talent for ramming through legislation."[1] Today she has been all but forgotten, even in the budding literature that addresses the accomplishments of the first postsuffrage generation of women politicians.[2] But Florence Prag Kahn was an important pioneer whose remarkable success in what was then an overwhelmingly male world can be attributed principally to three factors: the special character of San Francisco Jewry, the political exposure she received owing to the activities of both her mother and her husband, and her own formidable personality.

Born in 1866 Kahn was the daughter of two early San Francisco settlers, Conrad Prag, a merchant who was only intermittently successful, and Mary Goldsmith Prag, a teacher and administrator who became the economic mainstay of the family and went on to serve on the San Francisco Board of Education.[3]

Mary Prag was an important influence on her only surviving child's life, setting an example of educational and professional achievement. She proved that a woman could be a devoted mother and still have an active life outside of the home. She convinced her daughter to attend the new university across the bay in Berkeley instead of a normal school for teacher training. Kahn then graduated from the university in 1887, one of forty students to obtain a degree that year, only seven of whom were women.[4] Like her mother she became a teacher. The two women achieved public office within a few years of one another. In 1922 Mary Prag, approximately seventy-five years old, received a mayoral appointment as one of the first two Jews to serve on the San Francisco Board of Education. In 1925 her daughter won the first of several elections to Congress.

San Francisco is the key to understanding the remarkable careers of both mother and daughter. Founded as a European American community by Franciscan fathers, it was a village with only a few hundred souls at the time the Mexican War ended in 1846. In 1848 James Marshall discovered gold on the south fork of the American River, unleashing an explosive population growth throughout the region. By 1852 San Francisco claimed more than thirty thousand people, one of whom was the young Mary Goldsmith, a child around five years old when her family arrived in San Francisco that year.

Protestants built their first church in 1847, and Jews conducted their first services on Yom Kippur in 1849. Many Jewish immigrants—unlike the unfortunate Conrad Prag—did well during the gold rush and its aftermath, and they were thus able to build solid communal and religious institutions from the start. In addition to being the first city in the country to send a Jewish woman to Congress, San Francisco was also the first big city to elect a Jewish mayor, Adolph Sutro, in 1894. Levi Strauss, Sutro Tower, Fleishhacker Zoo, Zellerbach Auditorium at Berkeley—all of these well-known names and places in the Bay Area attest to the prosperity of Jewish families and to their cultural influence.

Mary Prag had positive memories of her childhood. After a difficult journey across the isthmus of Panama from their native Poland, the family encountered better times in San Francisco. They attended Sherith Israel, the synagogue founded by immigrants from England and Poland. Mary also attended Sabbath school at Emanu-El, the synagogue associated with German-Jewish immigrants. The idealistic Unitarian clergyman Thomas Starr King paid his young neighbor special attention and allowed her to browse in his library. Especially thrilling were all the theatrical performances in the opera-mad city of the 1850s. It was a culturally rich upbringing for a young girl, drawing upon San Francisco's fabled cosmopolitanism to prepare her well for a life devoted to education.[5]

In addition to being more integrated into mainstream cultural life than in most American cities—for example they belonged to the Masons as early as the Gilded Age[6]—San Francisco's Jews participated in its political life as well. During the years of Republican ascendancy from 1911 to 1963, the city's Jews, overwhelmingly Republican until the New Deal years, enjoyed an "extraordinary . . . influence in the government and politics of the city."[7] These were the years of Prag's and Kahn's public service.

Raised in a city where Jews played an active and visible role in civic and cultural life, reared by a mother who modeled high achievement, Florence Kahn was also fortunate in the man she married. Julius Kahn was born in Germany and, like Florence, raised in San Francisco. His family was too poor to provide him with an education beyond elementary school, but he found his way to New York, where he became a successful actor. The stage palled; he returned to California, studied law, and became active in Republican politics. At this juncture he looked up one of his old teachers, Mary Prag, and soon became interested in her daughter. Florence Prag was a successful woman in her own right, teaching high school English. She took her mother's advice and waited until Julius had settled his career before consenting to marry him. After his election to Congress in 1898 from one of the two districts in San Francisco, they became husband and wife.[8]

With the exception of a single term between 1902 and 1904, Julius represented the Fourth Congressional District until his death in 1924. Florence served as his secretary to economize. Their two sons, Julius II, born in 1902, and Conrad, born in 1906, spent much of their early lives in Washington. In a 1908 interview Florence Kahn described the busy and useful existence of a young mother who also happened to be a Congressman's helpmate. At that time, before the adoption of woman suffrage in California, she opposed suffrage. She mentioned that she was active in the Emanuel Sisterhood and was trying to start a branch in the East. Nothing in the article hints at the powerhouse to come.[9]

There is, however, a treasure trove of Florence's political and social ideas, formed while she was still a Congressman's wife rather than a politician herself, that foreshadows her later career. In 1919 and 1920, needing extra income as her two sons neared college age, she wrote columns signed "The Eavesdropper" for the *San Francisco Chronicle*. Far from light anecdotes about capital doings, they are closely argued analyses of both domestic and foreign policy issues, revealing a woman with a good education and a formidable intellect, who in her years as a congressional wife and secretary observed much and reflected deeply.

The political stance she presented was of a staunch party loyalist, not particularly sympathetic to labor, who approved of the infamous Palmer raids that launched the Red Scare of 1919. (Indeed she was a lifelong supporter of J. Edgar Hoover). Not surprisingly she endorsed the positions taken by her husband, especially his devotion to military preparedness. Julius, a member of the House Military Affairs Committee, had introduced the bill setting up the draft after American entry into World War I, and his wife was proud of that achievement.

A late twentieth-century feminist will find much that is alien in Kahn's opinions, but it is impossible not to admire the intelligence of the observations.

Especially striking is that the woman who had said in 1908 that she opposed woman suffrage had changed her mind by the time she wrote for the *Chronicle*. Many columns discuss the fate of political women, past and present. She writes about the role of women in the British Parliament, about the contribution made by American women to politics on the other side of the continent, and about current prospects for women candidates for Congress. On the founding of the League of Women Voters, she observed: "The success of the league and the effectiveness of the organization as a coercive element in legislation will depend on two things—the number of women that will join and the extent to which they will consider themselves bound by the edicts of the league."[10]

The columns exude a sense of ease with policy and politics. She was a mature and accomplished woman in her early thirties when she and Julius married. She had a university education, as he did not. Through her mother, appointed to the Board of Education in 1922, she had ties to the most influential people in San Francisco, such as Mayor James Rolph. Economic circumstance had made it expedient to serve as Julius's secretary, and she had spent many hours observing Congress from the gallery. All of these factors must have contributed to her comfort with politics. When Julius fell ill in 1924 and lingered for eight months before dying, she became the de facto representative herself. After he died, a "citizens' committee" of Republican leaders in San Francisco, headed by Mayor Rolph, approached her to run for the seat. However, she did not run unopposed; she overcame three opponents with only 48 percent of the vote in a very light turnout.[11]

At the time of Julius's death, there was scant room for optimism about the future for women in Congress. Jeannette Rankin had been elected as a Republican from Montana in 1916, had opposed American entry into World War I, and had served only one term. Alice Mary Robertson of Oklahoma was the second woman to serve in the House, again for only a single term, beginning in 1921. Rebecca Latimer Felton of Georgia had served in the U.S. Senate for a single day in 1922, as a sop thrown by the governor of that state to newly enfranchised women before the real senator was sworn in. Winnifred Huck of Illinois had served for a few months between November 1922 and March 1923. Mae Ella Nolan of San Francisco (the first Irish American woman and the first widow to serve in Congress) had replaced her husband following a special election in 1923, and then she had gone home saying that "[p]olitics is man's business."[12] Only a small group of women, such as New York's Belle Moskowitz, the right-hand woman of Governor Al Smith, and Illinois's Ruth Hanna

McCormick, daughter and wife of politicians, had Kahn's type of hands-on experience in the world of politics and policy.[13]

From all indications the superbly prepared Florence Kahn knew that she was up to the challenge. Announcing her candidacy in late December 1924, she said that during her husband's long illness, she had "carried on the work alone." The city's Republican newspapers endorsed her, with the *San Francisco Bulletin* arguing that it was not a matter of sentiment to support the widow Kahn, but rather a decision based "on the solid ground of character and competence."[14] Her supporters were not endorsing an unknown political quantity; in her *Chronicle* columns she had set forth her opinions on a wide range of important issues. Once elected Kahn immediately dedicated herself to hard work and to serving her constituents, as had her late husband. She also carried on the family tradition of devotion to military preparedness.

Her maiden speech to the House, in April 1926, showed Florence Kahn in characteristic form. Before addressing her main point—supporting reapportionment in favor of the nation's cities—she quoted from the book of Numbers in the Bible. She humorously implied that as her coreligionist Moses had conducted the world's first census, she was especially qualified to address this issue herself. (She loved a quip, and at a time of widespread anti-Semitism in American society, she also loved to call bantering attention to her religion.) Her speech was greeted by a "tremendous ovation."[15]

Her wit and force of personality had made her something of an insider—not easily achieved by a woman politician, then or now. Party loyalty helped, too. An observer writing in the *American Mercury* in 1929 said: "Gentlewoman Florence Prag Kahn is as regular a Republican as Gentlewoman [Edith Nourse] Rogers or Andy Mellon. She believes in a high tariff, is strong for National Defense, and has the confidence of the Republican members of the House." She was so regular "that you always know how she's going to vote, but only God has the slightest inkling of what she's going to say." She delighted in being outrageous, and people remembered the choice lines for years. The *American Mercury* writer summed her up: "It is probably the twinkle in her brown eyes that gets her by, though the high respectability of her politics helps."[16]

Given "the high respectability of her politics," certain of her stances are worth noting. A "wet" at a time when many Republican women were "dry," she invited—and received—opposition from other women, including one who ran against her in the 1926 primary, her "newness" that year attracting a total of four opponents. Since San Francisco was a center of opposition to Prohibition, being "wet" did not damage her: she outpolled her four opponents put together, including Raymond Burr, former secretary to Hiram Johnson. Burr had come within slightly more than two thousand votes of her total in 1925, but in 1926 neither he nor anyone else offered a serious challenge.[17]

Following in Julius's footsteps, she vigorously supported military preparedness. After the election of 1928, in which she performed the valuable partisan service of organizing women's groups for Hoover in forty-eight California counties, she was rewarded by being the first woman appointed to the House Military Affairs Committee.[18] Here she came into her own.

It is difficult in the post–Cold War world to develop a sympathetic and balanced understanding of the role that Florence Kahn played. Simply put, in the infancy of American military might, she worried that pacifism might fatally undermine the strength of her country. Since a stronger military was essential, then the greater Bay Area might as well be the beneficiary of the build-up; indeed the Pacific region had strategic importance. In a report to her constituents dated July 3, 1930, she outlined her vision for the Bay Area.[19] She then carried or cosponsored legislation establishing Moffett Field in Sunnyvale, Alameda Naval Air Station, and Hamilton Air Base in the North Bay.[20] She also carried the legislation that secured federal approval for building the Bay Bridge, linking San Francisco to the East Bay.[21] Others in the region, in government and in the business community, shared her vision,[22] but her own political skills played a very large role in turning that vision into reality.

The Kahn papers contain an undated newspaper clipping that details the way she operated. Headed "Navy Use of San Francisco Drydock to Continue/ Mrs. Kahn Defeats Move to Have Fleet Sent to Bremerton," the article explains the outcome of a vote that would have sent the fleet to the state of Washington. Florence Kahn trusted nothing to chance. "As the members were marching through the tellers, Mrs. Kahn posted herself in an advantageous position, urging her friends to join the line of the opposition."[23] Two things may be noted: at a time when the few women in Congress were likely to be patronized by their male colleagues, it took both courage and confidence for a woman member to behave so assertively; but she appealed to her "friends." Her vibrant personality ensured that she would have friends at a crucial juncture.

Her successes did not pass without notice at home. In 1934 the Democratic San Francisco Examiner rated her as one of "the important figures in Congress," to whom much credit should go for San Francisco's prosperity. Her "continuous and indefatigable labors" were instrumental in bringing new military facilities to the region.[24]

To accomplish what she did while getting reelected, Florence Kahn executed what can only be called a gender straddle—or maybe a gender minuet. "There is no sex in citizenship, and there should be none in politics," she proclaimed.

"I felt that I had a man's job to do and I wanted to fill it in a man's way, by attending to business." Yet she posed for photographs that played up her adherence to female gender norms. A picture of her buying chicken in 1926 is captioned: "In addition to being an able legislator, Mrs. Florence Prag Kahn, San Francisco congresswoman, is a capable housewife. She does most of her own shopping besides."[25] Other photographs depicted her with her sons or her mother. In a period in which "male" and "politician" went together as "naturally" as do "woman" and "mother," in which the very term "public woman" might still be considered an epithet, she was inventing a gender valence for the role of female politician as she went along.[26] The women of her hometown were proud of her, and she was the guest of honor at a San Francisco Soroptimist Club luncheon in August 1929, at which Mary Prag was also honored.

The woman who had opposed suffrage in 1908 but had become a competent congresswoman twenty years later might embrace her sister Soroptimists, but she made clear that she was not a feminist. "Mrs. Kahn in No Fear of Woman's Bloc," proclaimed the heading of an article in the *Chronicle.* "'American men are too nice to make the development of a woman's bloc necessary in American politics,' says Congresswoman Florence Kahn of San Francisco." She was quoted as saying that all four of the women members in the House agreed that there would never be such a group.[27] Yet a few months later she told a hometown paper about the letters she received from women all over the country, some fifty or sixty a day. "They seem to feel that they can call on a woman Congressman with less reserve."[28] She apparently believed that she had a responsibility to do constituent work for any American woman who needed her help. She "declared that the woman in political office must remember her responsibility toward other women."[29]

We should not be surprised that Florence Kahn was ambivalent about how to present her gender. In the 1970s, after the rebirth of feminism, there was still a well-documented "closet feminist syndrome": women running for office cloaked their support for feminist measures until they had won election. For women candidates to "run as women" is quite recent.[30] The issue of how a woman candidate can present herself as responsive to the needs of her female constituents while not alienating male voters is far from settled even now.

One qualified contemporary observer who thought well of Florence Kahn was Eleanor Roosevelt. Florence Kahn had met Franklin Roosevelt in 1915, at the Panama Pacific International Exposition in San Francisco. When the Roosevelts took occupancy of the White House, in 1933, Kahn was the first Republican invited for dinner. She voted for certain early New Deal measures, although her support waned over time as she became critical of the New

Deal.[31] Nonetheless FDR wrote warmly of Kahn in 1940, after voters had sent her back to San Francisco: "Mrs. Florence Kahn of California was an able and witty member, who would be welcomed back into the House with open arms."[32] Another member of the Roosevelt clan, the frequently acerbic Alice Roosevelt Longworth, had a similarly high opinion of Kahn: "Mrs. Kahn, shrewd, resourceful, and witty, is an all-around first-rate legislator, the equal of any man in Congress, and the superior of most."[33]

Kahn was definitely in ER's and Longworth's fields of vision, but her achievements largely escaped the attention of other observers of the period, as they have been ignored by historians. Representing a California district no doubt compounded the "invisibility" problem created by gender; she was better known at home than on the East Coast. One analyst assessing the women in Congress in 1930 specifically referred to this issue: "She [Kahn] goes about her job in Washington with great assurance, and while her work is quiet, it is very effective. Should she work for a national party with the understanding with which she works for the Republican party of California, many of us would be ready to call her a great politician."[34]

Those who now assess the history of women's involvement in partisan politics should take note of Kahn's achievements, because the Bay Bridge and the military bases she fought for have had a profound effect on the Bay Area. It is a telling indication of the way women's accomplishments are leached out of the record that at the very time she was toiling in this vineyard, some analysts were deprecating the contributions made by the early congresswomen. That tiny band of pioneers, lacking either a social movement to back them up or a tradition of public female authority, was supposed to make a protofeminist splash, and if they did not, then they were not doing much—that was the tenor of the criticism.[35]

In 1940 Eleanor Roosevelt wrote a more balanced assessment of the first twenty years of women's enfranchisement. She noted that the government's role had grown in humanitarian content since women had begun to vote. Nevertheless women were still not inured to the demands of a hard-fought campaign. Roosevelt prescribed a paradoxical formula for how political women should function in the future. Women must become more conscious of themselves as women, while in the larger world trying to drive from men's minds any thought of their group identity.[36] She was wrestling with issues we have not yet resolved. If Florence Kahn failed to reconcile fully her gender identity with her highly developed sense of herself as a politician, she still deserves to be remembered as one of the earliest women officeholders to leave an important legislative legacy. Florence Kahn provides a model of remarkable political effectiveness.

NOTES

1. *San Francisco Chronicle,* November 17, 1948, and November 18, 1948; *New York Times,* November 17, 1948.

2. See for example Kristi Andersen, *After Suffrage.*

3. Kahn Papers, Western Jewish History Center, Judah Magnes Museum, Berkeley, CA, box II, folder 5.

4. See Frances Parkinson Keyes, "The Lady from California," *Delineator* 118 (February 1931),

5 "Early Days," typescript in Kahn Papers; Keyes, "Lady from California."

6. Tony Fels, "Religious Assimilation in a Fraternal Organization."

7. David G. Dalin, "Jewish and Non-Partisan Republicanism in San Francisco," 1911–1963," 196.

8. Keyes, "Lady from California."

9. Clipping, Kahn Papers, box 2, folder 2.

10. *San Francisco Chronicle,* March 20, 1920.

11. *San Francisco Chronicle,* February 18, 1925.

12. As quoted in Linda Witt, Karen M. Paget, and Glenna Matthews, *Running as a Woman,* 31, 32.

13. On Moskowitz, see Elisabeth Israels Perry, *Belle Moskowitz.* On McCormick, see Kristie Miller, *Ruth Hanna McCormick.*

14. *San Francisco Bulletin,* December 22, 1924; February 11, 1925.

15. *San Francisco Daily News,* April 29, 1926; *Time,* May 10, 1926.

16. Duff Gelfand, "Gentlewomen of the House," *American Mercury* 18 (October 1929).

17. On San Francisco as a wet town, see Michael Paul Rogin and John L. Shover, *Political Change in California.* On the primary election in 1926, see the *San Francisco Bulletin,* September 1, 1926.

18. *Jewish Tribune,* December 28, 1928.

19. Kahn Papers, box 1, folder 14.

20. Harriet Hansen, "Woman Enters Politics," 24.

21. See Max Stern, "The Widow Kahn," *Today* (August 31, 1935).

22. See Roger W. Lotchin, *Fortress California.*

23. Kahn Papers, box 2, folder 2.

24. *San Francisco Examiner,* February 26, 1934.

25. Clipping dated March 26, 1928, Kahn Papers, box 2, folder 2; *San Francisco Examiner,* June 18, 1928; *San Francisco Bulletin,* October 7, 1926.

26. See Glenna Matthews, *The Rise of Public Woman.*

27. March 12, 1928.

28. *San Francisco Examiner,* June 18, 1928.

29. *New York Times,* March 8, 1929.

30. See Susan J. Carroll, "Women Candidates and Support for Feminist Concerns"; and Witt, Paget, and Matthews, *Running as a Woman.*

31. Hansen, "Woman Enters Politics," 19, 23.

32. Mrs. Franklin Roosevelt, "Women in Politics," *Good Housekeeping* 110 (January 1940).

33. Alice Roosevelt Longworth, "What Are the Women Up To?" *Ladies Home Journal* 51 (March 1934).

34. Clare Ogden Davis, "Politicians, Female," *North American Review* 229 (June 1930).

35. See for example Mildred Adams, "Congresswomen Are Just Congressmen," *New York Times,* June 19, 1932.

36. Eleanor Roosevelt wrote on this subject in the January, March, and April 1940 issues of *Good Housekeeping.*

CHAPTER FOURTEEN

ANNA WILMARTH ICKES
A Staunch Woman Republican

MAUREEN A. FLANAGAN

Chicagoan Anna Wilmarth Ickes (1873–1935) was a clubwoman turned politician who served three terms as a Republican representative in the Illinois General Assembly. She was also married to a famous political figure, Harold L. Ickes. Wilmarth Ickes's marital circumstance is relevant to a discussion of women's partisan politics for two reasons. First it contradicts the standard generalizations that women either followed their husband's political lead or were politically nonpartisan. Both Anna and Harold flirted with the Progressive Party. He moved inexorably into the ranks of the Democratic Party, eventually to become secretary of the interior in the Democratic administrations of Franklin D. Roosevelt. Anna not only became a staunch Republican, she entered formal politics before he did.

Her marriage is also relevant because her husband's numerous, typical male-hero biographies (and his autobiography) depict her political accomplishments either as adjuncts to her husband's politics or portray them, and her personally, in an adverse light.[1] Anna Wilmarth Ickes's politics derived not from her husband but from her mother and from her own experiences growing up within the milieu of Chicago women's activism. After Anna's father died when she was young, her mother, Mary Hawes Wilmarth, dedicated her life and considerable wealth to the women's activism swirling through Chicago in the late nineteenth and early twentieth centuries. She transmitted her ideals and her work to her daughter, and these were the formative political experiences that Wilmarth Ickes brought to her work, first in women's municipal organizations and then as a three-term representative in the Illinois House.

Wilmarth Ickes's political development within women's activism, and her

15. Anna Wilmarth Ickes as a young woman (Chicago Historical Society, Prints & Photographs Department).

career as a Republican politician, reveal important historical elements of the nature of women's political partisanship as they made the transition into formal politics in the 1920s. Women's partisanship then did not mimic male partisanship, and Wilmarth Ickes stands as an exemplar of the former, as she strove simultaneously to be a *woman* partisan and a partisan *woman.* Her political life encompassed a woman's strategy both for entering the male world of politics and once there, for pursuing a policy agenda that would draw upon the female models of achievement and politics that she had learned early in life from other women.

Mary Wilmarth was a close friend of Hull House cofounder Ellen Gates Starr. She provided considerable financial support for the settlement and its residents and was in constant attendance at its meetings and functions. She participated actively in the most important women's organizations in the city, helping to found in 1910 the Woman's City Club, the city's foremost women's municipal organization. She served as the WCC's first president, remained its honorary president until her death in 1919, campaigned actively for woman suffrage, fought for public education reforms, belonged to the Women's Trade Union League, and championed the rights of women workers to strike and of women teachers to unionize.

Anna Wilmarth grew up in her mother's world amidst a remarkable cohort of Chicago women engaged in social and political reform. From a young age she knew and worked with settlement house activists such as Jane Addams, Harriet Vittum, and Mary McDowell; clubwomen such as Louise DeKoven Bowen and Elizabeth Bass (who went on to chair the Women's Bureau of the Democratic National Committee); and working women and workers' activists such as Agnes Nestor and Margaret Dreier Robins. It was in Mary Wilmarth's living room in 1889 that Jane Addams and Ellen Gates Starr discussed their desires to found a social settlement. When Anna attended the University of Chicago in the 1890s, she was surrounded by many of the women students and professors who formed the vanguard of women's welfare and political work in the city across the first two decades of the twentieth century.

After leaving the university and marrying, Anna steadily followed her mother's example of municipal reform work. She opened her home to activists interested in discussing contemporary urban problems. She and her mother attended a meeting called at Hull House in 1908 to confront an episode of violent anti-Semitism in the city. In 1914 both Anna and Mary furnished bond money for striking women waitresses arrested while picketing, and Anna testified in court against the actions of the police during the strike. Whether she actually belonged to the Women's Trade Union League, as did her mother, is not certain, but she did attend the league's annual Halloween Ball in 1914, the profits from which were earmarked to furnish restrooms for the working "girls in the loop," Chicago's downtown business and shopping district. That same year she was scheduled to march in a massive woman suffrage parade in the city, although she does not seem to have been a member of the Chicago Political Equality League.[2] She belonged to the Chicago Woman's Club, serving as its president in the 1920s. In that decade she also sat on the independent Chicago Government Planning Commission, whose other women members were drawn from the leadership ranks of the city's most visible women's organizations.

Anna Wilmarth joined the Woman's City Club at its founding in 1910; it was the city's largest, most active women's municipal reform organization. The club conducted political campaigns both before and after suffrage, in order to implement new public policies on issues of municipal health, garbage disposal, clean air, public school reform, housing, and more. In all of its reform proposals, the WCC demanded that the city be made to work for the benefit of all of its citizens.[3] When Wilmarth Ickes formally entered politics, she would bring with her a political agenda shaped by her earlier experiences with these issues.

Her mother and this milieu of women's activism helped define her choice of political party. Along with Addams, Vittum, McDowell, and Bowen, Mary and Anna Wilmarth were "progressive" Republicans in the heady but brief period in the second decade of the century when reformers sought to reshape the Republican Party to their agenda. When these efforts failed, Wilmarth Ickes remained a Republican even as other Chicago "progressive" women strayed from the party. In the 1920s she ran for political office as a Republican, first for University of Illinois trustee and then for state legislator. Her partisanship held even as Harold Ickes moved steadily into the Democratic Party.

Yet Wilmarth Ickes's partisanship was not the same as that of Republican men. She was clearly a partisan *woman*. This difference can be seen by reflecting on how the prevailing assessment of women's political partisanship parallels the ways in which the biographies of famous men deal with their wives. Both assessments are generated by a male perspective on the subject. Harold Ickes's biographers have always depicted Anna by accepting her husband's assessment. In the case of political partisanship, men had defined *partisan* to describe their political world before they allowed women into it. When women entered the formal world of politics with suffrage, men then used their definition against women, declaring them unwilling to be partisan because they did not wholeheartedly agree with men about what it meant. If we shift focus to examine Wilmarth Ickes and what she learned from other women about politics and partisanship, we can see a very partisan party woman working to redefine the term.

When Anna Wilmarth Ickes entered politics, newly enfranchised Chicago women declared allegiance to one of the two parties, voted for that party in elections, and fought for women's appointments to party positions and for nominations for political office.[4] At the same time, the women of Wilmarth Ickes's generation had undergone their formative political experiences outside the party system. Thus they carried into partisan politics a political agenda whose legislative priorities and political styles were destined to clash with those of the men controlling the parties. In Chicago the application form of the Woman's Roosevelt Republican Club gives perhaps the best group expression of this women's partisanship. It declared its members to be Republicans, but that they stood ready "to conduct a coalition campaign by a union of Democrats and Republicans" if securing certain pieces of legislation required it.[5]

Wilmarth Ickes initiated her political party activities in the enthusiasm of the progressive revolt within the Republican Party. At the party convention in Chicago in 1912, the progressives bolted, held their own convention, and nominated Theodore Roosevelt for president under the banner of the new Progressive Party. Anna could not attend this convention, having recently given birth to her son Raymond. But her mother and husband attended, and it seems likely that had she been able, she would also have attended. Since the convention occurred only a year after her marriage to Ickes but after several years of her own activism, it also seems safe to conclude that her mother and the circle of activist Republican women in the city were the decisive influences in Anna's adherence to progressive Republicanism, not her husband. In fact Harold Ickes's only mention of the origins of Anna's political career was to note "her participation in the Progressive Party with her mother."[6]

As the Progressive Party faded from national prominence, her husband drifted steadily toward the Democrats. But Anna remained a Republican for the rest of her life. She perhaps occasionally deviated from a strict party line for the sake of her husband, although that is difficult to verify. One Ickes biographer says that Anna took "to the stump in South Dakota in support of the [Democratic] Cox-Roosevelt ticket" and that she along with her husband were on the executive committee of the Independent Dever Club in 1923 (William Dever was the Democratic candidate for mayor of Chicago in that year). This information may have come from Harold Ickes, but no newspaper accounts of these campaigns or other primary and secondary sources mention Anna's participation. If she did engage in some Democratic Party politicking, it was a transitory and not well publicized phenomenon.[7]

Notwithstanding her husband's political leanings and the fact that other Republican women bolted the party in the coming years over disgust with its corrupt municipal politics, Anna maintained her allegiance in local and state affairs. Lists of independent Republicans and progressives supporting the Democrats William Dever for mayor in 1927 or Henry Horner for governor in 1932, for example, do not contain her name. Nor is she listed as a contributor to the political campaign of Democratic activist Agnes Nestor, who ran for the state legislator also in 1928.[8] By the late 1920s, her husband stood firmly in the Democratic ranks, and she reportedly was not pleased with his support of Franklin D. Roosevelt. Until she died, in 1935, she remained a staunch Republican, even sticking with elements of the Republican Party that eventually drove out other progressive Republican woman.

In her formal political career, Wilmarth Ickes first ran for political office in 1924 as a Republican candidate for trustee of the University of Illinois. Accounts of her nomination describe her as the "hand-picked" candidate of Republican Governor Len Small, indicating that she belonged to a specific faction of the Illinois Republican Party.[9] She won this post, and when her term expired in 1928, she ran for the Illinois House of Representatives as a Republican from the Seventh Congressional District. She then served three terms in the Illinois legislature. She won her first two races handily, with the backing of the faction in the regular Republican Party headed by former Governor Charles Deneen. Her husband (who claimed to have encouraged her to run for office so that she would leave him alone!) managed her campaign. To do so he turned his back, at least temporarily, on his own political proclivities and supported the Republican ticket and publicly tolerated his wife's moderately "dry" position, although he was a "wet" on the prohibition issue.

By her 1932 campaign, Wilmarth Ickes had garnered "enough prestige in the Republican Party to command organizational backing . . . even though the Deneen organization, piqued at her husband's connection with [the Democratic Party], withdrew its support." That year she pursued her Republican politics even as her husband and her eldest son worked actively for Democratic candidates. Harold Ickes supported Roosevelt on the national ticket and the local Democratic candidate for state's attorney, Thomas Courtney. Anna's son from her first marriage, Wilmarth (Thompson) Ickes, was active in the Courtney campaign, as were some of her former female allies in Republican politics, including Jane Addams and Mary McDowell. Moreover despite the political tide turning against the prohibition stance of the Republican Party, Wilmarth Ickes remained a "dry" Republican, surviving an attack against her candidacy by the Women's Organization for National Prohibition Reform and winning a third term in the legislature.[10]

The documentary evidence that exists for Wilmarth Ickes's actual political experiences reveals her as a strong supporter of party politics. She appealed to women to vote for her as a party politician, arguing that party politics was good because parties were the best vehicle for exercising political power. Yet she balanced her fervent belief in party politics against her long experience in women's organization and women's municipal activities and refused to become just another party politician.

Her relationship with the League of Women Voters (LWV) exemplifies her sense of herself as a both a woman partisan and a partisan woman. Wilmarth Ickes seems to have kept her distance from the nominally nonpartisan LWV. Again an Ickes biographer says she belonged to the organization; but a search of the manuscript collection of the Illinois and Cook County branches does not yield her name. At the least this indicates that she played no prominent role in the organization, unlike other Chicago activists such as Nestor and Mc-Dowell. In her 1930 reelection campaign, she attacked the league for its anti-politics stance, telling female audiences that the LWV motto, "measures not men," was shortsighted, because politics was the "machinery without which measures can never be enacted by men, however well-intentioned." Women had to understand that they were entering a male world when they won political office and had to learn to operate in that world. She urged women to partic-ipate actively in the nomination and election processes as the political means through which they could take power away from the old political bosses. "If you refuse to help in the selection of candidates," she told women's clubs, "you will come to the November elections faced with the choice between a boss selected Republican candidate and a boss selected Democratic candidate."[11]

In office she certainly put her political instincts and the needs of her largely Republican district above those of the league. When the Illinois LWV presi-dent asked Ickes to support certain league-endorsed revenue amendments to the state constitution, Ickes responded that she could not support the amend-ments, because they would allow the legislature to levy taxes on Cook County (where her district was) without any guarantee that these revenues would be returned to the county taxpayers rather than being spent "down state" (as Chicagoans habitually refer to the rest of the state, whether north, south, or west of the city). She rejected the amendments as potentially harmful for her constituents and declared that she would not support any amendment unless it would "properly safeguard the interests of all parts of the State."[12] Simulta-neously, however, Wilmarth Ickes projected a woman's point of view into politics. By accepting that the two elements of political partisanship and wom-en's partisanship coexisted within her politics, we can discover a women's understanding of a broader partisanship.

During her first campaign for state representative, Wilmarth Ickes declared that her aim in entering politics was to accomplish "the greatest good for the greatest number," not to promote the Republican Party. She specifically appealed to women to support her, because she understood that the concerns once limited to the home, such as sanitation, pure food, education, and health, were now subject to public decision making. These were issues, she claimed, "upon which men are only too willing to consult with women as to what is what." They were also the issues that had most concerned the Woman's City Club since 1910, and her political aim of doing the greatest good for the greatest number was exactly what the WCC had been saying for years ought to be the highest priority of politicians. By electing her, she said, women could assure such a woman's voice and a woman's priorities in the legislature. In her next campaign, she asked women to send her back to the legislature because such issues were clearly the work of government, and "this certainly brings the work of the legislature near to women's hearts. Would we keep our rightful influence in these matters we must go to the polls. . . . send me back to Springfield." In Chicago the Woman's City Club supported her election, saying she was "interested in having government serve the human interests of the people and if she is elected her efforts will be to forward the welfare and social legislation which women have at heart."[13]

Wilmarth Ickes understood the endurance of male political behavior and partisanship as something to be challenged by women as they brought new ideas into politics. She told her audiences that one bill she had introduced during her first term had died in committee, "the argument being advanced against it being that it contained an 'entirely new idea.'" This extraordinary claim, she declared, was a "man's reason surely. . . . I cannot imagine a group of women calmly scrapping a bill because its contents were new." She regretted that any legislation she desired would fail if more traditional stalwarts in the Republican Party could exercise the clout to thwart it, no matter how much women voters might desire it.[14]

When Harold Ickes was appointed secretary of the interior in Roosevelt's first administration and moved to Washington, Anna faced a personal upheaval. She stayed in Illinois to serve out her third term, then followed her husband to Washington. Precisely why she decided to quit organized politics we cannot know; their relationship had always been a difficult one. Harold was a man of considerable political ambition but little money; Anna was a woman of considerable wealth, well-connected in Chicago's progressive Republican circles, and a formidable public figure in her own right when they married, in 1911. The marriage seems to have been filled with jealousy, mistrust, and acrimony generated by the clash of two strong egos and the fact that most of their money was Anna's. His biographers accept virtually at face value his evaluation of her and their marriage, despite the cautionary note of one of them that "what correspondence there might have been between [them] about their relationship has been removed" from the voluminous Ickes papers. Ickes says that his wife abandoned her political career because she found it more flattering to be the wife of a cabinet officer rather than a political figure in her own right.[15] Surely if Wilmarth Ickes desired to keep her marriage intact, the fact that she was receiving anonymous letters detailing an affair that her husband was having with an unidentified woman in Washington must have helped her decision.

Her own interests, in the meantime, had turned over the years to New Mexico and its Indian population. It is possible that had she lived, she would have turned her political energies in that direction. Whatever her reasons for declining to seek reelection, Anna Wilmarth Ickes did not live long enough to see how her relationship might have worked out, nor to find another political niche. In August 1935 she died in an automobile accident in New Mexico. At the time of her death, the New Deal programs of the Democrats were drawing more and more women into that party's ranks. As Robyn Muncy and other historians have shown, however, no matter how partisan women became they were never welcomed as political equals in either party.[16] The New Deal Democratic women discovered, as women have realized ever since, that women's formative experiences outside the party system endowed them with a legacy of women's political partisanship that has always looked different from men's. The life and career of staunch Republican Anna Wilmarth Ickes reveal important elements of this difference but also show clearly that political partisanship existed among the first generation of women voters in the 1920s.

NOTES

1. Harold L. Ickes, *The Autobiography of a Curmudgeon* (New York: Reynaland Hitchcock, 1943); Linda Lear, *Harold L. Ickes;* T. H. Watkins, *Righteous Pilgrim.*

2. Jane Addams, *Twenty Years at Hull House* (New York: MacMillan, 1910), 75; Mary Wilmarth to Ellen Gates Starr, June 2, 190[?], Ellen Gates Starr Ms Collection, box 12, folder 143, Sophia Smith Collection, Smith College Library, Northampton, MA; Watkins, *Righteous Pilgrim,* 96; *Chicago Tribune,* March 6 and 10, 1914 (for waitresses' strike), May 1, 1914 (for suffrage), and November 1, 1914 (for WTUL).

3. Maureen A. Flanagan, "Gender and Urban Political Reform"; and "The City Profitable."

4. Maureen A. Flanagan, "The Predicament of New Rights."

5. Membership application (n.d.), Emily Washburn Dean Ms Collection, folder 11, Chicago Historical Society.

6. Lear, *Harold L. Ickes,* 322 and 323 n. 1.

7. Watkins, *Righteous Pilgrim,* 404 and 197; *Chicago Tribune,* March 19, 22, and 25, 1923. Lear, *Harold L. Ickes,* 322, says that "after 1916 she had returned to the Republican Party,

never sharing Ickes' passion for independence." Anna and most Chicago Republican women stuck with the party candidate for mayor in 1923.

8. See the "Manifest of People's Dever for Mayor Campaign—1927," in Agnes Nestor Ms Collection, box 3, folder 3, Chicago Historical Society. This list includes the names of Harold Ickes, Harriet Vittum, and Jane Addams, for example; box 3, folder 5, records contributions to the Nestor campaign.

9. Unidentified newspaper clipping (1924), Ickes Scrapbooks, vol. 1, container #465, Library of Congress.

10. Lear, *Harold L. Ickes,* 351–52; and *Chicago Tribune,* April 4 and November 7, 1932.

11. Watkins (1990), *Righteous Pilgrim,* 201; "Notes for campaign speech to be given to women's clubs—1930," Harold L. Ickes Ms Collection, box 571, Library of Congress.

12. Letters of May 31 and June 4, 1930, between Anna Wilmarth Ickes and Mrs. Ralph Treadway, Illinois League of Women Voters Ms Collection, box 4, folder 31, Chicago Historical Society.

13. Unidentified newspaper clipping, April 28, 1928, Ickes Scrapbooks, vol. 1; Woman's City Club of Chicago, *Bulletin* (1928); "Notes for campaign speech," Ickes Ms Collection, box 571.

14. "Notes for campaign speech," Ickes Ms Collection, box 571.

15. Lear, *Harold L. Ickes,* 406.

16. Kristi Andersen, *After Suffrage;* Flanagan, "The Predicament of New Rights"; Cynthia Harrison, *On Account of Sex;* Robyn Muncy, *Creating a Female Dominion;* and Susan Ware, *Beyond Suffrage.*

CHAPTER FIFTEEN

"SHE IS THE BEST MAN ON THE WARD COMMITTEE"
Women in Grassroots Party Organizations, 1930s–1950s

PAULA BAKER

The story of the decline of political parties in United States is a familiar one to political historians and political scientists. Over the course of the twentieth century (scholars disagree about exactly when), voters became less likely to identify strongly with a party and more inclined to split their tickets between parties. Campaigns became more focused on candidates than their parties, and candidates fielded their own organizations and raised their own money. Parties became less and less relevant to ordering voters' decisions, conducting campaigns, and making law. Parties have hardly disappeared—in some ways the organizations have grown stronger in recent decades—but interest groups, candidates, and the mass media do much of the work parties used to do in defining issues, raising money, and educating and motivating voters.[1]

Women and gender are not normally mentioned in this story. This essay is an early exploration of what women's participation as party workers in the twentieth century can tell us about both women's partisan activism and the history of political parties. A substantial literature produced by political scientists and journalists during the middle decades of the twentieth century described party workers as the middlemen between the manufacturers of campaigns, issues, and candidates and the retail sale to voters. As volunteers for particular campaigns or regular year-round activists, they got out a party's or candidate's message on a one-to-one level, tried to inspire voters to get out and support their party, and took care of the endless mechanical tasks of a campaign. Whether they were the "cogwheels of democracy" or not, they were the human faces of party politics.[2]

If we think of those who have worked for candidates and parties as a

16. Burlington, Vermont, women active in party politics, 1944 (Special Collections, University of Vermont).

workforce, like those in industry or the service sector, we find that the work-force became smaller and increasingly female. It also became more stratified, with highly skilled and well-paid professionals at the top and workers stuffing envelopes, delivering literature, and reading canned appeals over the phone down below. Women came to dominate at the lower end of the workforce, and they gained control over areas that involved authority only over other women. Changes in the party workforce mirrored those in the clerical workforce; like clerks, women party workers encountered diminished chances for mobility and control over their work when compared to their nineteenth-century male counterparts. Those differing experiences illuminate women's slow rise in par-tisan politics and the apparent decline of political parties in the twentieth century.

There is no accurate count of the party workforce during the heyday of political parties, from the 1840s through the 1890s. We do know it was vast. Some men worked hard for their parties because their jobs demanded it—

postmasters and mail carriers, schoolteachers, policemen, firemen, laborers who maintained roads and canals or cleaned streets and offices, contractors and construction workers who got government work, and printers often held their posts because of political connections. Patronage alone, however, could not have sent thousands of men traipsing door-to-door, since there were hardly enough jobs to take care of all workers. For other men working on campaigns was an essential part of being a supporter of a political party and its principles. Party workers indicated in letters they wrote to politicians that they believed their work was important. They explained to state or even national candidates how things were going in towns or districts, how voters reacted to the party's appeals, and what troubles might lie ahead. Their labors made them "friends" of the candidate. Getting a job or a favor was something one friend might do for another—an exchange between equals—not a grant extended from the powerful to the powerless. So one man asked a Democratic politician for a thirty-dollar loan until his pension check arrived, because "Four years ago I labored for your nomination for the Presidency." Another writer explained to a Republican politician, "We have worked the best way we knew how in your favor, and we are proud to inform you that you got a majority of about 70. . . . [W]e trust you will reciprocate by doing all you can to bring about the mail route we deserve." These men believed there was a close and reciprocal relationship between politicians and themselves.[3]

Party workers had important responsibilities because nineteenth-century parties did things later taken care of by candidates, private groups, or government. There were rallies to organize, speakers to line up, campaign materials to produce, and voters to transport. By the 1880s there were polls to take, and since their version of scientific sampling meant contacting just about every voter in a competitive state, polling was labor intensive. States did not print ballots, so workers prepared them. On election days workers tracked down voters who needed to be paid for their trouble, organized what would be, with luck, a victory celebration, peddled the tickets, and watched the proceedings. Their efforts paid off; in the late nineteenth century, voter turnout reached the level of 80 to 90 percent.[4]

The party workforce began to change in the early twentieth century. For party leaders the workforce was expensive and often troublesome, even if it did get out the vote. The cost of everything from the day-long rallies, to excursions to country resorts, campaign paraphernalia, vote-buying, and the ballots were borne by the parties. To pay for campaigns they operated what was in essence their own tax system: those who accepted patronage jobs or contracts kicked back a portion of their pay to the party; candidates paid an "assessment" for the privilege of running; state representatives shook down corporations with threats of regulation; city officials took cuts from the vice trade. While they were profitable, these activities exploded into controversy at times. The mischief party workers could cause was even more serious; they had a good deal of power, and they knew it. They could prepare ballots as they saw fit, and if in a given district they wanted to honor a local man of the opposite party or if they objected to one of their own party's nominees, they "knifed" a candidate—replaced the name of the regular nominee with another name. "Knifing" on a large scale in even one state could bring down a potential president, which probably happened to Grover Cleveland in 1888. Party workers could as easily lose as win an election for their parties if they were so inclined.[5]

State party leaders determined that a large party workforce had outlived its usefulness by the early twentieth century. The political realignment of the late 1890s put the Republican Party firmly in national control, and there were few states left in which both parties were competitive. Meanwhile party leaders felt pressure from reformers to make elections more "honest," while corporations and many politicians had grown disgusted with periodic shakedowns for money. Civil service reform had begun to deplete the stock of patronage positions. So party leaders took advantage of necessity: state legislators passed on the costs of elections to the government. They did this in the name of honest elections, but these reforms also reduced the need for unpredictable party workers and made it more difficult for third parties to get a place on the ballot. The parties also cut back on campaign hoopla and looked to indirect contact with voters to get them to the polls. The outcome was a smaller but more controllable workforce and a smaller but more controllable electorate.[6]

The Nineteenth Amendment took effect as parties and campaigns began to change. New techniques were most prominent in national politics. By the 1920s individual candidates began to take charge of campaigns and to hire "consultants"—campaign specialists who provided everything from clipping services to "intelligence" and advertising, and this trend became more and more common over the course of the twentieth century, as nominees employing their own professional campaign staffs became the rule. The rise of interest groups has also changed campaigns and the place of party workers. Interest groups provided another way besides voting to get involved in politics. Someone interested in a particular issue—from ending child labor to improving municipal sanitation in the first decade of the twentieth century, from enforcing Prohibition to repealing it in the 1920s—could find a group that lobbied Congress and state legislatures on that issue. Interest groups wrote legislation in their specialty and funded their candidates and parties. Some interest groups—the AFL-CIO since the 1940s and groups such as the Christian Coalition more recently—have provided campaign workers to operate phone banks, construct mailing lists, and get out the vote. They have both supplemented and supplanted party organizations.[7]

Prevailing ideas about gender, as well as these somewhat smaller and more fragmented national party organizations, shaped women's places in party politics. The Democrats and Republicans created "women's divisions" and saved slots for women on their (generally insignificant) national committees. The parties assigned the women's committees the tasks of getting out the women's vote and attending to "women's issues," although the women rarely had access to patronage or money to accomplish these tasks. Still some women—India Edwards, Molly Dewson, Frances Perkins, and Emily Newell Blair, for example—rose through the party ranks by means of the women's divisions and their connections to independent women's reform organizations. More rarely women gained political influence in less traditional ways. Belle Moskowitz, who had been involved in reform politics in New York City at the turn of the century, was New York Governor (and presidential candidate) Al Smith's most trusted and important advisor.[8]

Women with an interest in party politics, however, usually started at the bottom of local organizations, where changes in nineteenth-century political patterns were subtle and uneven. The heyday of political machines in United States cities had passed, but some survived—some even came to life in the 1930s—into the middle of the twentieth century. Consider the case of Rose Popovits of Philadelphia. In that city candidates still paid for their place on the ballot, political appointees kicked back a portion of their salaries, patronage sustained the machines' health, and votes measured the success of ward and precinct leaders as they had in the nineteenth century. Five of the fifty Republican ward leaders were women in 1932; Rose Popovits was one of the 1,283 Republican precinct leaders. She entered politics in 1922, when the former precinct leader inspired the twenty-two-year-old to help on election day. Taking his place after his death, she carried "her division of 658 votes in her vanity case . . . because she chooses to carry a man-sized load of neighborhood troubles on her back." She continued to carry her division even in the teeth of the realignment that toppled the Republican machine. "You see," she explained, "the so called feminine claim does not mean a thing in politics, and jealousy is the chief obstacle in a woman's path to success." She was, according to her ward captain, "the best man on the ward committee."[9]

Popovits's experiences were matched in Chicago, where from the late 1920s to the mid-1930s, a growing number of women gained control of precincts. Women held 11 percent of the precincts in 1936 against only 5.1 percent in 1928. African American women made up 25 percent of the precinct leaders in African American districts. Party leaders' belief that women district leaders were essential if the machine were to attract women's votes accounted for some of these precinct captains. A Mrs. Smith, a "neat, elderly, garrulous woman," was cocaptain of Chicago's Fifteenth Ward in the 1930s, assigned the responsibility of getting women to the polls. She helped with washing and minded babies so that women in her district could get to the polls. She set up a women's club that sponsored card parties and dances and provided a space where women grew accustomed to talking about politics apart from men.[10]

Women involved in machine politics did more than cultivate the women's vote. Changes in the tasks and the resources of urban machines, while not yet as dramatic as those of the national parties, also explain the emergence of women at the base of the organizations. Precinct leaders were no longer personal purveyors of social services as much as they were links between citizens and the city bureaucracy. Popovits concerned herself chiefly with helping residents straighten out troubles with a magistrate or deal with forms in city offices. Chicago precinct leaders typically chased fewer fire engines and handed out fewer buckets of coal. Instead they pointed residents to social service agencies and intervened in the decisions of tax assessors, judges, and public welfare officials. Precinct leaders still put in long hours and occasionally acted as personal charity organizations, but they increasingly were the human face of local, state, and national government, not the political parties.[11]

As the job changed, so did the people who did it. Men and women of long residence and long records of political involvement became precinct leaders, and many hoped to get something for their work—a city or county job, perhaps. When a researcher in 1927 asked a female precinct leader in Chicago why she got involved in politics, she answered "To get some of the graft!" But precinct leaders, especially African Americans and residents of poorer areas, mentioned their desire to help their neighbors more than their own advancement in explaining their involvement in party politics. And it was just as well; even in the 1930s such jobs were becoming more scarce, and the machine had to rely on people who simply wanted to help or happened to love politics. People animated by goals other than personal reward grew in importance to the machines. Women, who were far less likely than men to get jobs on the public payroll, were increasingly valuable party workers. Changed duties and shrinking resources opened spaces in politics for women in machine cities.[12]

But party machines were not dead by a long shot. "Boss rule" in cities such as Chicago, Kansas City, Memphis, New Orleans, Jersey City, and Albany, New York, continued into the mid-twentieth century and even beyond in a few cases. But they were not the wave of the future. The future looked somewhat more like the political patterns in western states, where party organizations that were never terribly strong grew even more attenuated. Party leaders in

Washington found it difficult to fill county committee posts, much less find workers for election districts. Perhaps because of the lack of interest—and lack of reward—middle-class women filled most of these positions. In California the parties and their candidates relied more on mass media than on old-fashioned campaign organizations to reach voters. Impatient with the major parties, new voluntary groups related to the major parties but independent from them began to compete with the Democrats and Republicans as early as the 1930s. The clubmen—and women—wanted parties with a more pronounced ideological flavor; the clubs filled the organizational void left by the major parties.[13]

By World War II the trends set in western states spread across the rest of the country. With those trends a new party workforce had taken shape. At the top professionals ran campaigns. Replacing the newspapermen and public relations specialists borrowed from business who had helped candidates and the parties in the 1920s and 1930s, a new group of (male) political professionals crafted campaign appeals and candidate images and worked with the press. The Republican and Democratic National Committees employed such political professionals, as did individual candidates. "The propaganda function of politics has, more and more, moved out of the hand of the lay politician into those of propaganda specialists," according to a witness at a congressional hearing on campaign expenditures in 1952. Firms, notably Whitaker and Baxter, provided a full menu of services to candidates, including polling, fundraising, and strategy. Claiming to know more about modern, mobile Americans than the old-time bosses did, Whitaker and Baxter aimed not to provide services to voters but to identify issues that would create an entertaining contest. Technique and presentation, not contact with actual voters, now mattered in politics.[14]

While professionals provided skilled services, regular "core" workers kept local races in order, and low-level workers and volunteers did the ordinary office and campaign work. All of these workers, but especially those at the lower levels, tended to be middle class. Party workers could not expect to get much financial benefit for their efforts; between civil service rules and the unionization of some public employees, people who sought government jobs relied less on political connections than in the past. The Hatch Act, passed in 1939, and similar laws at the state level prevented government workers from taking part in campaigns, which wiped out another potential source of party workers. So the party workforce consisted of people with enough leisure and interest in politics to spend long days tending phones and the mail without much promise of tangible rewards coming their way.[15]

By the 1950s women filled the ranks at the lowest levels and did most of the ordinary campaign work. As a political scientist observed in 1947, "Whereas two decades ago the polling place on registration, primary, and election day was exclusively the province of the male, today, especially in urban communities, it is often the women who serve as election clerks and inspectors." They had the time for politics, according to one woman Democratic activist: "A load of phoning, canvassing, list checking and other partisan chores can be wedged between trips to the laundromat and Den Mother's Day by those who like politics." Women served as poll watchers, as baby-sitters and drivers, and as errand runners. At party headquarters women answered the phones, distributed literature, and mailed letters. According to one somewhat soured party activist, women "allowed men to shift much of the hard work in party organization to them for which they get small pay and small places of influence."[16]

Women were also present in the middle levels of party organization. According to a survey in the 1950s, 56 percent of Republican and 41 percent of Democratic core activists were women. This was enough to inspire some grumbling on the part of a male partisan, who warned in a *Harper's* article: "Men may think they are safely in control, but one of these mornings all of the district leaders will stroll down to their clubrooms, chomping their cigars. When they open the doors they will find the windows have been swathed in pastel curtains, the spittoons and pinochle decks thrown out, and the poker layouts converted into vanity tables." Despite such grousing party leaders believed women made excellent party workers; they happily performed routine tasks, and middle-class housewives had the time for it. Better still they did not demand much in return.[17]

Women had difficulty, however, rising out of the lower ranks or women's divisions. "Women have influence only when matters concerning women are being considered," one activist complained in the 1940s. "I do not consider the influence of the women important, and see no immediate prospect of it becoming anything more than personal and indirect," added another. Another believed that the "secret opinion" of party men was that "Women are fine in the precincts but out of place in the policy-making department." Although both major parties abolished their women's divisions in 1952, women remained in positions of limited responsibility that largely concerned women voters.[18]

This brief sketch of women and changes in the party workforce suggests, most obviously, that women *were* involved in the grubby work of party politics. Not only did a few women achieve recognition and political influence through their work in women's divisions and reform networks, but a large number became crucial workers for the political parties. By the 1940s women made up the majority of low- and middle-level party workers. These were women not especially driven by a reformist agenda or "women's issues." Some simply liked politics and public service; some even sought graft. Many of them enjoyed the masculine pleasures of the political "game"—the excitement of being part of a campaign team.

While women were important to the party organizations, they received few tangible rewards for their trouble. They filled positions in the political parties at a point when the structure and meaning of party work was changing in a way that did not benefit the low-level workforce. As the party workforce specialized, the low- and even middle-level posts that women usually filled did not normally lead to remunerative positions in the parties. Party work had become a stool, not a ladder; women might make contacts and even be offered a chance to run for office (usually in hopeless races), but it did not pay. It did not teach many skills, as hired professionals took care of policy, strategy, and technical tasks. There is no evidence that mid-twentieth-century party workers shared the belief of their nineteenth-century counterparts that candidates owed something to them and that they had knowledge that candidates were anxious to hear.

This survey of the party workforce suggests that some concepts drawn from labor history have a good deal to offer to the study of politics. Women in the party workforce gained a substantial presence as the work was becoming less skilled, more stratified, and except at the very top, less important. So it was with office work: at one time to become an office clerk was to become an apprentice businessman. When women moved into office work, however, the jobs were finely subdivided, less likely to demand more than a single, narrow skill and leading only to dead ends (the height of advancement was supervising other secretaries). A similar pattern developed in telephone work. Women's place in the party workforce paralleled many women's experiences in the wider workforce.

Finally historians might join with some political scientists in questioning the traditional story of party decline. Parties did not disappear. Their organizations changed, but they remained vital and staffed by women. Even the decay of voter attachment to the parties can be overstated. The tendency of most voters to identify with a party remained strong until the 1970s. Turnout lows in the 1920s and 1970s need not characterize the entire century. Furthermore we might speculate that the growing presence of women in party organizations was connected with the complaints about "weak" parties sounded in the 1950s. The presence of women in the political parties (and not, significantly, among political writers and political scientists) changed in the 1940s and 1950s, while the parties and their resonance with voters did not. In any event historians might do well not to simply dismiss twentieth-century political parties as hazy reflections of their nineteenth-century predecessors.

NOTES

1. Michael E. McGerr, *The Decline of Popular Politics.* On the political science literature, see Leon D. Epstein, *Political Parties in the American Mold,* chap. 2.

2. Sonya Forthal, *Cogwheels of Democracy.* A review of studies of party workers from the 1920s through the 1960s is Lyman Arthur Kellstadt, "Precinct Committeemen," chap. 1.

3. On connections between party workers and politicians, see Paula Baker, *The Moral Frameworks of Public Life,* chap. 2. A good deal of work on nineteenth-century politics—at least that which relies on personal papers—draws upon material produced by party workers. See for example William E. Gienapp, *The Origins of the Republican Party.*

4. John F. Reynolds and Richard L. McCormick, " 'Outlawing Treachery' "; and John F. Reynolds, *Testing Democracy* cover the work of campaigns. On turnout see Paul Kleppner, *Who Voted?,* chap. 3.

5. See Clifton K. Yearley, *The Money Machines,* on the party tax system; Reynolds and McCormick, " 'Outlawing Treachery,' " covers unruly party workers.

6. On changing campaign styles, see McGerr, *The Decline of Popular Politics;* and Silbey, *The American Political Nation.* On the resolution of financial problems, see Yearley, *The Money Machines.*

7. On changes in party organizations, see Stanley Kelley, Jr., *Professional Public Relations and Political Power;* and Melvyn H. Bloom, *Public Relations and Presidential Campaigns.* On the increasing importance of candidates, see McGerr, *The Decline of Popular Politics.*

8. Sophonisba P. Breckinridge, *Women in the Twentieth Century;* Marguerite J. Fisher, "Women in the Political Parties"; and Martin Gruberg, *Women in American Politics,* chap. 2. On individual achievement, see for example Elisabeth Israels Perry, *Belle Moskowitz;* Susan Ware, *Partner and I;* and India Edwards, *Pulling No Punches.*

9. J. T. Salter, *Boss Rule,* 194, 196, 203, 193.

10. Evelyn Brooks Higginbotham, "In Politics to Stay"; and Harold Foote Gosnell, *Machine Politics,* 62–63.

11. Gosnell, *Machine Politics,* chap. 4; Salter, *Boss Rule,* 193–207; and Leon Weaver, "Some Soundings on the Party System."

12. Forthal, *Cogwheels of Democracy,* 21.

13. Hugh A. Bone, "New Party Associations in the West"; and Hugh A. Bone, *Party Committees and National Politics.*

14. Kelley, *Professional Public Relations and Political Power,* 2.

15. On the Hatch Act and the fate of mid-twentieth-century party organizations, see Sidney Milkis, *The President and the Parties.*

16. Fisher, "Women in the Political Parties," 87; Marion K. Sanders, *The Lady and the Vote,* 31; Gruberg, *Women in American Politics,* 49–53; and Marguerite J. Fisher and Betty Whitehead, "Women and National Party Organization," 902.

17. Dwaine Marvick and Charles Nixon, "Recruitment Contrasts in Rival Campaign Groups," 205; *Harper's* quote in Sanders, *The Lady and the Vote,* 31.

18. Fisher, "Women in the Political Parties," 88.

CHAPTER SIXTEEN

SOLEDAD CHÁVEZ CHACÓN, ADELINA OTERO-WARREN, AND CONCHA ORTIZ Y PINO

Three Hispana Politicians in New Mexico Politics, 1920–1940

ELIZABETH SALAS

Soledad Chávez Chacón, Adelina (Nina) Otero-Warren, and Concha Ortiz y Pino employed cultural and familial strategies to advance themselves into the political arena in New Mexico and address issues of ethnic, gender, and political identification as well as bilingual/bicultural education and economic advancement for Hispanos. However, death, personal and familial divisions, and crises resulted in these Hispana officeholders encountering resistance from their families in seeking office at the national level. Nevertheless Hispanas still managed to play a crucial role in helping women find places in local and state politics from 1920 into the 1940s.[1]

Chávez Chacón was the first Democratic woman of Spanish-American ancestry to win election as secretary of state in New Mexico, in 1922. Written material relating to her political career is sketchy at best. She was born on August 11, 1892, and died in her forties in 1936. Chávez Chacón was from an old pioneer family and had been one of the first Hispanas to be graduated from Albuquerque High School and Albuquerque Business College. She was put up by the Democrats in the 1922 election by young politicians on the rise such as Dennis Chávez, John E. Miles, and Thomas J. Mabry. The Democrats selected a woman to run for this state position as a way of challenging the selection of Adelina Otero-Warren as the Republican candidate for the national office of U.S. representative in the same election. Democrats hoped to deflect criticism by Republicans that they were "anti-woman" and yet insure that the office selected for a woman candidate would not be a powerful position.

Cultural and familial ideologies were at work in the selection of Chávez

17. Adelina Otero-Warren (left), crisscrossing New Mexico in her 1922 bid for the U.S. House of Representatives (Bergere Family Collection, photo no. 21252, New Mexico State Records Center and Archives, Santa Fe, NM).

Chacón. Hispano and Anglo politicians liked her because of the way she responded to their request. She first asked permission of her father and husband to run for the office, thereby reaffirming Hispano patriarchal notions that women were subject to the will of their fathers before marriage and should seek their husband's consent in making decisions after marriage. Chávez Chacón was a woman candidate who emphasized her role as wife and mother.

When she heard that she had been nominated for the office of secretary of state, she was "baking a cake" in the kitchen. She always insisted on being called "Mrs." when introduced at public rallies and emphasized that she was the mother of two children. Chávez Chacón belonged to Spanish-speaking, literary, issues-oriented, and women's clubs such as El Club Literario, El Club Latino, the Minerva Club, and the Women's Club. She emphasized education as the next generation's strategy for improving themselves. Whereas she completed the accounting curriculum at the Albuquerque Business College, her daughter was the only Hispana graduate in the 1932 graduating class of the University of New Mexico, and her son was a 1934 graduate of the National Law School in Washington, D.C.[2]

Chávez Chacón was the "eighth highest vote-getter" in the field of twelve candidates (seven were Anglos and five were Hispanos) running that year for state and national office. She missed being the highest Hispana/Hispano vote-getter by fifty-two votes. As secretary of state she was described as "painstaking and careful, prompt and courteous and inspired."[3] She won reelection and served in the office twice from 1923 to 1926. Perhaps her most trying time in office involved having to certify a disputed election for the position of sheriff in San Miguel County. Confidently she tallied the votes, and with her official poll books in hand, declared Lorenzo Delgado the winner of the election by six votes over rival Cleofas Romero.

When Governor James F. Hinkle was out of town from June 21 to July 5, 1924, she served as "acting governor." She signed requisition orders for government monies, gave a partial pardon for one convicted criminal, and signed extradition papers for the return of a man charged with grand larceny in Kansas.

Chávez Chacón was a role model for many Hispanas seeking political office. In fact the position of New Mexico secretary of state has often been filled by Hispanas, including Jesusita (Mrs. E. A.) Perrault, a Republican (1929–30); and the Democrats Marguerite P. Baca (1931–34); Elizabeth F. Gonzales (1935–38); Jessie M. Gonzales, (1939–42); Cecilia Tafoya Cleveland (1943–46); Alicia Romero (1947–50); Ernestine D. Evans (1967–70 and 1975–78); and Rebecca Vigil-Girón (1987–1990). Chávez Chacón's daughter, Adelina Chacón Ward, was a candidate for the post in 1948. The position of secretary of state is generally considered an "honorific" post with little political leverage. But for many

Hispanas working their way up through the local political system, winning election as secretary of state has been considered an important achievement.[4]

So well liked was Chávez Chacón that she won election to the New Mexico state legislature from Bernalillo County in 1935, the fourth Hispana to be elected to the legislature. The other three were Mrs. Ezequiel Gallegos, from Mora County (1931–32); Mrs. P. Saiz, from Socorro and Catron Counties (1931–32); and school teacher Mrs. Susie Chávez, from San Miguel County, for two terms (1933–36). While Chávez Chacón was in the state legislature she was put on the following committees: Rules and Order of Business Committee (served as chair); Appropriations and Finance; Ways and Means; Education; and Irrigation, Drainage and Conservancy.[5] Unfortunately, during her second year in office, she fell ill and died of peritonitis. Many Hispano political observers believed that if she had lived she might well have won higher office, either as governor, U.S. representative, or U.S. senator.

Chávez Chacón's success in New Mexico politics came from familial connections to Democratic politicians. Her best friend was the wife of future U.S. Senator Dennis Chávez. She also represented the kind of woman politician the Democrats could support wholeheartedly, because of her emphasis on being a devoted daughter, wife, and mother in her campaigns. Her political style was decidedly understated. She claimed her identity as an Hispana and a Democrat and confined her behavior within the boundaries of Hispano norms and expectations for women politicians.

Such was not the strategy of Adelina Otero-Warren, who like Chávez Chacón, ran for political office in 1922. She was at once a very conservative Catholic, a proud Hispana, a firm surrogate mother to her half-sisters and brothers, a staunch Republican progressive politician, and an educator. Otero-Warren challenged conventional ideas about women by divorcing her husband, Lt. Rawson Warren, after a brief marriage and by running for office at a time when divorced individuals in general had little acceptance in the political world. Where Chávez Chacón's writings are sparse, Otero-Warren was a prolific writer. As an educator she wrote extensively about Hispanos, Native Americans, and Puerto Rican educational needs, and as a folklorist she wrote the book *Old Spain in Our Southwest* (1936) and several articles.

Born into an old, prominent, and wealthy family in 1881, Otero-Warren's most important role model was her mother, Eloisa Luna. Her mother had attended a convent school in New York City, married twice, and had twelve children. Her first marriage was to an Hispano, her second to an Anglo. She was the sister of a well-known Republican leader, Solomon Luna, and offered her home in Santa Fe as a gathering place for politicians to discuss important issues. She attended most of the sessions of the first legislative assembly, when

New Mexico became a state in 1912. In addition to being a member of the Woman's Christian Temperance Union, she also was appointed as a member of the Santa Fe School Board.[6]

In many ways Otero-Warren followed in her mother's footsteps by going off to a convent school and one year of college in St. Louis, Missouri. Her mother had died in 1914, and Otero-Warren, who was living in New York City, returned home to become a surrogate mother for her nine half-siblings. While her mother had left her a trust fund, Otero-Warren knew she had to work to supplement her income nonetheless. Just as her mother had sat on a school board, so too did Otero-Warren. Her appointment in 1917 to the position of Santa Fe County superintendent of schools was made by Democratic Governor Ezequiel Cabeza de Baca, which suggests that initially Hispano families put aside partisan politics to promote the appointment of Hispanas and Hispanos to public office, regardless of whether they were Democrats or Republicans. Otero-Warren, a Republican, then ran for that office in 1918 and was consistently reelected until 1929, when she retired from politics.

Otero-Warren's participation in suffrage politics was considerable. She was asked by Congressional Union organizer Ella St. Clair Thompson in 1917 to head the state CU chapter. Otero-Warren's skill as an advocate of suffrage led to her appointment as chairperson of the Women's Division of the Republican State Committee for New Mexico as well as chairperson of the Legislative Committee of the New Mexico Federation of Women's Clubs.

By 1922 Otero-Warren had decided to run for national office as the Republican candidate for the U.S. House of Representatives. Part of her campaign consisted of advocating a secretary of education at the cabinet level and promoting federal aid for education throughout the country.[7] While all Republican national and state candidates lost to Democrats in New Mexico in 1922, Otero-Warren's campaign was shaken by her misrepresentation of herself as a "widow" rather than a divorcée. While Hispana women in New Mexico have a centuries-long history of calling themselves "widows" rather than acknowledging abandonment or divorce, Otero-Warren must have known that she would not have been allowed to be nominated for office if she had stated that she was divorced.

Former Democratic Governor Miguel Otero, her cousin, was responsible for divulging information about her divorce. It seems that by 1922 the Oteros and other Hispano families had split into Democratic and Republican factions, with bitter feuding finding its way into the political arena. Besides wanting to reenter politics, former Governor Otero's motives might have included conservative Catholic views about divorce and his chagrin at being snubbed by Otero-Warren in her campaign speeches when she spoke about her famous relatives.[8]

Convinced in 1922 that she could never again run for national office without her divorce becoming an issue of contention, Otero-Warren changed strategies and redirected her political ambitions to state appointed offices. She was more than ever committed to developing an educational system in New Mexico that considered the needs of Native Americans, Hispanos, and illiterates.

Education for Native Americans came under her scrutiny in 1923, primarily because of her appointment as inspector of Indian schools in Santa Fe County. In speeches about Native American education, Otero-Warren announced that "the Indians are not a vanishing race, as many suppose."[9] Changes in American Indian education that Otero-Warren sponsored included special attention given to educating mothers and closer cooperation between the school and the home. Her efforts to "Americanize" Indians were balanced by her view that a Native American student "must be taught to appreciate the history and traditions of his own race and thus inspired to continue the native arts of his own people as well as acquire a new type of learning."[10] Otero-Warren's ideas about combining Americanization and the retention of ethnic identity also applied to her observations about the educational needs of Hispanos.

In the 1930s Otero-Warren complained that "constant political changes . . . which are necessary in a political office" often "made it impossible" to bring about educational reform that would benefit Spanish-Americans.[11] Her concerns were echoed by other Hispanos such as George I. Sánchez and Joaquin Ortega, both noted educators in New Mexico. Ortega, a professor at the University of New Mexico, explained that the problems Spanish-Americans faced in New Mexico "related not so much to discrimination as to poor economic and health conditions," and that solutions involved "further educational and vocational training."[12]

Rather than seek reelection for a twelfth term as Santa Fe superintendent of schools in 1930, Otero-Warren decided to retire from political office. She cited the increasing power of the Democrats and thought that her reelection as a Republican was in jeopardy. She did, however, want the position to remain in the family; she and the conservative old-guard Republicans of Santa Fe sponsored her half-sister Anita Bergere for the post. Bergere held the office for just one term and was then defeated by Democrat Manuel Lujan, Sr. According to Otero-Warren's biographer, Bergere's loss was "no great disappointment"; "she simply wanted to please Nina and felt duty-bound to try to help the Republicans cling to some vestige of power in Santa Fe."[13] The death of Otero-Warren's brother Eduardo in 1932, a very influential Republican and her consistent backer, also affected the decision of Otero-Warren and her female relatives to leave political office.

Otero-Warren's attention during the 1930s focused more than ever on investigating strategies that would reaffirm her commitment to the educational needs of New Mexicans. Despite her own checkered political past and the loss of key familial political supporters, Otero-Warren nonetheless remained innovative in her attempts to better the lives of Hispanos through bilingual/bicultural education. She sought funding for educational reform through the Laura Spellman Rockefeller Foundation. Otero-Warren became convinced that Hispanos should become an integral part of the United States as Spanish-Americans, proud and knowledgeable about their Spanish heritage, speakers of the Spanish language, and as artisans securing a more promising economic future.

In a 1930 letter to Dr. Herman M. Bumpus, an educational consultant, Otero-Warren stated that:

In an effort to preserve the Spanish-American people and their culture I feel this can best be accomplished through education. Heretofore, there has been a neglect of the great opportunity to incorporate the culture of these people—their arts, crafts and literature—in our educational work throughout the country. Therefore, with the combination of the most progressive American educational methods, together with the stimulus to preserve their culture, the Spanish-Americans can be put on a sound economic basis.[14]

While Otero-Warren's efforts to protect and promote the culture of Spanish-Americans were genuine and represent some of the first steps in the creation of an "ethnic identity," it has to be remembered that she, like many others who called themselves "Spanish-Americans" or "Hispanos" did not reflect the complex ethnic mix of Indian, African, and European ancestry of most New Mexicans of Hispanic heritage.

Philip B. Gonzalez has stated that the use of the "Spanish Fantasy Heritage" by Hispanos served to undercut the negative connotations of the label "Mexican" so often voiced by Anglo-Americans. Emphasizing Spanish ancestry, according to Gonzalez, did however serve as a "political device allowing its adherents to act in their collective interest."[15]

Otero-Warren's presence and influence in local politics continued with her appointment as director of literacy education for the state-directed Civilian Conservation Corps in the 1930s. She cited the 1930 population census of New Mexico as 314,370 persons and the number of illiterates (ten years of age or older) in the population as 41,845, or 13.3 percent. One of Otero-Warren's remedies for Hispano illiteracy was to promote the bilingual approach of teaching Hispanos in both Spanish and English. In a 1938 report, she defined a "politically or a civic illiterate person" as one who "cannot take a sane, sensible informed place in the politics of his precinct, county, state and nation."[16] The goal of teaching for Otero-Warren was to link "literacy" with citizenship and as a "means of discovering answers . . . for health, social, economic and civic problems."[17]

While Otero-Warren's political life had stabilized as that of an appointed officeholder, writer, and educational consultant, her personal life continued to challenge standard Hispano and Anglo notions about women's roles as wife and mother. Throughout her life Otero-Warren had to navigate between rigid Catholic beliefs about "right conduct—piety, devotion to duty and deportment—and the proper roles for women in church and community," and her own personal desires and actions.[18] As an Hispana Otero-Warren grew up with religious and cultural values that were very orthodox with regard to marriage and divorce but quite relaxed in relation to smoking cigarettes, drinking, and gambling. She had been educated in the Midwest and had lived for awhile in New York and had traveled extensively, oftentimes with non-Hispanic companions. But Otero-Warren's attention to "appearances" resulted in calling herself a "widow" rather than a "divorcée" in her 1922 campaign, all her elections as school superintendent, and on all her applications for appointed offices.

Her cosmopolitan behavior and attitudes were reenforced by liberal-minded Anglo-Americans who came to live in Santa Fe. Otero-Warren became friends with Alice Corbin Henderson, Mary Austin, Ruth Laughlin, and Witter Bynner. Austin urged Otero-Warren to write books about Hispanos, and Bynner, a "self-described homosexual," was a constant companion of Otero-Warren and her half-sisters, "invited weekly for tea, cocktails, dinners and pleasant evenings of animated conversation and bridge."[19]

It is within this social milieu that Otero-Warren began her thirty-year relationship with another woman, Mamie Meadors. Like other people suffering from tuberculosis, Arkansas-born Meadors relocated to Santa Fe in 1918 to recover her health. After graduating from the University of Arkansas she worked as a clerical assistant. In New Mexico she joined woman suffrage campaigns and volunteered in the Otero-Warren campaign of 1922. Carroll Smith-Rosenberg's description of the "new woman" as college educated and willing to "experiment with alternative lifestyles and institutions," aptly describes Otero-Warren and Meadors.[20] With her appointment as inspector of Indian schools in 1923, Otero-Warren hired Meadors as a paid assistant, a job she held during most of the 1930s as well. Charlotte Whaley, Otero-Warren's biographer, has said this about the relationship:

Las Dos (the two) was the name Nina and Mamie had acquired in Santa Fe, given to them by Hispanic friends and business associates who saw them as a devoted twosome, always together in their trips around town and to the outlying county schools. The two women had developed a close friendship based on mutual support and affection, and together they had created an environment in which they could live and work independently. Their sustaining and secure relationship became the basis of a productive partnership that lasted for more than thirty years. With Nina, Mamie felt loved and accepted even though she had little status or power. And Nina knew she could rely on Mamie for loyalty and devotion, for companionship without confrontation.[21]

Otero-Warren's forceful personality was reaffirmed in her relationship with Meadors and represents one of the few examples of an Hispana dominating an Anglo woman during this period. But we must rely primarily on inferences, since Otero-Warren, according to Whaley, "was a woman who generally avoided self-revelation and recoiled from intimate discussions of personal matters."[22]

From 1932 to 1935 Otero-Warren took a hiatus from politics and appointed office to homestead 1,257 acres with Meadors about twelve miles northwest of Santa Fe. Calling their land "Las Dos Ranch," Otero-Warren and Meadors had two adobe ranch houses built next to each other. They moved into their homes in 1932 and remained there until 1935, when they gained full title to the land. During their sojourn at the ranch, Otero-Warren wrote her book on New Mexico folklore, *Old Spain in Our Southwest,* which many scholars think romanticized life in New Mexico and ignored the class conflicts between elite Hispano families and the majority of Hispanos in the state.[23]

After Otero-Warren and Meadors returned to Santa Fe, Otero-Warren rarely appointed her as an assistant when she secured government jobs. In 1941 Otero-Warren was appointed an educational consultant for the Works Progress Administration program in Rio Piedras, Puerto Rico. She assessed the educational problems of Puerto Ricans in relation to school attendance of children, adult education, bilingual education, and hiring new teachers. Her recommendations were very much in keeping with her views about the importance of bilingual education not only for retaining the linguistic heritage of Puerto Ricans, but also for teaching United States military officers the Spanish language.[24]

At the time when Otero-Warren shifted her ambition to the area of education and government appointments, a young Hispana, Concha Ortiz y Pino, blazed a brilliant path for Hispana politicians in the New Mexico state legislature. Born in 1914 Ortiz y Pino represented Santa Fe County for three terms from 1937 to 1942, while in her twenties. Her introduction to politics came as a result of familial duty and obligation. Her family had sworn loyalty to the

United States at the end of Mexican War of 1846–48 by stating that an Ortiz family member would run for election in every generation. She recalled that her family's philosophy was "to be of service first to one's church, then to one's country and to one's family."[25] Her father had only two children; rather than train his son to become a politician, he selected his only daughter. Ortiz y Pino's father decided that his son would be the manager of the family ranch of over 100,000 acres. At the age of twelve, Ortiz y Pino was taken from the care of her grandmother in Galisteo, a small village near Santa Fe. For Ortiz y Pino, leaving Galisteo was difficult, as her grandmother was the matriarch of the village and acted as a caregiver for everyone in the village needing help.[26]

In Santa Fe Ortiz y Pino attended Loretto Academy in the mornings and during the afternoons she attended legislative sessions. At the age of twenty-one Ortiz y Pino, initially a Republican, was put up for election as a Democrat by her very powerful and influential relatives in the state legislature. She won the election and during her first term received mentoring by prominent state politicians in the workings of the state legislature during breakfast meetings twice a week. Ortiz y Pino quickly made a name for herself by becoming majority whip of the legislature. She introduced bills in favor of women sitting on juries and students in the seventh and eighth grades learning Spanish as well as the regulation of small loans and the state personnel system.

Ortiz y Pino's views on bilingual education are interesting. Although she was an American born in New Mexico, Spanish was her first language, and she felt strongly that Spanish-Americans should not have to give up their primary language in the United States. One of Ortiz y Pino's most traumatizing memories was of being punished by nuns for speaking and singing in Spanish in the classroom. She also knew that the 1848 Treaty of Guadalupe Hidalgo and the 1912 New Mexico state constitution protected the rights of Spanish-Americans. According to the New Mexico constitution:

Section 3 of Article VII protected, among other things, the right of a citizen to vote regardless of his 'religion, race, language or color,' and regardless of his inability to handle effectively either the English or Spanish languages 'except as may be otherwise provided in this constitution.' Section 10 of Article XII declared that 'children of Spanish descent' would never be denied the right of admission to the public schools, nor ever 'classed in separate schools, but shall forever enjoy perfect equality with other children in all public schools.'[27]

Ortiz y Pino was well aware that Hispanos still represented the majority of people in New Mexico and that Hispano politicians were practiced in the art of politics and very able at protecting their rights as bilingual and bicultural ethnic Americans through their state constitution.

In February of 1941 Ortiz y Pino wrote a letter inviting Otero-Warren to attend a roundtable discussion on Senate Bill No. 3, which called for the teaching of Spanish in the public schools. Otero-Warren noted in her response that bilingualism was "not only desirable but necessary," because it would bring about "closer cooperation between the home and the school" and constitute "a step forward in progressive education."[28] The letters between the two Hispana politicians underscored the continuity of resolve and political will that successfully connected these two "new women" with progressive ideas of the twentieth century without giving up the language and culture of the Hispanos of New Mexico.

Like other politicians, including Otero-Warren, Ortiz y Pino believed that New Mexican Hispanos could operate as a "bridge" in U.S. Latin American relations by retaining the language and culture of Spain and Mexico. One of the bills Ortiz y Pino sponsored in the legislature was the creation of the School of Inter-American Affairs at the University of New Mexico. Ten years after its creation, Ortiz y Pino became the program's first Bachelor of Arts graduate.

While Otero-Warren argued for the inclusion of arts and crafts in school curricula, Ortiz y Pino advocated vocational schools to create artisans. From 1930 to 1935, she owned and operated a vocational school in her hometown of Galisteo. Spanish-American artisans in her school were part of the revival of Spanish colonial arts and crafts in New Mexico. The intent behind the establishment of vocational schools of this kind was to reaffirm Spanish American culture and provide skills that would allow artisans to create and market their own work.

In 1942 Ortiz y Pino left the state legislature. By her own admission, her stint as a legislator had not been that of a personal avocation but rather of a dutiful daughter maintaining the family honor. She declined to run for the position of secretary of state when approached to do so. In fact she sneered at the idea, saying that she would not only never run for that position but that "the job should go to some mother with a family to support, or to one with a boy in Bataan."[29] In 1943 Ortiz y Pino married University of New Mexico Professor Victor E. Klevan and spent the rest of the 1940s living in Albuquerque with her husband and participating in local civic committees. Ortiz y Pino considered her primary goal to be a good wife to Klevan and only then to participate in civic culture.

Chávez Chacón, Otero-Warren, and Ortiz y Pino are linked by their political activism and commitment to the improvement of Hispanos in New Mexico, especially through bilingual/bicultural education. Familial ideals and support for these women were strong, except in the case of Otero-Warren's Democratic cousin. While the idea for Chávez Chacón and Ortiz y Pino to run for office came from other family members, these two women embraced campaigning and did very well as politicians at the state level. Otero-Warren, who ran for national office, was challenged both by familial divisions and by conflicting views about her private life and political ambitions. Perhaps the most enduring legacy of these three Hispana politicians is the precedent they set for hundreds of Hispanas to participate in politics and successfully win elections at the village, town, city, and state levels.

NOTES

1. Ethnic terms such as Hispano/Hispana, Spanish-American, Anglo-American, and Anglo all refer to persons born in the United States.

2. Dan D. Chávez, *Soledad Chávez Chacón,* 9.

3. Ibid.

4. State of New Mexico, *Official New Mexico Blue Book* (Santa Fe: Secretary of State, 1987/1988), 41–45.

5. Chávez, *Soledad Chávez Chacón,* 14.

6. A. M. Bergere Family Papers, State Records Center and Archives, Santa Fe, New Mexico, folder 117; Joan M. Jensen, "Disfranchisement is a Disgrace."

7. [Santa Fe] *New Mexican,* April 11, 1965.

8. *Magee's Independent,* November 23, 1922.

9. Bergere Family Papers, folders 40, 105.

10. Ibid.

11. Ibid., folder 41.

12. Gerald D. Nash, *The American West Transformed,* 126; George I. Sanchez, *Forgotten People.*

13. Charlotte Whaley, *Nina Otero-Warren of Santa Fe,* 131–32.

14. Bergere Family Papers, folder 41.

15. Philip B. Gonzalez, "Spanish Heritage and Ethnic Protest in New Mexico," 29.

16. Bergere Family Papers, folder 506.

17. Ibid.

18. Whaley, *Nina Otero-Warren,* 105.

19. Ibid., 123.

20. Carroll Smith-Rosenberg, "Discourses of Sexuality and Subjectivity," 266.

21. Whaley, *Nina Otero-Warren,* 138–39.

22. Ibid., 193.

23. Ibid.

24. Bergere Family Papers, folder 55.

25. Women of New Mexico Collection no. 303, University of New Mexico, General Library, Special Collections, box 1, folder 9, items 1–3.

26. Ibid.

27. Robert W. Larson, *New Mexico's Quest for Statehood,* 279.

28. Bergere Family Papers, folder 43.

29. Ortiz y Pino Scrapbook no. 336, University of New Mexico, General Library, Special Collections.

18. Molly Dewson's successful efforts to link women into far-reaching networks aided the growth of the fifty-fifty movement (Democratic Digest, *June 1935*).

CHAPTER SEVENTEEN

LEGISLATED PARITY
Mandating Integration of Women into California
Political Parties, 1930s–1950s

JACQUELINE R. BRAITMAN

California Democrats ran a strong female candidate for governor in 1992 and currently the Golden State approaches the twenty-first century with two female Democratic senators. The electoral presence of Democratic women in a state generally dominated by Republicans grows out of a strong tradition of Democratic women's partisan activism. Present-day opportunities stem from earlier accomplishments of female partisans, who set the stage for the unprecedented visibility of contemporary female candidacies and campaigning. This chapter explores California women's twentieth-century local- and state-level activism, primarily within the Democratic Party, as part of recent scholarship challenging traditional notions about women's historical place in the world of partisan politics.

California is a noteworthy state for studying women in the political arena because of the high degree of female participation in all of the state's parties. The post–World War Two revival of California's competitive two-party system, after decades of Republican hegemony, provided new opportunities for recruitment of both men and women into partisan ranks. Both factors, as well as California's electoral importance and its close relationship to the national Democratic Party, help us to examine traditional assumptions about women's political marginality while at the same time revising accounts of the state's indigenous political past.

It has generally been assumed that women's experience in mainstream political parties has been either marginal or negligible. While this conclusion rests on the work of many scholars who have grappled with diverse questions about women's political participation, both behind the scenes and in elective or appointed office, recently scholars have begun to reexamine the stereotype of marginality to provide more subtle interpretations about the range of women's behavior in the guise of partisanship. But in doing so the most important phenomenon of women's twentieth-century political evolution has been only superficially treated or simply ignored: that is, the legislatively mandated, or party-designated, equal representation of women in the nation's state political parties through the national "fifty-fifty" movement.[1]

Scholars have generally been inattentive to the nationwide movement of state-level campaigns for equal representation during the first half of the twentieth century, which mandated women's integration into state political parties. This oversight has hindered our ability to fully understand the dialectical transition from the nineteenth-century tradition of women's nonpartisanship to the late twentieth-century "gender gap" in political party allegiance. Nor have scholars assessed the implications of women's legally required or party-designated political integration either for what it says about women's pre-WWI political culture or the women's movement of the mid-twentieth century and their subsequent political evolution. Incorporating structural parity into a historical analysis should shed new light on the gendered nature of power and the impact this has for women's political efficacy, participation, and electability.

Colorado was the first state to pass a fifty-fifty law, in 1906.[2] By 1936 sixteen states had established equal representation either by state law or party rule; twenty-five other states had partial representational parity, usually on appointed state central committees. In California women won partial parity in 1937, during the tumultuous years of the Depression.

The campaign for California's fifty-fifty law accelerated in the wake of the unsuccessful gubernatorial "End Poverty in California (EPIC)" campaign of Upton Sinclair, in 1934. Thousands of Democratic women partisans cut their political teeth on EPIC, while others supported the subsequent victory of Governor Culbert Olson, in 1938, and then went on to influence the state's political evolution for decades. As some women moved up the party hierarchy they set the stage for subsequent electoral victories, and they did it within the context of women's equal status on the state parties' central committees.

The California Federation of Women's Democratic Study Clubs (CFWDSC) initiated a drive not only to "win back" what was lost in the 1934 elections but to build a new party from the bottom up, just as the nationwide momentum for state fifty-fifty laws was growing.[3] The chairman of the Democratic National Committee, James A. Farley, issued a call to county chairmen throughout the country to "take the necessary steps to secure" fifty-fifty in their states by the end of the year.[4] He attended a conference sponsored by the CFWDSC, and met with its state president, Mrs. Mattison Boyd Jones, a notable Glendale clubwoman and former president of the Los Angeles branch of the California Federation of Women's Clubs (CFWC), who was the leading force behind the California fifty-fifty movement.[5] When the national FWDSC met in San Francisco in July, the group passed a resolution endorsing the fifty-fifty plan and called for "the drafting of a bill"[6] under the direction of Mrs. Jones. Jones galvanized the CFWC, the state Federation of Business and Professional Women's Clubs (CFBPW), the Parents and Teacher's Association (PTA), business leaders, and the Young Democrats, along with Republican women's groups, to support the legislation.[7]

Bipartisan support for a fifty-fifty law came from legislators in both houses, particularly two assemblywomen who had pledged to collaborate on legislation of special interest to women, Jeannette Daley, a San Diego Democrat, and Republican Eleanor Miller, of Los Angeles.[8] After Jeannette Daley introduced the Assembly bill, national leaders Farley and Molly Dewson of the U.S. Department of Labor effectively lobbied for passage of the bill by applying their "charms, which unlocked the Assembly doors and started the bill on its practical way," passing 66–1.[9] When the Senate Elections Committee blocked the bill, Senators Sanborn Young (Republican), William F. Knowland (Republican), and R. R. Cunningham (Democrat) argued from the floor as telegrams, telephone calls, and letters poured in demanding that legislators dislodge the bill, which then went on to win on a 30–5 vote.

Republican Governor Frank Merriman signed the bill into law on June 17, 1937.[10] The new law required equal representation of men and women on all legally recognized state party central committees. In California state central committee members are appointed by the assemblyperson elected in each Assembly district. A male legislator had to appoint one man and two women to the state central committee. A female official then had to appoint one woman and two men. After the bill's passage, State Democratic Party Chairman Cliff A. Anglim heralded the legislation as constituting "one of the most important political developments in recent history," telling an audience that "for women, this legislation is almost of equal importance with that which gave the right of suffrage."[11]

Within one year California's fifty-fifty law dramatically increased women's membership in political parties. Scores of women were ready to pledge "A Democratic State in '38!"[12] Women were no longer only allowed participation in auxiliary women's divisions and informal clubs or reliance on "influence." Women had achieved full party member status.

Party membership or structural integration did not necessarily translate into increased power or influence, however. Nevertheless the 1937 fifty-fifty mandate reflected the tremendous progress women as political actors had made in

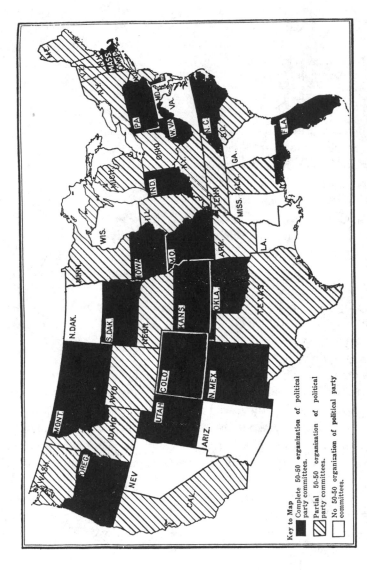

FIFTY-FIFTY—THE FIRST STEP FOR '40

19. The Democratic Digest kept its readers up to date on the fifty-fifty movement (Democratic Digest 1939).

the preceding decades. As one observer correctly predicted, fifty-fifty was a necessary first step, "which may be followed later by actual participation in policy formation."[13] With time the fifty-fifty law contributed to what political scientist Marjorie Lansing calls "the major shift toward the general acceptance of the legitimacy of the female vote," and "*of a participant role as appropriate for women.*"[14] But with fifty-fifty in place, this shift began earlier than Lansing and other scholars had assumed. Women demanded and won entry into male bastions of party membership because dedicated partisans had also been in the vanguard of women's clubs and state and national suffrage and women's rights campaigns. And subsequent partisans continued their integrationist efforts.

Regardless of the tremendous impact fifty-fifty had on women's political power, its legacy is ambiguous. Contemporaries and subsequent observers diminished the impact of women's legal equality by arguing that women were largely window-dressing or were displaced by their husbands or other men who acted as their proxies. However, available evidence does not bear this out. The majority of women listed on party rosters were identified by a feminine first name rather than a "Mrs." followed by their husbands' first and surnames, as was common for married women at the time. Nor did the vast majority of women's addresses match those of men. Admittedly it is still unclear if husbands gave their recorded place to women and acted through them.

The ranks of Republican women increased by about 400 percent from 1934 to 1938, while Democratic women increased by 700 percent. By 1954 women made up 46 percent of both Republican and Democratic Parties, whereas they had only accounted for 5 percent in the Democratic Party and 6 percent in the Republican Party in 1934.[15] Women were making inroads into elective party offices as well as in party membership tallies.[16] The *Democratic Digest* reported that "for years the chairmanship of a political committee was considered a man's job. But not now. . . . Fifty-fifty makes it possible for a woman to be state or county chairman."[17] Women were, in fact, heading political committees and being elected as county and state chairs in Oregon, Washington, Wyoming, and Montana, for example.[18]

Unlike the appointed positions on state central committees, county committee members were elected and thus fell outside of California's fifty-fifty law. When published rosters of California county chairs first appeared, in 1948, the Republicans had elected four women and the Democrats two. By 1954 each party had three female county chairs, and in 1962 the Democrats seated six and the Republicans eight.

The postwar years accelerated women's political progress, if only as a consequence of the realization that women were now a majority of the voting constituency.[19] In this context the numbers of women elected as county chairs exploded around the country, from twelve in 1940 to one hundred in 1944, although relative to men this number still represented a minuscule amount. Nevertheless by the end of the decade all but eight states had passed fifty-fifty laws or party rules whereby women were equally represented on state and local party committees. Along with fifty-fifty integration, the war had encouraged women to take civilian and government jobs, which served as the chief training grounds for women's shift into politics.[20]

Parity in the state partisan arena meant that women faced increasingly competitive races against both men and women when they sought party elective and appointed office. In California activist women vied for chair and vice chair positions in the party's northern and southern regions, as well as for national committeewomen posts and their traditional jobs as northern and southern directors of the party's Women's Division. Party service usually meant moving up the hierarchy from women's auxiliaries to the party proper. But sometimes women insiders were challenged by charismatic newcomers, such as was the case in 1940, when Mrs. Mattison Boyd Jones was overlooked in favor of Helen Gahagan Douglas by Governor Olson for appointment as national committeewoman.[21]

Even though the Cold War cultural climate tended to encourage conformity to traditional middle-class notions of male and female roles, during the 1950s these intraparty contests increasingly represented volatile ideological schisms and personality power plays between party leaders. One example is the vociferous war waged by opponent Dick Richards against Elizabeth Snyder in her unprecedented 1954 victory as the first woman in the state (and possibly the nation) to be elected outright as chair of a state political party.

While these fights raged on the state level, political scientists and historians have tended to focus more on the national "humdrum" political climate of the Eisenhower years. This was a time when only about 3 percent of Americans belonged to a political club or organization, as opposed to the generally assumed 4–8 percent of the population who usually participate in party or candidate work. As one author writes, "one of the central facts of political life is that politics, local, state, national, and international, lies for most people at the outer periphery of attention, interest, concern, and activity."[22] But this national perspective masks important events and trends on the local and state levels, especially with regard to the advances women were making. These gains are frequently discounted, however, due to the generally higher standard applied to women when assessing levels of political involvement.

Amid the widespread climate of disinterest among voters of both sexes, women's national partisan activism achieved higher levels by 1952 than in any previous year. In California this included the institution of a legislative committee by northern women, in the hopes of building a Democratic women's lobby. Southern California activists sought to establish standards of performance for women state central committee members.[23] More dramatic, however, was the increase in constituent involvement sparked by the inspirational oratory of the 1956 Democratic presidential candidate, Adlai Stevenson. State Democratic Party worker Cyr Copertini says that in fact, "it wasn't Jack Kennedy who should be credited" with reigniting interest in the Democratic Party, but rather Adlai Stevenson, who made the troops "ready for Kennedy" to use when his time came. She says that "without this earlier awakening," perhaps the momentum would not have been there "to elect a president in 1960."[24]

The California Stevenson campaign relied on the skills and talents of both men and women, new enthusiasts and long-time activists alike. Two notable women at the head of this effort were Elizabeth Snyder and Florence (Susie) Clifton. Snyder, as head of the state party's Women's Division recounts that the campaign "unleashed all the good efforts of good people," and that "this is when we formed many of the women's clubs that are still in existence today."[25]

Stevenson lost the presidency, and state Democrats managed only one victory, that of Edmund G.(Pat) Brown, Sr., as attorney general. But in the wake of defeat, the state Democratic Party's Women's Division thrived through its educational, fund raising, and outreach activities as it looked toward the next election.[26] Sometimes networking and fund raisers led to regionwide activities, such as the one-day interstate "campaign workshop" for Democratic women campaign leaders from western states, held in Las Vegas in October of 1955. Snyder, then Democratic Party state chair, other California activists, and representatives from Nevada, Utah, Arizona, New Mexico, and Wyoming attended this event, the theme of which was "Politics is Every Woman's Business."[27]

Cyr Copertini captures the mood: "1950's was an era when there were women's committees and women who shared leadership for the party," and "women were always recognized, and the legislators who had appointments to the state central committee had to make them 50–50."[28] Recognition of women increased their visibility on the national level as well, such as the record high number of women in attendance at the party's national convention in 1956, with California having the largest female delegation, at 18 percent.

According to historians Leila Rupp and Verta Taylor, even though women were not necessarily associated with women-specific goals or feminist groups, in the 1950s "the activities of women's organizations and individual women in the political parties had some impact in winning recognition, if only grudging, of the importance of women in politics."[29] Snyder, Clifton, and others actually attest to much more. Women's partisan activism allowed them to make inroads into male-dominated bailiwicks of power and policymaking. While it is true that men most often won the prize of officeholding and took credit for party triumphs, in reality women shared party administration and the running of campaigns through their gender-specific and/or integrated organizations.[30] But women also crossed over into nontraditional, leadership positions, allowing them to exercise their talents at "hard-core" politicking. While integrationist and appearing gender-neutral in practice, these activities paradoxically resulted in actually promoting the creation of feminist-oriented policies and access for women to party apparatuses, electoral office, and government appointments.

These growing opportunities paralleled women politicos' increased ability and inclination to represent women's interests. The establishment of the California State Commission on the Status of Women in 1965 was a culmination of that trend. State commissions were spun off from President John F. Kennedy's Commission on the Status of Women of 1961, and both are partly credited with sparking the formation of a mass-based woman's movement by inspiring social, political, and economic change through the creation of communication networks and opportunities for raising consciousness about discrimination.[31] Members of commissions came from the very ranks of women who may have eschewed specific feminist identification but who often parlayed their partisan connections into policy formation. Even so the transition was less than smooth.

The establishment of California's Commission on Women illustrates the long-standing tension among partisan women between their dual loyalties of partisanship and gender-related strategies of change. Two historians, Joan Jensen and Gloria Ricci Lothrop, argue that "mainstream politicians ignored women's new place in California because the liberal Democrats who controlled state politics under Governor Brown from 1956 to 1967 saw no need to work with women as a specific group or to recognize the need for attention to the changes already taking place within women's lives."[32] California did lag behind other states, but this characterization disengages the conflict from the dialectical relationship between the participation of women in politics on behalf of other women and women acting as partisans. Mid-twentieth-century Democratic women politicos, who were part of the 1930s liberal coalition, may have encouraged an ambivalence about the creation of female-specific institutions, in as much as throughout their political careers they identified themselves as partisans first, women second. While valuing women's separate party auxiliaries, women's mandated integration through the fifty-fifty law and their increasing presence in appointed and elected positions was a victory for these advocates who sought full equality within the mainstream party apparatus. Many of these women embraced the Equal Rights Amendment and other goals of the new feminist agenda. But creating women-centered bureaucracies contradicted the move toward integration into male-dominated political institutions, clashing with their goal of equal competition in the political arena. What's more the goals of different women's groups themselves contributed to a less than united women's front.

Many of the proponents of the Commission on Women, for example, were stalwart Democrats who also had memberships in nonpartisan women's groups such as the League of Women Voters (LWV) and the California Federation of Business and Professional Women (CFBPW). The CFBPW, in particular, generated wide support among women-only groups for the creation of the State Commission on the Status of Women. Ruth Church Gupta, after becoming a member of the Democratic State Central Committee in 1956 and unsuccessfully running for assemblywoman two years later, served as the legislative advocate and later president of the CFBPW. Gupta was a woman of many firsts in the legal profession, and she became one of Sacramento's most highly respected lobbyists on behalf of the commission and women's legal causes. Over the years Gupta served on numerous state commissions and boards, while maintaining her behind-the-scenes, elder stateswoman status in northern California politics.[33]

Gupta's lobbying on behalf of the CFBPW closely allied her with other partisans. For example the Democratic Women's Forum (DWF) of Los Angeles often held workshops in practical politics. Most of the women speakers on one DWF program supported the establishment of the women's commission and were part of the network of activists dating back to the 1930s, but there were also younger party members such as Mrs. Madale Watson, vice president of the DWF, and Carmen H. Warschaw, member of the state Fair Employment Practices Commission and southern vice chair of the Women's Division, who led a session on "New Frontiers in Politics for Women." Ruth Lybeck, a campaign leader for Helen Gahagan Douglas in the 1940s, explained party structure on the national, state, and local levels.[34] This meeting of the DWF illustrates the continuity of Democratic women partisans such as Gupta, Snyder, and Florence (Susie) Clifton, who although stemming from different organizations with different agendas, were united in their overall desire to increase women's political awareness and to work with younger women promoting women-centered, state-level policies.

Susie Clifton campaigned for Upton Sinclair and Culbert Olson in the 1930s and then went on to run campaigns for James Roosevelt and Helen Gahagan Douglas in the 1940s. She joined the state Democratic Central Committee in 1938 and was active on it for eighteen of her thirty-one years in politics. Because of her talents on the campaign trail, Pat Brown selected her as the southern

California coordinator for his successful 1958 gubernatorial election. He then appointed her to head the state's Industrial Welfare Commission, which regulates wages and industrial conditions for California workers.[35] He consulted with her about the Commission on Women and then asked her to be its transitional chairperson. The policies Clifton upheld on the IWC put her in direct opposition to the antiregulatory philosophy promoted by the CFBPW. But her prominence allowed her significant input into the creation and mandate of the commission. In fact at the time Clifton was described as a mother of four and a grandmother who was "California's #1 woman in position and political savvy."[36]

Thus despite their differences, women like Clifton, Snyder, and Gupta were integrated party stalwarts who promoted and headed mainstream party, government, and female-centered organizations, and they mentored new recruits into women-centered activism. The 1960s and 1970s generation of women activists who carried on the tradition of ideological diversity were able to move even further into the electoral arena, in large part due to the precedents set by these and scores of other early female politicos.

California offers ample evidence to alter the notion that women were marginalized political players. Following suffrage women's partisan activism led to their fifty-fifty membership in political parties, which eventually fostered the creation of women-centered policies and bureaucracies and the increasing visibility of women in the electoral arena. Several recent studies have concluded that women are no longer hindered by their sex for party support in their efforts to run for office; rather they are hindered or supported in the same ways that men are. But women are still reluctant to run for public office. By shifting attention to the nation's fifty fifty movement and contextualizing women's current electoral victories in a broader historical perspective, we can better understand the opportunities and limitations afforded by women's partisan integration and thus the implications for women candidates throughout the twentieth century.

NOTES

1. Elisabeth Israels Perry, "Women's Political Choices after Suffrage: The Women's City Club of New York, 1915–1990," does not address the process whereby New York achieved legislated partial fifty-fifty for women in 1939. What role did the Women's City Club play in this effort? Kristi Andersen's *After Suffrage* ends before the big push in the 1940s and Maureen Flanagan's "The Predicament of New Rights" ends four years before 1934, when the Illinois Federated Clubs successfully presented an amendment for full fifty-fifty representation, implemented in 1935.

2. Colorado Republicans appointed women as early as 1894, and Democrats actually elected women in 1906. Helen L. Sumner, *Equal Suffrage: The Results of an Investigation in Colorado Made for the Collegiate Equal Suffrage League of New York State* (New York: Harper and Brothers, 1909).

3. *Democratic Digest* (February 1935): 8.

4. Letter from James Farley August 1, 1935, reprinted in *Democratic Digest* (August 1935): 31.

5. *Democratic Digest* (October 1936): 24. Jones's supporters admonished the governor for going outside party stalwarts for his selection of Douglas and for not recognizing Jones's service to the party.

6. *Democratic Digest* (May 1936): 8.

7. *Democratic Digest* (1937): 28.

8. *Sacramento Bee,* January 3, 1937.

9. *Democratic Digest* (July 1937): 28.

10. AB 2298 process started January 22, 1937; *Los Angeles Times,* June 11, 1956.

11. *Democratic Digest* (1937).

12. *Democratic Digest* (December 1937): 30.

13. Marguerite J. Fisher, "Women in the Political Parties" 90.

14. Emphasis added; Marjorie Lansing, "The American Woman," 6.

15. State of California, *Officers and Members, State Central Committees* [various parties] (Sacramento: Secretary of State, 1934–62).

16. For example a Mrs. O. Bauresfeld was elected chair of her county central committee in Kansas in 1937, which was attributed to her invaluable expertise (even as a housewife with three children) and "the fifty-fifty bill giving women equal representation on party committees." *Democratic Digest* (June 1937): 12.

17. *Democratic Digest* (March 1941): 25.

18. *Democratic Digest* (September 1938): 25, 37.

19. Fisher, "Women in the Political Parties," 93.

20. Jacqueline R. Braitman, "Partisans in Overalls: New Perspectives on Women and Politics in Wartime California," paper delivered at California and World War Two conference at the Huntington Library, San Marino, CA, November 1995.

21. Mrs. Willoughby Rodman to Culbert L. Olson, July 22, 1940, Culbert Olson Papers, C-B 442, box 2, folder 1, Bancroft Library, University of California, Berkeley.

22. Gabriel A. Verba and Sidney Verba, *The Civic Culture,* 188.

23. *Democratic Digest* (March-April 1950): 29–31; (May 1949): 10.

24. Gabrielle Morris, "Cyr Copertini: Campaign Housekeeping 1940–1966," in *California Democrats' Golden Era, 1958–1966.* Berkeley: Berkeley Regional Oral History, University of California, 1987. 11–12.

25. Elizabeth Snyder, interview by author, 1990, 79.

26. Malca Chall, *Elizabeth Snyder, California's First Woman State Party Chairman,* Berkeley: Women in Politics Oral History Project, Regional Oral History Office, University of California, 1977, 83.

27. [Los Angeles] *Herald and Express,* October 10, 1955.

28. Copertini does add that "lots of men walk[ed] around with their wives' proxies"; Gabrielle Morris, "Cyr Copertini: Campaign Housekeeping 1940–1966." 14.

29. Leila J. Rupp and Verta Taylor, *Survival in the Doldrums*, 189.

30. See Abraham Holtzman, "Campaign Politics: A New Role for Women," 314–20.

31. The other two events were Betty Friedan's *The Feminine Mystique,* in 1963, and Title VII of the Civil Rights Act of 1964; Rupp and Taylor, *Survival in the Doldrums.* See also Jo Freeman, *The Politics of Women's Liberation,* 52–53.

32. Joan M. Jensen and Gloria Ricci Lothrop, *California Women,* 128.

33. *National Business Woman* (January 1958): 24.

34. Helen Gahagan Douglas was the honorary chairperson; Democratic Women's Forum of Los Angeles Truthsayers Course flier, 1963, California State Democratic Party, Women's Division, Oviatt Library, California State University at Northridge, Special Collections and Archives Section.

35. Florence (Susie) Clifton, interview by author, 1994.

36. Democratic Women's Forum of Los Angeles Truthsayer's Course flier, Sept. 16, 1965, Oviatt Library, California State University at Northridge, Special Collections and Archives Section.

WORKS CITED

Andersen, Kristi. *After Suffrage: Women in Electoral and Partisan Politics before the New Deal.* Chicago: University of Chicago Press, 1996.

Argersinger, Peter H. *Structure, Process and Party: Essays in American Political History.* Armonk, NY: Sharpe, 1992.

Baker, Paula. "The Domestication of Politics: Women and American Political Society, 1780–1920." *American Historical Review* 89 (1984): 620–47.

——. *The Moral Frameworks of Public Life: Gender, Politics, and the State in Rural New York 1830–1930.* New York: Oxford University Press, 1991.

Bloom, Melvyn H. *Public Relations and Presidential Campaigns: A Crisis in Democracy.* New York: Thomas Y. Crowell, 1973.

Bone, Hugh A. "New Party Associations in the West." *American Political Science Review* 45 (December 1951): 1115–25.

——. *Party Committees and National Politics.* Seattle: University of Washington Press, 1958.

Bordin, Ruth. *Frances Willard: A Biography.* Chapel Hill: University of North Carolina Press, 1986.

Breckenridge, Sophonisba P. *Women in the Twentieth Century: A Study of Their Political, Social, and Economic Activities.* New York: McGraw-Hill, 1933.

Brown, Elsa Barkley. "Negotiating and Transforming the Public Sphere: African American Political Life in the Transition from Slavery to Freedom." *Public Culture* 7 (1994): 107–46.

Brown, Joseph G. *History of Equal Suffrage in Colorado, 1868–1898.* Denver: New Jobs Printing Co., 1898.

Brown, Norman D. *Hood, Bonnet, and Little Brown Jug: Texas Politics, 1921–1928.* College Station: Texas A & M University Press, 1984.

Buenker, John D. "Illinois and the Four Progressive-Era Amendments to the United States Constitution." *Illinois Historical Journal* 80 (1987): 222–25.

Carroll, Susan J. "Women Candidates and Support for Feminist Concerns: The Closet Feminist Syndrome." *Western Political Quarterly* 37 (1984): 307–23.

Chafe, William. *The American Woman: Her Changing Social, Economic, and Political Roles, 1920–1970.* New York: Oxford University Press, 1972.

———. "Women's History and Political History: Some Thoughts on Progressivism and the New Deal." In *Visible Women: New Essays on American Activism,* ed. Nancy Hewitt and Suzanne Lebsock. Urbana: University of Illinois Press, 1993.

Chávez, Dan D. *Soledad Chávez Chacón: A New Mexico Political Pioneer, 1890–1936.* [New Mexico]: n.p., 1996.

Cott, Nancy F. *The Grounding of Modern Feminism.* New Haven, CT: Yale University Press, 1987.

Dalin, David G. "Jewish and Non-Partisan Republicanism in San Francisco, 1911–1963." *American Jewish History* 68 (1979): 492–516.

Dinkin, Robert J. *Before Equal Suffrage: Women in Partisan Politics from Colonial Times to 1920.* Westport, CT: Greenwood, 1995.

Disbrow, Donald. "Reform in Philadelphia under Mayor Blankenburg." *Pennsylvania History* (September 1960): 379–96.

Dreier, Mary. *Margaret Dreier Robins: Her Life, Letters and Work.* New York: Island Press Cooperative, 1950.

DuBois, Ellen Carol. "Outgrowing the Compact of Fathers: Equal Rights, Woman Suffrage, and the United States Constitution, 1820–1878." *Journal of American History* 74 (3) (December 1987): 836–62.

Duster, Alfreda, ed. *Crusade for Justice: The Autobiography of Ida B. Wells.* Chicago: University of Chicago Press, 1972.

Edwards, India. *Pulling No Punches: Memoirs of a Woman in Politics.* New York: Putnam's, 1977.

Edwards, Rebecca. *Angels in the Machinery: Gender in American Party Politics from the Civil War to the Progressive Era.* New York: Oxford University Press, 1997.

Epstein, Leon D. *Political Parties in the American Mold.* Madison: University of Wisconsin Press, 1986.

Eyre, John R., and Curtis Martin. *The Colorado Preprimary System.* Boulder, CO: Bureau of Governmental Research and Service, 1967.

Fels, Tony. "Religious Assimilation in a Fraternal Organization: Jews and Freemasonry in Gilded-Age San Francisco." *American Jewish History* 74 (1985): 360–403.

Fisher, Marguerite J., "Women in the Political Parties." *Annals of the American Academy of Political and Social Science* 251 (1947): 87–93.

Fisher, Marguerite J., and Betty Whitehead. "Women and National Party Organization." *American Political Science Review* 38 (October 1944): 895–905.

Fitzpatrick, Ellen. *Endless Crusade: Women Social Scientists and Progressive Reform.* New York: Oxford University Press, 1990.

Flanagan, Maureen. "Chicago Women and Party Politics, 1914–1932: The Historical Perspective." Paper presented at the annual meeting of the American Political Science Association, Chicago, Illinois, 1995.

———. "The City Profitable, the City Livable: Environmental Policy, Gender and Power in Chicago in the 1910s." *Journal of Urban History* 22 (2) (1996): 163–90.

———. "Gender and Urban Political Reform: The City Club and the Woman's City Club of Chicago in the Progressive Era." *American Historical Review* 95 (4) (October 1990): 1032–50.

———. "The Predicament of New Rights: Suffrage and Women's Political Power from a Local Perspective." *Social Politics: International Studies in Gender, State and Society* 2 (3) (1995): 305–30.

Forthal, Sonya. *Cogwheels of Democracy: A Study of the Precinct Captain.* New York: William-Frederick Press, 1946.

Fox, Bonnie. "The Philadelphia Progressives: A Test of the Hofstadter-Hays Thesis," *Pennsylvania History* (October 1967): 372–394

Fredman, L.E. *The Australian Ballot: The Story of an American Reform.* East Lansing: Michigan State University Press, 1968.

Freedman, Estelle. "Separatism as Strategy: Female Institution Building and American Feminism, 1870–1930." *Feminist Studies* (5) (fall 1979): 512–29.

Freeman, Jo. *The Politics of Women's Liberation.* New York: David MacKay, 1975.

Gable, John Allen. *The Bull Moose Years: Theodore Roosevelt and the Progressive Party.* Port Washington, N.Y.: Kennikat Press, 1978.

Gatewood, Willard B. *Aristocrats of Color: The Black Elite, 1880–1920.* Bloomington: Indiana University Press, 1990.

Gienapp, William E. *The Origins of the Republican Party, 1852–1856.* New York: Oxford University Press, 1987.

Ginzberg, Lori D. " 'Moral Suasion is Moral Balderdash': Women, Politics, and Social Activism in the 1850s." *Journal of American History* 73 (3) (December 1986): 601–22.

Goldberg, Michael Lewis. *"An Army of Women": Gender and Politics in Gilded Age Kansas.* Baltimore: Johns Hopkins University Press, 1997.

Gonzalez, Philip B. "Spanish Heritage and Ethnic Protest in New Mexico: The Anti-Fraternity Bill of 1933." *New Mexico Historical Review* 61 (1986): 281–99.

Gordon, Felice D. *After Winning: The Legacy of the New Jersey Suffragists, 1920–1947.* New Brunswick, NJ: Rutgers University Press, 1986.

Gosnell, Harold. *Machine Politics: Chicago Model,* 2d ed. Chicago: University of Chicago Press, 1937, 1968.

———. *Negro Politicians: The Rise of Negro Politics in Chicago.* Chicago: University of Chicago Press, 1935.

Gould, Lewis L. *Progressives and Prohibitionists: Texas Democrats in the Wilson Era.* Austin: University of Texas Press, 1973.

Graham, Sara Hunter. *Woman Suffrage and the New Democracy.* New Haven, CT: Yale University Press, 1996.

Gruberg, Martin. *Women in American Politics: An Assessment and Sourcebook.* Oshkosh, WI: Academia Press, 1968.

Gustafson, Melanie. "Partisan Women in the Progressive Era: The Struggle for Inclusion in Political Parties in the United States." *Journal of Women's History* 9 (2) (Summer 1997): 7–30.

Hansen, Harriet. "Woman Enters Politics: San Francisco's Pioneer Congresswoman, Florence Prag Kahn." Master's thesis, San Francisco State University, 1969.

Harrison, Cynthia. *On Account of Sex: The Politics of Women's Issues, 1945–1968.* Berkeley: University of California Press, 1988.

Harvey, Anna L. *Votes Without Leverage: Women in American Electoral Politics, 1920–1970.* Cambridge: Cambridge University Press, 1998.

Hendricks, Wanda A. "Ida B. Wells-Barnett and the Alpha Suffrage Club." In *One Woman, One Vote: Rediscovering the Woman Suffrage Movement,* ed. Marjorie Spruill Wheeler. Troutdale, OR: NewSage Press, 1995.

——. " 'Vote for the Advantage of Ourselves and Our Race': The Election of the First Black Alderman in Chicago." *Illinois Historical Journal* 87 (1994): 171–84.

Hewitt, Nancy. *Women's Activism and Social Change: Rochester, New York, 1822–1872.* Ithaca, NY: Cornell University Press, 1984.

Higginbotham, Evelyn Brooks. "In Politics to Stay: Black Women Leaders and Party Politics in the 1920s." In *Women, Politics, and Change,* ed. Louise A. Tilly and Patricia Gurin. New York: Russell Sage, 1990.

Holtzman, Abraham. "Campaign Politics: A New Role for Women." *South Western Social Science Quarterly* (March 1960): 314–20.

James, Edward, Janet Wilson James, and Paul Boyer, eds. *Notable American Women, 1607–1950: A Biographical Dictionary.* Cambridge, MA: Belknap Press, 1971.

Jensen, Joan M. "Disfranchisement is a Disgrace: Women and Politics in New Mexico, 1900–1940." *New Mexico Historical Review* 56 (1981): 5–36.

Jensen, Joan M., and Gloria Ricci Lothrop. *California Women: A History.* San Francisco: Boyd and Fraser, 1987.

Johnson, Donald Bruce, and Kirk Porter, eds. *National Party Platforms, 1840–1973.* Chicago: University of Illinois Press, 1973.

Johnson-McGrath, Julie. "The Civic Club of Philadelphia" and "The Octavia Hill Association." In *Invisible Philadelphia: Community through Voluntary Organizations.* Philadelphia: Atwater Kent Museum, 1993.

Katz, Sherry Jeanne. "Dual Commitments: Feminism, Socialism, and Women's Political Activism in California, 1890–1920." Ph.D. diss., University of California, Los Angeles, 1991.

——. "A Politics of Coalition: Socialist Women and the California Suffrage Movement, 1900–1911." In *One Woman, One Vote: Rediscovering the Woman Suffrage Movement,* ed. Marjorie Spruill Wheeler. Troutdale, OR: NewSage Press, 1995.

——. "Socialist Women and Progressive Reform." In *California Progressivism Revisited,* ed. William Deverell and Tom Sitton. Berkeley: University of California Press, 1994.

Keller, Morton. *Affairs of State: Public Life in Late Nineteenth Century America.* Cambridge, MA: Harvard University Press, 1977.

Kelley, Jr., Stanley. *Professional Public Relations and Political Power.* Baltimore: Johns Hopkins University Press, 1956.

Kellstadt, Lyman Arthur. "Precinct Committeemen in the Philadelphia Metropolitan Area: An Analysis of Role." Ph.D. diss., University of Illinois, 1965.

Kirkendall, Richard S. *A History of Missouri,* vol. 5. Columbia: University of Missouri Press, 1986.

Kleppner, Paul. *Who Voted?: The Dynamics of Electoral Turnout, 1870–1980.* New York: Praeger, 1982.

Knupfer, Anne Meis. *Toward a Tenderer Humanity and a Nobler Womanhood: African American Women's Clubs in Turn-of-the-Century Chicago.* New York: New York University Press, 1996.

Koven, Seth, and Sonya Michel. "Mother Worlds." In *Mothers of a New World: Maternalist Politics and the Origins of Welfare States,* ed. Seth Koven and Sonya Michel. New York: Routledge, 1993.

Lansing, Marjorie. "The American Woman: Voter and Activist." In *Women in Politics,* ed. Jane S. Jaquette. New York: John Wiley & Sons, 1974.

Larson, Robert W. *New Mexico's Quest for Statehood, 1846–1912.* Albuquerque: University of New Mexico Press, 1968.

Lear, Linda. *Harold L. Ickes, the Aggressive Progressive, 1874–1993.* New York: Garland, 1981.

Lemons, J. Stanley. *The Woman Citizen: Social Feminism in the 1920s.* Urbana: University of Illinois Press, 1973.

Lotchin, Roger W. *Fortress California, 1910–1961: From Warfare to Welfare.* New York: Oxford University Press, 1992.

Lovell, S.D. *The Presidential Election of 1916.* Carbondale: Southern Illinois University Press, 1980.

Marvick, Dwaine, and Charles Nixon. "Recruitment Contrasts in Rival Campaign Groups." In *Political Decision-Makers,* ed. Dwaine Marvick. Glencoe, IL: Free Press, 1961.

Matthews, Glenna. *The Rise of Public Woman: Woman's Power and Woman's Place, 1630–1970.* New York: Oxford University Press, 1992.

McGerr, Michael. *The Decline of Popular Politics: The American North, 1865–1928.* New York: Oxford University Press, 1986.

——. "Political Style and Women's Power, 1830–1930." *Journal of American History* 77 (1990): 864–85.

Milkis, Sidney. *The President and the Parties: The Transformation of the American Party System Since the New Deal.* New York: Oxford University Press, 1993.

Miller, Kristie. *Ruth Hanna McCormick: A Life in Politics 1880–1944.* Albuquerque: University of New Mexico Press, 1992.

Mitchell, Franklin D. *Embattled Democracy: Missouri Democratic Politics, 1919–1932.* Columbia: University of Missouri Press, 1968.

Monoson, S. Sara. "The Lady and the Tiger: Women's Electoral Activism in New York City before Suffrage." *Journal of Women's History* 2 (2) (Fall 1990): 100–135.

Muncy, Robyn. *Creating a Female Dominion in American Reform, 1890–1935.* New York: Oxford University Press, 1991.

Nash, Gerald D. *The American West Transformed: The Impact of the Second World War.* Bloomington: Indiana University Press, 1985.

Paulissen, May Nelson, and Carl McQuery. *Miriam: The Southern Belle Who Became the First Woman Governor of Texas.* Austin, TX: Eakin Press, 1995.

Perry, Elisabeth Israels. *Belle Moskowitz: Feminine Politics and the Exercise of Power in the Age of Alfred E. Smith.* New York: Oxford University Press, 1987; New York: Routledge, 1992.

——. "Women's Political Choices after Suffrage: The Women's City Club of New York, 1915–1990," *New York History* (October 1990): 417–34.

Reynolds, John F. *Testing Democracy: Electoral Behavior and Progressive Reform in New Jersey, 1880–1920.* Chapel Hill: University of North Carolina Press, 1988.

Reynolds, John F., and Richard L. McCormick. " 'Outlawing Treachery': Split Tickets and Ballot Laws in New York and New Jersey, 1880–1910." *Journal of American History* 72 (1986): 835–58.

Rogin, Michael Paul, and John L. Shover. *Political Change in California: Critical Elections and Social Movements, 1890–1966.* Westport, CT: Greenwood Press, 1970.

Rupp, Leila J., and Verta Taylor. *Survival in the Doldrums: The American Women's Rights Movement, 1945 to the 1960s.* Columbus: Ohio State University Press, 1990.

Salas, Elizabeth. "Ethnicity, Gender and Divorce: Issues in the 1922 Campaign by Adelina Otero-Warren for the U.S. House of Representatives." *New Mexico Historical Review* 70 (1995): 367–82.

Sallee, Shelley. " 'The Woman of It': Governor Miriam Ferguson's 1924 Election." *Southwestern Historical Quarterly* 100 (1996): 1–16.

Salter, J. T. *Boss Rule: Portraits in City Politics.* New York: Whittlesey House, 1935.

Sanchez, George I. *Forgotten People: A Study of New Mexicans.* Albuquerque: University of New Mexico Press, 1940.

Sanders, Marion K. *The Lady and the Vote.* Boston: Houghton Mifflin, 1956.

Shaffer, Ralph Edward. "A History of the Socialist Party of California." Master's thesis, University of California, Berkeley, 1955.

——. "Radicalism in California, 1869–1929." Ph.D. diss., University of California, Berkeley, 1962.

Shepsle, Ken, and Mark Bonchek. *Analyzing Politics.* New York: W.W. Norton, 1996.

Sicherman, Barbara, and Carol Hurd Green, eds., with Ilene Kantrov and Harriet Walker. *Notable American Women: The Modern Period.* Cambridge, MA: Belknap Press, 1980.

Silbey, Joel H. *The American Political Nation 1838–1893.* Stanford CA: Stanford University Press, 1991.

Sitton, Tom. "John Randolph Haynes and the Left Wing of California Progressivism." In *California Progressivism Revisited,* ed. William Deverell and Tom Sitton. Berkeley: University of California Press, 1994.

Sklar, Kathryn Kish. *Florence Kelley and the Nation's Work: The Rise of Women's Political Culture, 1830–1900.* New Haven, CT: Yale University Press, 1995.

——. "The Historical Foundations of Women's Power in the Creation of the American Welfare State, 1830–1930." In *Mothers of a New World: Maternalist Politics and the Origins of Welfare States,* ed. Seth Koven and Sonya Michel. New York: Routledge, 1993.

——. "Two Political Cultures in the Progressive Era." In *U.S. History as Women's History,* ed. Linda Kerber, Alice Kessler-Harris, and Kathryn Kish Sklar. Chapel Hill: University of North Carolina Press, 1993.

Skocpol, Theda. *Protecting Soldiers and Mothers: The Political Origins of Social Policy in the United States*. Cambridge, MA: Harvard University Press, 1992.

Smith-Rosenberg, Carroll. "Discourses of Sexuality and Subjectivity: The New Woman, 1870–1936." In *Hidden from History: Reclaiming the Gay and Lesbian Past*, ed. Martin B. Duberman, Martha Vicinus, and George Chauncey, Jr. NY: Meridian, 1989.

Spear, Allan H. *Black Chicago: The Making of a Negro Ghetto 1890–1920*. Chicago: University of Chicago Press, 1967.

Stanton, Elizabeth Cady, Matilda Joslyn Gage, Susan B. Anthony, and Ida Husted Harper, eds. *History of Woman Suffrage*. 6 vols. (vols. 1–4, Rochester, NY: Susan B. Anthony, 1881–1902; vols. 5–6, New York: National American Woman Suffrage Association, 1922; reprint ed., New York: Arno, 1969).

Thompson, Mildred. *Ida B. Wells-Barnett: An Exploratory Study of an American Black Woman, 1893–1930*. vol. 15 of *Black Women in United States History*, ed. Darlene Clark Hine. New York: Carlson Publishing, 1990.

Tilly, Louise A., and Patricia Gurin, eds. *Women, Politics and Change*. New York: Russell Sage Foundation, 1990.

Varon, Elizabeth R. "Tippecanoe and the Ladies, Too: White Women and Party Politics in Antebellum Virginia." *Journal of American History* 82 (1995): 494–521.

Verba, Gabriel A. and Sidney Verba. *The Civic Culture: Political Attitudes and Democracy in Five Nations*. Boston: Little Brown and Company, 1965.

Ware, Susan. *Beyond Suffrage: Women in the New Deal*. Cambridge, MA: Harvard University Press, 1981.

——. *Partner and I: Molly Dewson, Feminism, and New Deal Politics*. New Haven, CT: Yale University Press, 1987.

Watkins, T. H. *Righteous Pilgrim: The Life and Times of Harold L. Ickes, 1874–1952*. New York: Henry Holt, 1990.

Weaver, Leon. "Some Soundings on the Party System: Rural Precinct Committeemen." *American Political Science Review* 34 (February 1940): 76–84.

Whaley, Charlotte. *Nina Otero-Warren of Santa Fe*. Albuquerque: University of New Mexico Press, 1994.

Wheeler, Adade Mitchell, and Marjorie Stein Wortman. *The Roads They Made: Women in Illinois History*. Chicago: Charles H. Kerr Publishing Company, 1977.

White, Deborah Gray. "The Cost of Club Work, The Price of Black Feminism." In *Visible Women: New Essays on American Activism,* ed. Nancy A. Hewitt and Suzanne Lebsock. Urbana: University of Illinois Press, 1993.

Wiebe, Robert H. *The Search for Order, 1877–1920*. New York: Farrar, Straus, Giroux, 1967.

Witt, Linda, Karen M. Paget, and Glenna Matthews. *Running as a Woman: Gender and Power in American Politics*. New York: Free Press, 1993.

Yearley, Clifton K. *The Money Machines: The Breakdown and Reform of Governmental and Party Finance in the North, 1860–1920*. Albany: SUNY Albany Press, 1970.

INDEX

NOTES ON CONTRIBUTORS

KATHRYN ANDERSON is a professor at Fairhaven College, an interdisciplinary cluster college of Western Washington University, and a member of the Women Studies faculty. She has published articles on women and politics and women's oral history and is currently working on a biography of Emily Newell Blair.

PAULA BAKER is an associate professor of history at the University of Pittsburgh. She has written on the history of women and politics and is the author of *The Moral Frameworks of Public Life: Gender, Politics, and the State in Rural New York, 1870–1930* (1991). She is at work on a history of the party workforce and party finance from the 1840s through the 1970s.

JACQUELINE R. BRAITMAN is research associate in the Department of History at the University of California, Los Angeles. Under the auspices of the John and Dora Haynes Foundation, she is completing her manuscript on California progressive Katherine Philips Edson. She continues her revision of California political history through a forthcoming biography of partisan Elizabeth Snyder.

REBECCA EDWARDS received a Ph.D. in history from the University of Virginia in 1995. She is assistant professor of history at Vassar College in Poughkeepsie, New York, and the author of *Angels in the Machinery: Gender in American Party Politics from the Civil War to the Progressive Era* (1997).

MAUREEN A. FLANAGAN is associate professor of history at Michigan State University. She has published several essays on Chicago women and urban politics in the early twentieth century and is currently completing a manuscript, *Chicago Women and Politics, 1871–1932: From Social Vision to Political Action.*

MELANIE GUSTAFSON is assistant professor of history at the University of Vermont and is currently working on a study of women in the Republican and Progressive Parties at the turn of the last century. She received her Ph.D. from New York University in 1993.

ANNA L. HARVEY is assistant professor of politics at New York University and author of *Votes without Leverage: Women in American Electoral Politics 1920–1970* (1998). She has also been published in *Social Science History* and *Studies in American Political Development* and on the politics of school desegregation. Professor Harvey is currently working on the politics of minor parties in the United States.

WANDA A. HENDRICKS, associate professor of history at Arizona State University, received her Ph.D. from Purdue University and is the author of *Gender, Race, and Politics in the Midwest: Black Club Women in Illinois* (1998). She has also published articles and essays in the *Illinois Historical Journal* and the *Illinois History Teacher*, as well as in the edited volumes *One Woman, One Vote: Rediscovering the Woman Suffrage Movement*, and *African-American Orators: A Bio-Critical Sourcebook*.

SHERRY J. KATZ received her Ph.D. from the University of California, Los Angeles. She currently teaches United States history at San Francisco State University and California State University, Hayward. Her forthcoming book on socialist women, social reform, and the welfare state in Progressive-Era California will be published by Routledge.

GLENNA MATTHEWS is a research associate at the Institute of Urban and Regional Development at the University of California, Berkeley. The author of three previous books, including two on women and politics, she is currently writing *The Young Oxford Companion to U.S. Women's History* and is also working on *Silicon Valley Women and the California Dream*, forthcoming from Stanford University Press.

KRISTIE MILLER is an independent historian, author of *Ruth Hanna McCormick: A Life in Politics 1880–1944* (1992). She has published articles on women in politics and is working on a biography of Arizona Congresswoman Isabella Greenway.

ROBYN MUNCY is associate professor of history at the University of Maryland–College Park. She is the author of *Creating a Female Dominion in American Reform, 1890–1935* (1991) and coeditor with Sonya Michel of *Engendering America: A Documentary History, 1865-the Present*, forthcoming from McGraw-Hill.

ELISABETH ISRAELS PERRY earned her Ph.D. in history at the University of California at Los Angeles in 1967. Her recent books include *Belle Moskowitz: Feminine Politics and the Exercise of Power in the Age of Alfred E. Smith* (1987) and *The Challenge of Feminist Biography: Writing the Lives of Modern American Women* (1992).

ELIZABETH SALAS is associate professor in the Department of American Ethnic Studies at the University of Washington. She is the author of *Soldaderas in the Mexican Military: Myth and History* (1990). Her research areas include women and minorities in the U.S. military, Hispana politicians in New Mexico, and Chicanas in the Pacific Northwest.

DREW E. VANDECREEK received his Ph.D. in American History from the University of Virginia in 1996. He is Director of the Abraham Lincoln Historical Digitization Project at the University of Northern Illinois.

MOLLY M. WOOD earned her Ph.D. from the University of South Carolina in 1998. She holds a post-doctoral fellowship in the history department at the University of South Carolina where she is revising her dissertation, "An American Diplomat's Wife in Mexico: Gender, Politics, and Foreign Affairs Activism, 1907–1927," for publication.

NANCY BECK YOUNG, a historian of twentieth-century politics and women, received her Ph.D. from the University of Texas at Austin and is assistant professor of history at McKendree College. She coauthored *Texas, Her Texas: The Life and Times of Frances Goff* (1997) with Lewis L. Gould.